OUTSOURCING EMPIRE

Outsourcing Empire

HOW COMPANY-STATES MADE
THE MODERN WORLD

Andrew Phillips and
J. C. Sharman

PRINCETON UNIVERSITY PRESS

PRINCETON AND OXFORD

Requests for permission to reproduce material from this work
should be sent to permissions@press.princeton.edu

Published by Princeton University Press
41 William Street, Princeton, New Jersey 08540
6 Oxford Street, Woodstock, Oxfordshire OX20 1TR

press.princeton.edu

All Rights Reserved
ISBN 978-0-691-20351-5
ISBN (pbk.) 978-0-691-20619-6
ISBN (e-book) 978-0-691-20620-2
Library of Congress Control Number: 2020934560

British Library Cataloging-in-Publication Data is available

Editorial: Sarah Caro, Hannah Paul, and Josh Drake
Production Editorial: Karen Carter
Jacket/Cover Design: Lorraine Doneker
Production: Erin Suydam
Publicity: James Schneider and Kate Farquhar-Thomson
Copyeditor: Erin Hartshorn

Jacket art: Benjamin West, "Shah 'Alam, Mughal Emperor, Conveying the Grant
of the Diwani to Lord Clive," 1774 © British Library

This book has been composed in Miller

Printed on acid-free paper. ∞

Printed in the United States of America

10 9 8 7 6 5 4 3 2 1

CONTENTS

ACKNOWLEDGMENTS

WE BEGAN THIS BOOK while visiting the Centre for International Studies at the London School of Economics in the autumn of 2015, a visit made possible by Kirsten Ainley and George Lawson, who went well above and beyond both in their hospitality and their intellectual engagement with the project, at that time and since. Sharman also thanks Jeff Chwieroth for helping to make the visit possible. Our first public presentation of the project in the same year was at the School of Oriental and African Studies, generously hosted by Meera Sabaratnam.

Sharman is very grateful for feedback and support from colleagues at Griffith University during his time there until the end of 2016, especially from Ian Hall and Pat Weller. From 2017 the blend of International Relations and history expertise in Cambridge has made the Department of Politics and International Studies the perfect environment for thinking about and working on this project. In particular, Mette Eilstrup-Sangiovanni, Brendan Simms, and Ed Cavanagh provided very helpful corrections and pointers. More broadly, fellow Brisbane-to-Cambridge transplant Maja Spanu has been tireless in building a community of like-minded scholars in historical International Relations, a community that has had an important influence in shaping this book, and here particular thanks also to Ayse Zarakol and Duncan Bell. The Lauterpacht Centre for International Law also hosted a very positive session on the draft argument, thanks here to Sharman's King's College colleagues Megan Donaldson and Surabhi Ranganathan.

Later in the project Sharman was invited to the present the argument at the Minnesota International Relations Colloquium, and thanks to Nisha Fazal, Pedro Accorsi Amaral, Nicauris Heredia Rosario, and Carly Potz-Nielsen for both their hospitality and comments on the project.

Over the years Hendrik Spruyt and Jesse Dillon Savage have been very discerning sounding-boards for many of the ideas that have gone into the book. Jon Pevehouse was kind enough to give us a good deal of considered feedback on a shorter version of our argument.

Phillips thanks his colleagues at the School of Political Science and International Studies at the University of Queensland for their insightful and constructive critical feedback over several years as the book's argument evolved through successive iterations. Special thanks are due to the participants of the St. Lucy's History and Theory reading group and to Chris Reus-Smit especially for his continued mentorship and championing of International Relations scholarship working at the nexus of theory and history.

Scholarship depends on the selflessness of peer reviewers, and we were very fortunate to have two anonymous reviewers who spent a lot of time and effort in thoughtfully reading and responding to the draft manuscript in full. Thanks also to our incredibly professional indexer Dave Prout.

Kye Allen provided fantastic research assistance in sharpening the text and the bibliography; we could not have asked for more here.

We also acknowledge the Australian Research Council for crucial financial support through Discovery Project grant DP170101395.

At Princeton University Press thanks are due to Sarah Caro and Hannah Paul. We would also like to thank our agent James Pullen for his crucial support and advocacy.

Finally, Sharman thanks Bilyana for her steadfast support and general calming effect, all the more appreciated during and in the wake of the big move. Phillips thanks his mother and father for their love and support, as well as his surrogate Brisbane family—Daniel Celm and Sophie Devitt, and Joseph and Juliet Celm.

OUTSOURCING EMPIRE

Introducing the
Company-State

SOME OF THE most important actors in the crucial formative stages of the modern international system were neither states nor merchant companies, but hybrid entities representing a combination of both. For almost two centuries, "company-states" like the English and Dutch East India Companies and the Hudson's Bay Company combined spectacular success in amassing power and profit in driving the first wave of globalization. They were the forerunners of the modern day multinational corporation, but were at the same time endowed with extensive sovereign powers, formidable armies and navies, and practical independence. In some cases, company-states came to wield more military and political power than many monarchs of the day, as they exercised corporate sovereignty over vast territories and millions of subjects. The company-states were thus both engines of imperialism and engines of capitalism. Here we seek to explain the rise, fall, and significance of these hugely important yet often neglected actors in creating the first truly global international system.

To understand the creation of the modern international system we need a comparative study of the company-states. Yet such a study has been missing. Today we see rule, governing, and war as synonymous with states. But European states largely stood aloof from the initial wave of Western expansion that first made it possible to think of politics, economics, and many other forms of interaction as occurring on a global scale. As agents of exchange, company-states transformed the world through the inter-continental arbitrage of commodities, people, and ideas. A key theme of this book is that these actors were the primary mediators linking Europe with the rest of the world. Similarly, many European states were surprisingly reticent during the "new imperialism" of the late nineteenth century to directly assume the responsibilities of overseas expansion. Instead, of all the strategies and institutional expedients Europeans used to bring the rest of world under their sway from the seventeenth to the twentieth centuries, none was more common and consequential than that of the company-state. After initial spectacular successes, this form quickly became generic, being widely copied among diverse European states, from Scotland to Russia. Company-states dominated vast swathes of Asia and North America for more than a century, while also acting as the vanguard of European imperialism in Africa, much of the rest of the Americas, and in the South Pacific. While some company-states went on to great fame and fortune, many others were ignominious failures. Even now that company-states have gone, their legacies live on from Alaska to Zimbabwe.

By contemporary standards, these enterprises seem to be syncretic Frankenstein monsters in the way they combine quintessential sovereign prerogatives with the classic features of the modern corporation. But company-states and related hybrid actors were more the rule than the exception in European imperialism. Rulers that were unable or unwilling to provide the necessary fiscal, administrative, and military resources for extra-European expansion often created company-states via charters granting monopoly trading rights and endowing them with a brace of sovereign powers. By contrast, what we now take to be the normal way of exercising political authority, through the sovereign state, was comparatively rare in most regions outside Europe until quite recently. The great significance of this point is that international politics has long been a game played by a diverse range of actors, not just sovereign states, especially outside Europe.

The state and the company are the defining institutions of modernity. Rather than being somehow timeless or natural, what are now taken-for-granted conceptions of the different identities and roles of states in providing security, and companies in seeking profit, often reflect bitter historical struggles over the powers and prerogatives of the company-states. The consequences of these struggles extend to the bedrock divisions of modernity: "By serving as touch points between states, markets, and publics, the companies helped define the boundaries of what we now recognize as public and private."[1] Company-states epitomize a historical fluidity that is alien to us today, but entirely unremarkable to rulers and ruled a few centuries ago, when the division between *public* and *private* was blurred or entirely lacking. Functions now divided between private companies and the public authorities were in the past split, shared, swapped, and recombined. Core features of the modern corporation, like the separation of management from ownership, legal personality, limited liability, and joint-stock form were all pioneered by the company-states. To this extent, even hundreds of years later, company-states may share more with twentieth and twenty-first century multinational corporations than early modern contemporaries such as guilds and ad hoc merchant partnerships. The management of public debt, the foundations of later colonial empires, and current views and controversies regarding the state's monopoly on the legitimate use of organized violence were all shaped by or in response to the company-states.

What do the company-states tell us about big changes in the constitution of international society? These actors both helped form and were shaped by this society. A proper appreciation of their importance refutes the idea that the history of international politics can simply be understood in the same terms as the present, that is, that it can be reduced to interactions between sovereign states. As we show, it is impossible to see the company-states as merely mercantile concerns. Though they certainly were interested in profit, company-states were also inherently political actors, engaged in diplomacy, fighting wars, and governing substantial domains. What do the hybrid nature and motives of these actors mean for the conduct of international politics, and the character of the international society that they played such an important role in building? What does the rise and fall of company-states tell us about the broader forces that underlie and transform successive international orders? Disproportionately focused on Europe, scholars of international

1. Erikson and Assenova 2015: 11.

politics have had little to say in response to such questions—a lacuna that we rectify in this book.

Company-States: Their Rise and Fall, Failures and Successes

As hybrid institutions of expansion and imperialism, company-states were uniquely European institutions. This is not because, as is commonly thought, Europeans were the only, or even necessarily the most important, empire-builders of the era. Asian powers from the Ottomans, the Mughals in South Asia, and the Manchu Qing Dynasty in China constructed huge land-based empires in the early modern era. Yet none hit upon or mimicked the European company-state form.

Though the company-states in some cases amassed greater resources than the sovereigns that had initially chartered them (e.g., the English East India Company came to rule over a fifth of humanity), many more failed, or eked out a precarious, hand-to-mouth existence. Excellent studies of individual company-states (usually the success stories), or of particular regions, don't give us enough purchase to explain this variation in fortunes. Different chartered companies saw varied success across regions, within individual regions, but also across time. The greatest successes tended to be in the East rather than the Atlantic, but this was by no means uniform. After a period of decline and obsolescence in the late 1700s and 1800s, company-states seemed to enjoy a brief period of renewed popularity in the late nineteenth century, with the rise of the "new imperialism." Yet these later examples of the genre turned out to be pale imitations of their forebears, nowhere rivaling their early modern counterparts. Without understanding the reasons for failure, we may be blind to the true causes of success of some company-states relative to others, but also relative to other institutional forms, not least the sovereign state.

Closely related to the need to explain varying performance are unresolved controversies in accounting for the rise and fall of the company-states. What was the relative importance of functional concerns, like managing transaction costs, aligning the incentives of subordinates, and providing protection efficiently, versus

broader shifts in the climate of opinion inimical to the authority
and acceptance of company-states? Did this form fade and eventually disappear because it could no longer compete, especially with
the increasingly powerful sovereign state and its extra-European
imperial emanations? Or did the decline of the company-states
occur because this form became delegitimated as an outmoded and
troubling throwback to a previous era, out of keeping with modern
divisions of public and private?

Company-States Defined

What were company-states, these strange (to our eyes at least)
hybrid entities? How did they differ from more familiar institutions, like sovereign states or contemporary companies? Before we
launch into our story of their rise, spread, fall, and resurrection, it
is important to lay out the key features of the company-state, drawing closely on the pioneering work of the historian Philip Stern,
who first coined this term.[2] The defining characteristic was their
hybridity: company-states were granted what are now regarded as
fundamental sovereign prerogatives, most notably the authority to
wage war and make peace, while also being companies devoted to
making profit through trade, owned by and answerable to private
individuals. As we discuss later in the book, this hybrid identity,
and the existential balancing act it entailed, was both a source of
great strength and important vulnerabilities for the company-states
at different points in their history. Although by today's standards
it is incongruous for an institution to have such a combination of
public and private prerogatives, it is important to understand that
during the early modern period, sovereign powers were routinely
delegated and shared, while companies in their modern sense were
almost unknown.

Given that the concepts and divisions we take for granted today,
especially public and private, were understood differently centuries
ago, if at all, does it really make sense to apply these same terms
in a time when people had very different understandings of these
words? Acknowledging the dangers of anachronistic usage, we

---

2. Stern 2008, 2011.

nevertheless defend our use of these terms throughout this book on two grounds.

First, to fulfill our central goal of making an unfamiliar and historically distant phenomenon like company-states intelligible to a broad modern readership, we are compelled to use contemporary language and concepts. To a degree, the resulting risk of anachronism is both unavoidable and common in any study of historical international relations, where modern concepts like *globalization* and *international* are routinely invoked to communicate past realities to contemporary audiences.

Second, we have deliberately followed the standard practice of specialist historians. Thus Stern, from whom we take the term *company-state*, repeatedly and explicitly refers to these actors as being distinguished by their hybrid sovereignty.[3] The invocation of *public*, *private*, and *hybrid* in a manner consistent with our usage is likewise ubiquitous in a range of other specialist studies.[4] The trade-off between anachronism and accessibility is a challenge all students of the past confront, but is one that we have engaged here by following the best practice of the historians most familiar with the character and background of the company-states.

Mindful of the risks of anachronism, we nevertheless try to guard against its greatest dangers. We do so by recognizing and highlighting both the divergences as well as the parallels between historical and contemporary understandings of the public/private divide where they are relevant to our argument. Thus, the late medieval opposition between what we would now see as "public" versus "private" spheres was less sharply drawn, and configured around different polarities. Accordingly, we stress this difference as a crucial condition enabling the company-states' later emergence. Conversely, by the late eighteenth century, we see the rise of a recognizably modern "grand dichotomy"[5] separating the public realm of sovereign authority from the private realm of the self-regulating market. This development was crucial for helping to explain the

---

3. Stern 2008: 257, 283; 2009: 1157; 2015: 27.

4. See for example Weststeijn 2014: 14; Cavanagh 2011: 27–28; Wagner 2018: 15; van Meersbergen 2019: 882.

5. Bobbio 1997: 1.

company-states' subsequent decline, as well as for understanding their abortive late-nineteenth-century resurrection.

Company-states were a type of chartered company, in that they were created by a charter issued by the monarch or the legislature, with this charter functioning much like a constitution in specifying rights, powers, and privileges. The category of chartered companies was, however, an expansive one, encompassing a larger variety of actors than just company-states alone. Thus, while all company-states were chartered companies, many chartered companies were not company-states.[6]

Early regulated companies, such as those formed in England to trade with Scandinavia, Muscovy, and the Levant in the 1500s, generally kept capital and trading accounts separate with individual merchants.[7] In this sense, then, they did not actually have the legal form of companies, being rather closer to partnerships, and the label *regulated companies* is therefore something of a misnomer.[8] Conversely, company-states *were* bona fide companies, in that their members pooled capital and trading accounts, and the company-state acted as a coherent artificial person with its own separate and perpetual legal personality.

The most fundamental marker distinguishing company-states from the larger genus of chartered companies, however, was the scope of their sovereign powers. Company-states possessed powers normally associated with sovereign states, including the capacity to mint currency and administer civil and criminal justice within their forts and factories, as well as to raise military forces, wage war, and conduct diplomacy with non-European powers.[9] Company-states' charters typically granted them monopolies over trade in particular commodities (for example spices or slaves) in a given geographic area. The prospect of monopoly profits was seen as necessary to provide a sufficient incentive for investors to pay the substantial

6. Most famously, though it was later nationalized, the Bank of England began its life in the seventeenth century as a chartered company—origins reflected to this day in the fact that UK currency is still issued in the name of "The governor and company of the Bank of England."

7. Davies 1957: 28; Mather 2009: 5; Wagner 2018: 45, 119.

8. Mather 2009: 60.

9. Wagner 2018: 8.

up-front capital required for such a risky venture as long-distance trade. The geographic area over which exclusive trading privileges was often immense, such as all the lands and seas between East Africa and the west coast of the Americas.

Not merely historical curiosities, company-states pioneered the defining institutional features of the modern corporation that help to underpin the architecture of contemporary capitalism. The first of these was legal personality: in law, the company-states were regarded as a person, distinct and separate from their owners, and a person that outlived any individual owners. Closely linked to this was the notion of limited liability: debts or losses incurred by the company-state could not be assigned against the personal assets of owners. A further piece of the ensemble was the joint-stock owner-ship form, the modern conception of shareholding, whereby por-tions of the enterprise could be bought and sold among private par-ties. Each of these attributes was notably distinct from the typical merchant partnerships of the day, in which capital was temporarily pooled for individual voyages, and the partners risked all in every mission.

Rather than management being undertaken by all shareholders, company-states were run by a governing board in the metropole, often assisted by specialized committees working on particular aspects of business and administration. These boards issued direc-tions to subordinate officers in the field, who were responsible for day-to-day operations. Given the technology of the times, and the huge distances that separated central management from agents in the field, giving and receiving orders and reports might take many months in each direction. As a result, local agents enjoyed substan-tial practical autonomy. Managing this autonomy constituted per-haps the major governance challenge for company-states.

With their rather modern-looking corporate features, many scholars writing about the company-states have simply portrayed them as for-profit mercantile concerns. In contrast, we argue that it is essential to appreciate the importance of company-states' sov-ereign powers as well. Perhaps most obvious among these was the ability to declare and wage war. This power was often legally limited to fighting non-Christian powers, though in practice company-states often fought other Europeans. Another essential element was the ability to use violence to uphold their monopoly trading privileges against competing traders from Europe or elsewhere. Company-states often made enthusiastic use of these provisions of their charters, in some cases raising huge and potent armies and navies to carve out maritime and territorial empires. Relatedly, company-states had the authority to engage in diplomacy and make treaties with foreign powers, though once again reflecting the distinction between relations among and beyond European powers, this was often limited to non-Christian polities. Having conquered or settled territories, company-states had the powers to govern these areas and the inhabitants within them by administering criminal and civil justice, raising taxes, and minting coin.

Given these prerogatives, the company-states cannot be reduced to just a for-profit commercial enterprise along the lines of the modern-day corporation. But given the corporate features, and the profit imperative, neither can these actors be seen as just a state. Indeed, it was the combination of their powers that both accounts for much of their institutional success in conquest and commerce, but also was a major contributor to their later decline. In an environment where people subsequently came to see states and companies as fundamentally different sorts of actors with fundamentally different goals, company-states found themselves increasingly under pressure to fit a template of either a public or a private actor. Their hybrid institutional identity turned from an asset to a liability.

The Argument Summarized

Why did company-states emerge in the seventeenth century as a qualitatively new means of advancing European expansion? Why did they then spread throughout Asia, Africa, and the Americas, and experience such variable success in these different regions? Having been vanguards for European expansion for over 150 years, why did the company-state subsequently slide into irrelevance and then extinction in the mid-nineteenth century? And finally, why did company-states then enjoy a late but abortive resurrection with the onset of intensified European inter-imperial rivalries from the late nineteenth century? In providing summary answers to these questions we foreshadow the broad brushstrokes of our argument.

THE ORIGINS AND RISE OF THE COMPANY-STATE

Company-states emerged from a particular historical conjunction: a permissive ideational environment, the spur of increasingly globalized European geopolitical competition, and European rulers' limited capacity to project power across the seas.

For company-states to emerge as a distinct institutional form, Europeans first had to be able to even imagine the idea of granting sovereign powers to profit-seeking entities. They could do so because such arrangements accorded with a composite conception of sovereignty as a bundle of separate privileges rulers could delegate, sell, or otherwise alienate to privileged subjects that was predominant throughout early modern Europe. Consequently, an exploration of this mental universe forms our starting point.

By the early seventeenth century, Europeans were thoroughly familiar with rulers' assignment of what we would now classify as sovereign privileges to merchant and aristocratic elites, and also with the delegation of rights and responsibilities of conquest. This medieval inheritance made the idea of the company-state possible. But it was the sustained uptick in geopolitical competition in early modern Europe, especially following the rise of the globe-spanning Habsburg imperial conglomerate, that sparked concrete Anglo-Dutch efforts to translate this possibility into reality.

European rulers scrambled to win control over extra-European resources to help meet the challenges of military competition. However, early modern European rulers lacked the means to project power across continents. Consequently, this period spawned diverse institutional experiments. Company-states emerged from the early 1600s as the most prominent and consequential means of bridging this gap between rulers' grasp and their reach. These entities assumed the financial risks and provided the military muscle for exploration and trade. In theory, if often not in practice, the extension of monopoly privileges to company-states underpinned their profitability.

Individual company-states varied dramatically in their longevity and profitability. The stunning early successes of the first company-states from the 1600s inspired widespread imitation among European powers. What accounts for these successes?

By dint of their hybrid character, company-states possessed a range of institutional advantages. In their limited liability corporate structure, company-states had the potential to mobilize the substantial sums of "patient" capital necessary to fund highly risky overseas enterprises. Company-states also innovated mechanisms for aligning the incentives of far-flung and self-interested individual agents with those of their corporate employer. Finally, in an age in which trading often required fighting, these institutions benefited from developing a formidable in-house capacity for organized violence.

Nevertheless, these institutional advantages needed the right kind of environment in which to fully flourish. Maritime Asia provided such a milieu. As it was more distant from the Atlantic locus of European geopolitical competition, maritime Asia provided company-states with a degree of insulation from the interference of home-state sponsors (both rulers and corporate boards of governors). The risk that company-states would have their profits destroyed by being co-opted into the disputes over their state sponsors was correspondingly reduced. Besides the empowering effects of distance, political conditions in early modern Asia also contributed to the company-states' early success. In exchanging local powers' protection in return for ritual submission, company-states were able to inveigle their way into Asian commercial networks, and skim vast profits as arbitrageurs mediating the Europe-Asia trade.

THE SPREAD OF THE COMPANY-STATE

How and why did the institutional form of the company-state diffuse so widely? As noted, one of the reasons that this form is so important is because it was so common: almost every major European ruler chartered at least one company-state at some point, and the resulting institutions were active in almost every region of the world. The early successes of the English and Dutch East India Companies served as a dazzling precedent and model. Rulers calculated that in replicating the form of these trail-blazing company-states, they could also replicate their success. The resulting multiplication of company-states was especially prominent in the Atlantic. On both the African and American shores of this ocean, Dutch and English rulers reproduced the same template they had used earlier to create new company-states, while many other nations made their own bids using this same model. Despite being almost exact institutional copies of the company-states of the East, the results were far more varied in the Atlantic. This variation reflected two main factors.

First, to be commercially successful, the company-states had to have enough autonomy from their chartering home states to focus on commercial success, including the use of violence in achieving this end, rather than being subordinated into unprofitable strategic missions at the behest of rulers. Without this autonomy, company-states tended to fall into a vicious circle. A lack of autonomy meant that they were used as instruments of rulers' geopolitical and military aims, which meant that the companies were commercially unviable, which made them more financially dependent on rulers, who were then even more likely to use company-states as instruments of national policy in loss-making missions.

The second major factor was the international political context in which company-states operated, which was different in the Atlantic compared with in the East. In particular, geopolitical competition among Europeans in the Atlantic region was more intense at an earlier stage than in the East. This environment of intense military competition complicated the existential balancing act inherent in company-states: reconciling the pursuit of profit and power. After all, for company-states, violence had to be a means to a particular end, specifically commercial success. To the extent that company-states pursued war or geopolitical aims for their own sake (as a matter of choice, or as was forced upon them by circumstance), they made losses, which ultimately meant they went broke, or were bailed out by the state, with a corresponding loss of autonomy.

THE FALL OF THE COMPANY-STATE

Whereas the early modern period was dominated by the company-states' rise and worldwide spread, from the late eighteenth century onward they progressively vanished from the international stage. The forces that conspired to destroy the company-states were geopolitical as well as ideational, but also reflected the company-states' increasing redundancy in the face of European states' growing capacities for direct overseas expansion and rule.

From the mid-eighteenth century, the global dimensions of European inter-state rivalries intensified, complicating company-states' trade-off between power and profit. There was also a more general ideational shift in European (especially British) conceptions of political legitimacy from the mid-late eighteenth century. With the East India Company's metamorphosis into a power ruling more people and territory than the British monarch, British elites had to rethink the character of sovereignty, and with it, the legitimacy and limits of company-states' exercise of sovereign powers. Sharper, more rigid, and more recognizably modern demarcations between the public and the private sphere consolidated, leaving ever less legitimacy for hybrid sovereigns such as the company-state. From their very beginnings, company-states had faced their share of critics jealous of the company-states' enjoyment of lucrative monopoly privileges. But from the late eighteenth century, the legitimacy of the companies themselves became an object of controversy.

Finally, the company-states declined as a result of their growing functional redundancy. In the early 1600s, rulers' powers for governance and transcontinental power projection were positively anemic. By the late eighteenth century, however, successive waves of European warfare had helped forge military-fiscal states, which could mobilize credit to pay for powerful national navies and armies that served as an instrument of the sovereign's will. At the same time, company-states had ironically helped hasten their own redundancy through their successes. The infrastructure company-states had built throughout Asia, Africa, and the Americas lay ripe for the plucking by aggrandizing and increasingly powerful European states. This combination of geopolitical competition (and a resulting sharpening of company-states' existential trade-offs), delegitimation, and creeping redundancy thus pushed the companies to seemingly permanent extinction by the mid-nineteenth century.

THE RESURRECTION OF THE COMPANY-STATE

With the fading out of the company-states, it might have been expected that this form vanished forever. In fact, however, a second wave of company-states was created in the context of the "new imperialism," the scramble for colonies in Africa and elsewhere in the late nineteenth century, a comeback that surprised even many observers at the time. Yet these second-wave company-states turned out to be only shadows of their early modern predecessors. None had anything like the commercial success, still less the military power or political influence, of the Dutch or English East India Companies. Although some second-wave company-states managed to survive for decades, they did so only at the expense of relinquishing their governing powers to in effect become "normal" private companies, or as a result of de facto or de jure nationalization. Why was there a new wave of company-states? Why were the achievements of these new company-states so modest by comparison with the earlier era?

Though there were many idiosyncratic, one-off factors at particular times and places, the primary answer to the first question was the combination of the new geopolitical environment both reflected in and produced by the scramble for colonies, and the corresponding promise of using company-states to exploit these new opportunities via imperialism on the cheap. Analogous to the early modern period, once again a new geopolitical environment created the opportunity, for some observers perceived as a necessity, to acquire extensive extra-European holdings. Governments sought to satisfy this perceived imperative, and gain the prestige and security benefits of overseas empires, while deflecting the costs to self-financing chartered companies. The reasoning, or at least the hope, was that the prospect of profits on the frontiers would draw in private capital to fund the new empires, in lieu of direct government spending.

Yet this revived enthusiasm for company-states was tempered by a deep ambivalence among governments when it came to delegating sovereign prerogatives. Unlike in the 1600s, understandings of the separate and distinct roles of companies and states, private and public entities, were much more clear and fixed by the late nineteenth century. Governments sought to deflect the costs of empire on to company-states, but were reluctant to cede powers of war, peace, diplomacy, and many other governmental prerogatives as they once had. Governments were now accustomed to conducting inter-state affairs and wielding monopoly public control of the means of organized violence. Both metropolitan government bureaucrats and frontier settlers were often hostile to the new chartered companies, challenging their authority and legitimacy.

The company-states themselves were often keen to pass the costs of protection and administration back to the public purse. Many sank under the burden of the costs of rule, or only survived as dependent instruments of their respective governments. In this sense, the new company-states were crippled at birth. States delegated fewer powers, and were much more willing and able to interfere even in relation to those they had. The company-states themselves were far more willing to slough off the responsibilities of sovereignty in favor of the single-minded pursuit of profit, or perhaps even more commonly the pursuit of government subsidies.

THE BROADER SIGNIFICANCE OF
THE COMPANY-STATES

In combination, the arguments about company-states presented above force a major re-think of how we conceive international politics. First, we emphasize the company-states' centrality as cross-cultural mediators in the creation of the world's first global international system. Company-states pioneered distinct but parallel practices for mediating inter-polity relations among European polities, versus those between European Christian and "infidel" polities.

Important earlier scholarship has identified the bifurcation between relations among European polities, versus relations between Europeans and civilizational "others."[10] We build on this scholarship by demonstrating the indispensable role company-states played in managing the latter, and in overcoming the formidable barriers of geographic distance and cultural difference in European expansion. As they spread throughout the Americas, Asia, and Africa, company-states proved remarkably versatile in adapting their commercial, diplomatic, and legitimation strategies so as to best ingratiate themselves with local allies and patrons. Adhering to a divisible conception of sovereignty and to territorially non-exclusive conceptions of rule, company-states were relatively well suited to strike diverse bargains with powerful non-European polities. This chameleon-like ability to adapt to local circumstances yielded a variety of accommodations with indigenous political

---

10. See, for example, Keene 2002; Stern 2008: 270.

and commercial elites. It was via these bespoke bargains—not through the unilateral imposition of European diplomatic or legal practices—that company-states helped knit the world together into ever-tighter webs of interconnection after 1600.

The second fundamental implication concerns the changing constitution of international society. For centuries, company-states were a crucial component of international society. Now they are absent and almost unthinkable. Tracing the arc of these actors reveals the inter-play between evolving conceptions of the public/ private divide, and shifting membership of international society. The most basic questions of international relations concern not so much the outcomes of particular games, or even particular rules of the game, but who counts as a participant. Early modern international society was a permissive environment in which various hybrids and semi-sovereign entities were prominent alongside sovereign states. In the course of the nineteenth century as a matter of law, political sentiment, and practice, international politics, especially war and diplomacy, was increasingly restricted to sovereign states. By the twentieth century this trend had resulted in the extinction of the company-states, and a more general prohibition on hybrid actors in international society.

Finally, and directly following on from the last point, the current international system may be exclusively composed of sovereign states, but that does not mean it was built by them. Despite a widespread amnesia, company-states were crucial in knitting together previously isolated regional international systems to build the first global international society. We now study this system without really understanding where it came from or who built it.

Plan of the Book

Having introduced the central puzzles and sketched out our answers, the rest of this book proceeds in a broadly chronological and thematic fashion.

Chapter 1 briefly examines the historical antecedents to the company-state. We analyze their constitutive features, and explore the reasons for the emergence of company-states as a discrete institutional form in early-seventeenth-century England and the United

Provinces of the Netherlands. Company-states sprung out of long-established traditions of delegating rulers' prerogatives. Nevertheless, company-states were precociously modern, and distinct from medieval antecedents.

Company-states emerged at a particular historical juncture in Western Europe's development. Their rise was facilitated by the conjunction of a permissive ideational context, powerful geopolitical pressures spurring European empire-building, and immediate functional needs arising from European rulers' anemic capacities for overseas expansion. For Europe's beleaguered Protestant polities in particular, the looming specter of Habsburg hegemony demanded an effective riposte. This threat demanded that the Habsburgs' opponents find a way of tapping into extra-European sources of wealth to ensure their own protection, prosperity, and survival. It was out of this disconnect between geopolitical necessity and Protestant rulers' puny capacities for expansion that the world's first company-states—the English and Dutch East India Companies—were born.

The remainder of this chapter focuses on examining and explaining the English and Dutch East India Companies' success in infiltrating the courts, ports, and bazaars of early modern Asia. We also explain why the Dutch company was so successful here in smashing its main European state-based rival, the Portuguese *Estado da India*. The vast geographic distances separating company-states from their faraway European sponsors made control of self-interested subordinate agents particularly difficult, and proved especially enervating for rigidly centralized hierarchies like the Estado da India. At the same time, the distance partially inoculated the companies against the interference and encroachment from state sponsors that too often doomed them to bankruptcy in theaters closer to Europe. Finally, conditions in Asian host polities themselves favored company-states' expansion. In the Spice Islands, the Dutch East India Company overcame indigenous resistance with genocidal violence, and won control over commodities (nutmeg, mace, and cloves) that were uniquely profitable. At the other extreme, the vast power of Asian terrestrial empires sheltered European company-states from local predation. This enabled them to establish fortified networks of self-governing city-colonies across the Indian Ocean littoral, providing toeholds for more far-reaching territorial conquests once Asia's empires faltered from the early eighteenth century.

Chapter 2 examines company-states' spread into the Atlantic and their varied fortunes in this region. As in Asia, company-states played a pivotal role in driving European expansion. The English Royal African Company and the Dutch West India Company were crucial facilitators of the trans-Atlantic slave trade. Both established networks of forts in West Africa, and entered into diplomatic and commercial relations with local rulers to win access to slaves. Further north, the Hudson's Bay Company sought to monopolize control over the fur trade, and at one point was nominally suzerain of territories approximating almost 10 percent of the world's land surface.

Notwithstanding their prominence as agents of European expansion into the Atlantic world, company-states did not fare nearly as well as they did in the East. They often faltered in the Atlantic world as a result of the interaction between company-states' innate institutional vulnerabilities and the political interference of European sponsors, which were closer and thus more able to exert direct influence. Distance did not insulate company-states from overbearing European sponsors to the same degree as in the East. This made the contest between company-states and Iberian statist offshoots far more even in the Americas, raising company-states' security costs in ways that proved ruinous for profitability.

A contrast was the relative success of the Hudson's Bay Company, which retained its charter powers and remained profitable for most of its existence until surrendering its sovereign prerogatives in 1869. It had largely refused to take up the military prerogatives allowed in its charter, consistently pursuing pacific relations with American Indian nations, and ducking combat with the French wherever possible. Its geographic isolation (the Bay was frozen over most of the year), and the fact that it never drew on state support, generally insulated it from both government pressure and political controversy.

Highly variable though their success undoubtedly was in different parts of the world, company-states were both ubiquitous and generally unremarkable agents of European colonial expansion at this time. By contrast, from the late eighteenth century to the mid-nineteenth, some of the world's most prominent company-states either went broke (the Dutch companies and English Royal African Company), or lost their sovereign prerogatives to metropolitan governments (the English East India Company and the Hudson's Bay Company). Accordingly, whereas chapters 1 and 2 respectively trace company-states' rise and diffusion, chapter 3 focuses on their decline.

Concentrating on the English East India Company's contested evolution following its conquest of Bengal in the mid-eighteenth century, decline reflected in part delegitimation in the face of changing conceptions of sovereignty and the division of the political and economic spheres. As noted earlier, company-states rose in an environment in which composite understandings of sovereignty predominated, and hard binaries between the public and private domains did not exist. But by the late eighteenth century, such ideas of sovereignty were yielding to more monolithic ideas that vested exclusive public power in the sovereign state alone. At least in Britain, the scandals accompanying the EIC's seizure of Bengal and ensuing misrule there forced British elites to engage far more systematically with conceptions of sovereignty, and distinctions between public and private power, than had previously been the case.

In 1800 most of the world remained outside of European colonial control. But from the Seven Years' War onward (1756–63), the entire globe was becoming increasingly integrated as a theater of conflict, marked by large-scale increases in the tempo, scope, and range of European geopolitical competition. This geopolitical consolidation—which quickened further with the onset of the revolutionary and Napoleonic Wars—made it ever harder for company-states to escape interfering metropolitan governments, and to reconcile the perennially competing imperatives of security and profit. In combination with progressive ideational delegitimation, sharpening geopolitical competition aggravated tensions inherent in the hybrid identity of the company-states, driving their decline.

The late nineteenth century saw various forms of chartered imperialism revived, as the globalized rivalries of the era pushed European colonialists into hitherto unconquered frontiers in sub-Saharan Africa, Southeast Asia, and the South Pacific. The resulting company-states were uniformly less successful in both commerce and conquest than their early modern predecessors. Nevertheless, their resurrection—however ephemeral—does beg the question as to why Europeans remained so persistently attracted to company-states.

With this concern in mind, chapter 4 addresses the company-states' abortive resurrection and the causes of their failure. Not only did the British return to the idea of company-states, but the Portuguese belatedly adopted this model, and so too in various forms did colonial newcomers like the Germans, Italians, and Belgians, from West Africa to the islands of the South Pacific. At a time of heightened geopolitical competition, company-states again seemed to offer rulers the prospect of conquest without cost. Governments could supposedly enjoy the benefits of colonialism, while deflecting the burdens of conquest and imperial administration onto privileged subjects empowered by charter.

Yet the company-states of the late nineteenth and early twentieth centuries were nearly all costly failures. Most had to be bailed out by home-state governments at considerable financial (and sometimes diplomatic) expense. While these tensions between profit and power were perennial, the normative constraints present by the late nineteenth century mandated a degree of home-state control over chartered companies that made this tension almost impossible to reconcile. The sharpening differentiation between the public and private spheres that had helped drive the original company-states' demise placed a normative straitjacket on their late-nineteenth-century successors. Nineteenth-century company-states were vulnerable precisely because they were anomalous—exceptional deviations from an increasingly fixed understanding of sovereignty. Humanitarian scandals such as that surrounding the abuses of King Leopold's Congo Free State merely compounded suspicion of private imperialism.

We conclude by first briefly revisiting our historical findings, before successively considering the significance of contemporary forms of company "rule," and drawing out the book's key findings and implications. These include the central role of company-states in mediating cross-cultural relations; the successive changes in the rules of membership of international society, which increasingly excluded hybrid actors in line with a sharpening public/private divide; and, finally, the degree to which the current sovereign state order has been built on now-forgotten company-states. In the past couple of decades especially, hybrid actors such as private military companies have attracted a great deal of attention (and sometimes opprobrium) as potential harbingers of renewed forms of corporate imperialism. The same is true of speculations about the viability of privately governed charter cities as a potential solution to the governance problems of fragile states. But claims of an imminent return to a world of corporate sovereigns are overblown. More importantly, their exaggerations are generally built on misunderstandings of the true magnitude and significance of company-states as the vanguard agent of European expansion, and the particular historical conditions that once made them possible.

A discussion of the study's larger implications, both for how we understand the "rise of the West" and how we might more accurately theorize the expansion of the modern international system, rounds out the inquiry. To the extent that we still live in a Western-dominated international order, this is at least as much the legacy of corporate imperialism as state conquest. Though many have theorized about the links between capitalism and colonization, very few appreciate quite how intimately these are embodied in the company-state. And while talk of companies ruling the world is currently a rather loose metaphor, surprisingly recently this was much closer to being a statement of historical fact.

The Rise of the Company-States

WHAT WERE THE ORIGINS of the first company-states? What explains their spectacular success as the spearhead of Western infiltration into maritime Asia? We begin by considering the conditions that made company-states possible as an institutional form. While company-states are an early modern phenomenon, their antecedents extend back to the late medieval innovation of the corporation, and more broadly to understandings of sovereignty as a bundle of divisible prerogatives, capable of delegation to a wide variety of actors. Company-states emerged from the patchwork sovereignty arrangements of medieval Europe, where rulers routinely shared power with a host of other actors, from the Church to universities, urban municipalities, and merchant guilds.[1] Power was neither territorially exclusive, nor bounded by the strict demarcations between public and private that later emerged in Western political thought.[2] In this sense, rulers' authority was "heteronomous," in contrast to the definite borders sharply delineating the domestic and foreign realms which define contemporary sovereign states. Likewise, medieval rulers commonly delegated responsibilities for coordinating long-distance trade and conquest to what we would now anachronistically call non-state actors.[3] The historical legacy of divisible sovereignty, coupled with rich traditions of

1. Harris 2009: 613.
2. Ruggie 1993: 150.
3. Bartlett 1994: 308.

corporate trade and conquest, together enabled actors to invent the company-state.

The next section outlines the early modern catalysts for the birth of the company-states. The rise of the Habsburg Empire, roughly coinciding with the confessional polarization of the Reformation, provided the immediate impetus for the creation of the first company-states in Protestant northern Europe. For England and the Netherlands, the Habsburg Empire represented a grave strategic and ideological threat, but also an exemplar of the immense benefits that could be had from extra-European commerce and conquest. Accordingly, rulers in both countries scrambled to develop institutions that could help them maximize their wealth and power across the seas. Lacking the wherewithal necessary to finance and direct long-distance trade and conquest themselves, English and Dutch rulers opted for a hybrid alternative, one that combined the powers of a sovereign with the commercial imperatives and financial resources of a merchant enterprise. Thus the company-state was born.

Next we analyze the company-state's institutional advantages over its chief alternatives, namely more statist forms of direct overseas expansion epitomized by the Portuguese, and ad hoc groups of merchant adventurers. The focus here is on the success of the Dutch and English East India Companies (the VOC and the EIC). Between them, these two company-states exemplified a revolutionary new form of "extended polity,"[4] that proved more capable of projecting European sovereignty claims over oceanic distances than its institutional rivals. Company-states internalized their own protection costs; mobilized the large sums of patient capital necessary to finance long-distance commerce; innovated new ways to manage the principal-agent problems entailed in governing far-flung networks of factories and forts; and customized their diplomatic strategies to insinuate their way into Asian host polities, either as suppliants, partners, or suzerains. In combining all of these advantages within a single institution, the Dutch and English East India Companies established a potent new means to extend their commercial and political influence to the farthest ends of the earth,

4. Greene 1986.

allowing them to access what were at the time the world's largest and wealthiest markets. It was the spectacular success of this first wave of company-states in Asia that proved their worth, and helped catalyze widespread imitation and the ensuing replication of the company-state form in the following two centuries.

Finally, we explain why maritime Asia proved a congenial environment for the company-states, and what this meant for the subsequent course of both Western expansion and Eurasian political development.

The Medieval Antecedents to Company-States

To understand the origins of the company-state, we must first examine the mental universe of the late medieval era, as well as the more specific intellectual innovation of the corporation. Institutional vanguards of long-distance trade and conquest in the late Middle Ages also served as important precursors for the company-states.

The combination of sovereign powers with profit-seeking is the signature feature of company-states.[5] Incongruous from today's vantage point, this combination becomes intelligible once it is located within the larger traditions of heteronomy prevalent in late medieval Europe. Heteronomy refers to a condition in which multiple centers of power and authority overlap and intersect within the same territorial space.[6]

The concept of heteronomy captures a European political order in which two fundamentally modern distinctions—the domestic/foreign divide and the public/private divide—were either absent or ill-defined. Political authority in Western Europe was defined by the prevalence of territorially non-exclusive forms of rule. The Church and Empire stood at the apex.[7] Beneath were a plethora of kings, aristocrats, city-states, city-leagues, merchant guilds, and other forms.[8] Diverse claimants asserted authority over subjects

5. See, for example, Stern 2011; Weststeijn 2014.

6. As an organizing principle, heteronomy differs from both the singular hierarchies that define imperial international systems, as well as the sovereign anarchy that characterizes state systems. Ruggie 1993: 150–51.

7. Folz 1969: 81–89, passim.

8. Bartlett 1994: 308; see also generally Strayer 1970.

within particular issue areas, rather than aspiring to an indivisible and absolute sovereignty within a clearly demarcated territory, as is the norm today.

Besides territorially non-exclusive rule, medieval heteronomy was also marked by the absence of anything approaching today's public/private divide. Modern conceptions of the market as an asocial and self-regulating domain of impersonal exchange between rational egoists were still centuries away. The largely feudal system instead assumed a fusion between what we would now distinguish as political and economic forms of power. Powerful actors, such as the Church, the Emperor, and kings, derived their political and military power in large part from their possession of landed wealth, and asserted extensive seigneurial power over the peasants who tilled the land.[9] The late medieval commercial revival fueled a proliferation of new institutions, from the Hanseatic trading league in the Baltic through to monopoly merchant partnerships, to help coordinate and manage long-distance trade.[10] These and other institutions had commerce as their core focus. But they nevertheless disposed of significant civil and judicial authority over their members, blurring distinctions between public and private power.[11]

The medieval era therefore allowed for diverse forms of governance, combining what we now see as sovereign prerogatives with extensive economic power. Early modern Europeans later drew freely from this heritage in developing new institutions such as the company-state. Even more directly, company-states were shaped by prior conceptions of the corporation within Western political thought. We understand the corporation as follows:

> A corporation is an association of individuals that has a legal entity distinct from the identity of these individuals. It has the capacity to own property separate from its individual members, can contract with third parties in its corporate capacity, and can regulate its internal affairs, discipline its members and resolve their disputes. A corporation has a

9. Duby 1978: 118.
10. See, for example, Spruyt 1994; Cavanagh 2016.
11. Cavanagh 2016: 498.

hierarchical and centralized governance structure through which regulations and decisions are made and agents are empowered.[12]

As early as the twelfth century, Western Europe had seen the resurgence of the corporation (*universitas*) as a distinct category of rights-bearing entity within the Western legal tradition.[13] The main impetus for the rise of the corporation (or at least its reconstruction out of revived Roman law) remains contested. Some historians attribute the corporation's rise to the growth of universities, cities, merchant guilds, and other organizations that had need of a secure legal personality at this time.[14] Others focus on debates within the Church, both concerning its independence and supremacy from the Empire, and also between advocates of papal monarchy and their opponents.[15] Setting aside this debate, the late medieval proliferation of collective associations soon entrenched the idea of the corporation in the legal and social fabric. The idea that groups could collectively claim the status of corporations, and exercise powers of governance, soon became integral to Western conceptions of political and legal authority.[16] The corporation would eventually provide an essential legal building-block for the company-state. It combined in the one form an artificial legal person that was constitutionally separate from temporal rulers, enjoyed a longevity surpassing that of any of its members, provided a means for members to pool their assets, and provided a delegated but hierarchical governance structure through which they could coordinate for common purposes.[17]

In its territorially non-exclusive rule, and the frequent fusion of political and economic functions, medieval heteronomy provided the permissive context from which something like the company-state could emerge. The corporation provided a constitutional and legal prerequisite for the company-state. Medieval forms of long-distance trade and conquest, typically spearheaded by what we would now call non-state actors, also provided precedents for the

12. Harris 2009: 612.
13. Berman 1983: 215.
14. Harris 2009: 612.
15. Harris 2009: 612; see also Ryan 2011: 236.
16. Harris 2018: 113.
17. Harris 2018: 113.

company-states. The High Middle Ages saw Latin Christendom's dramatic commercial and military expansion. During this time, its frontiers extended into Iberia, northeastern Europe and (temporarily at least) into the eastern Mediterranean and the Levant. It was not Christendom's most powerful monarchs that undertook this expansion. Instead, an eclectic consortia of actors took the lead. Bartlett notes: "It was thus the knightly-clerical-mercantile consortium, not the apparatus of kingly power, that orchestrated the most characteristic expansionary movements of the eleventh and twelfth centuries."[18]

The predominance of non-state actors in driving medieval colonial expansion is hardly surprising. For well into the late medieval period, there *was* no state to speak of in Europe. Kings had few powers of direct rule within the territories they claimed. Due to the dearth of literate administrators, bureaucracies remained rudimentary at best, and rulers had little capacity to raise the troops and funds necessary to wage wars of conquest.[19] Kings instead cobbled together makeshift forces from feudal levies and freebooters as needed.[20] As the economy remained primarily an agrarian and subsistence-based one, there were definite limits on the taxable wealth that could be channeled into warfare.[21]

These constraints together severely limited rulers' reach, motivating them to delegate responsibilities for both conquering and administering new territories. The issuance of royal charters thus emerged as a favored means for monarchs to outsource conquest and extend their nominal authority to new lands.[22] Royal charters also helped rulers to assert at least some control over a restive warrior autocracy, curbing the centrifugal tendencies that unfettered expansion might otherwise have brought.[23]

Besides territorial conquest, medieval Europeans expanded their involvement in long-distance trade. In particular, a Eurasia-wide commercial expansion during the *Pax Mongolica* drew Europeans

18. Bartlett 1994: 308.
19. Mann 1986: 393.
20. Mann 1986: 393.
21. Bean 1973: 217–18.
22. Hsueh 2010: 21.
23. Hsueh 2010: 21.

more deeply into much more extensive trading circuits.[24] This integration helped spur new institutions to coordinate commercial transactions over long distances, and to also manage the significant protection costs that came with them.[25] Elsewhere, unarmed trading diasporas served as the main conduits for long-distance trade.[26] But trading routes in the Mediterranean had long been violently contested, and increased trade here brought with it new forms of armed trading networks that often operated autonomously of their sponsoring rulers. Medieval Venice and Genoa in particular were famed for their far-flung networks of colonies throughout the eastern Mediterranean from the thirteenth century.[27] Especially pertinent to this inquiry, in Genoa's case responsibility for administering many of its overseas territories was outsourced to the Bank of St. George, a financial entity distinct from the republic itself.[28] These early experiments in armed commercial expansion provided important precedents for the company-states that forcibly extended European commerce into Asia, Africa, and the Americas from the seventeenth century.[29]

Finally, the late medieval commercial revival spawned other entities that anticipated the company-states in important aspects. In the Low Countries in particular, foreign merchants organized themselves into "nations" to enhance their negotiating power with local rulers.[30] The most pertinent example is the Merchant Adventurers that monopolized England's cloth trade to northwestern Europe down to the late seventeenth century.[31] As a regulated company it lacked the joint-stock form and the limited liability that eventually came to define the company-states, and in this sense was closer to a partnership.[32] Nevertheless, the Merchant Adventurers matured as a means of self-government for the English merchant diaspora. Empowered by a charter of privileges granted from the

24. Abu-Lughod 1991: 137.
25. See generally Lane 1958.
26. Curtin 1984: 146.
27. Curtin 1984: 116–17.
28. Verlinden 2008: 195.
29. Verlinden 2008: 195; see also Lane 1966; Lambert 2018.
30. Sutton 2002: 45.
31. Butman and Targett 2018: 4.
32. Davies 1957: 25.

Duke of Brabant, the Merchant Adventurers were allowed to hold assemblies, elect their own officials, and even "punish offences among themselves unless they involved life or limb."[33] Additionally, the Adventurers also served as the primary conduit for negotiating market access to the Low Countries and eventually also the German states.[34] In exercising some powers of diplomacy and self-government, the Adventurers thus foreshadowed the more extensive sovereign powers of the company-states.

Habsburg Imperialism, European Expansion, and the Rise of the Company-States

From 1500, three fundamental developments jointly created conditions for the emergence of the company-state. The first was a dramatic extension of Europeans' late medieval expansion, this time drawing them into interaction with American, African, and Asian societies. With the Iberian powers in the lead, Western Europeans steadily advanced into the Americas, their progress made easier by New World societies' catastrophic susceptibility to Old World diseases.[35] In Asia, meanwhile, Portugal carved out an extensive maritime protection racket throughout the Indian Ocean littoral in a bid to monopolize Europe's trade with more prosperous and commercially sophisticated Asian polities.[36] European expansion during this time also connected it more durably into African trading networks, laying the foundations for the trans-Atlantic slave trade.[37]

Second, sixteenth-century Christendom witnessed major geopolitical consolidation as the Habsburgs became Europe's dominant power. Through a series of dynastic alliances, they secured dominance over Iberia, the Low Countries, and swathes of central Europe, including title to the Holy Roman Empire.[38] In the case of Spain and Portugal (united in a personal union from 1580–1640),

---

33. Sutton 2002: 33.
34. Lloyd 2002: 312.
35. McNeill 1977: 208.
36. Crowley 2015.
37. Green 2011: 177–78.
38. Blockmans 2002: 36.

Habsburg authority brought with it possession of these kingdoms' vast empires in the Americas and Asia, thus dwarfing the wealth of European enemies.[39]

Third, from 1517, the Reformation bitterly polarized existing rivalries along religious lines. As England entered the ranks of the Protestant powers, the spread of Calvinism in the Spanish Netherlands fueled an eighty-year rebellion against the Habsburg monarchy, which ended only with recognition of the Dutch Republic's independence in 1648.[40] Successive French Huguenot rebellions at the same time plunged one of Europe's most powerful kingdoms into civil war, removing a major obstacle to Habsburg hegemony.[41]

For the beleaguered Protestant polities of England and the Netherlands, Habsburg power posed an existential danger. The Spanish Armada's botched effort in 1588 to support an invasion of England marks merely the most well-remembered instance of Anglo-Spanish antagonism from this time. As a weak and marginal kingdom on Europe's northern periphery, Elizabethan England lacked the extensive colonial possessions that would later make England a global power. Likewise, the monarchy itself remained weak, the English state yet to develop the key institutions that would later enable it to finance extensive wars on the Continent and beyond.[42] The Dutch—locked in their seemingly interminable rebellion against Spain—were in an even more precarious position.

The Habsburgs' empire also served as a compelling demonstration of the immense power and profit that could be wrung from overseas commerce and conquest. Their control over the silver mines of New Spain provided an enormous source of revenue to fund Philip II's wars of conquest. Spanish silver likewise enabled the Habsburgs to vastly expand their trade with Asia, particularly following the Ming Dynasty's serendipitous decision to convert China to a silver-based monetary system.[43] During the period of Iberian union (1580–1640), the Habsburgs were also able to skim profits from the Portuguese Estado da India, reaping lucrative

39. Parker 2000: 3.
40. See generally Koenigsberger 1955.
41. Koenigsberger 1955; see also Nexon 2009: 235.
42. Scott 2011: 3–4.
43. See generally Flynn and Giráldez 1995.

benefits from its dominance of the import of fine spices into western Europe. With an empire stretching from Mexico to Manila, the Habsburgs plundered vast resources from outside Europe.[44]

For powers such as England and the Netherlands, both threatened by Habsburg power and constrained by the limited military and fiscal resources available domestically, overseas expansion exercised a powerful attraction. In response, both powers resorted to privateering, another hybrid public/private solution that demonstrates the highly malleable character of this distinction that, like the company-states, was used to compensate for the scarcity of military resources under rulers' direct control.[45] Privateering was publicly authorized but (predominantly) privately funded and operated naval raiding against enemies' commerce. Private ships were granted an official letter of marque to pursue such action, often with a proportion of the resulting proceeds owed to the ruler.

Privateers collectively known as the Sea Beggars constituted the primary maritime arm of the Dutch revolt against Habsburg Spain.[46] English privateer-led commerce raiding inflicted significant destruction on the Spanish empire, as well as sometimes yielding massive financial returns for investors.[47] Thus private English vessels were authorized "to anoye the Kinge of Spayne and his subjects, and to burne, kill, and slaye, as just and needful cause shall require."[48] To cite the most famous example, Sir Francis Drake's 1577–1580 circumnavigation of the world was not merely a huge navigational achievement, but also an audacious smash and grab raid against the Habsburgs. Drake's predation netted a Spanish silver galleon off the coast of Peru, as well as a spice-laden ship in the Moluccas.[49] These assets together totaled 600,000 pounds on Drake's return to England, the equivalent of twice the Crown's annual revenues.[50] They also yielded the voyage's financiers (including Elizabeth herself) a return of 4,700 percent on their

44. Parker 2000: 3.
45. Starkey 2011.
46. Anderson 1995: 184.
47. Kyriazis et al. 2018: 346.
48. Rodger 2014: 9.
49. Kyriazis et al. 2018: 346.
50. Kyriazis et al. 2018: 346.

initial investment.[51] Indeed, so successful was Drake's adventure that the Crown authorized between 100 to 200 privateer vessels a year to raid Spain's Caribbean possessions between 1585 and 1604, while plundered Spanish cargo is estimated to have accounted for up to 15 percent of England's annual imports during this time.[52]

Privateering thus offered a lucrative and often effective means for England and the Netherlands to harry their Habsburg nemesis. But it was ill-suited to establishing a permanent presence beyond Europe. The Habsburgs' insistence on monopolizing trade with their colonies created enormous friction with other European powers. And for the English and Dutch in particular, it sparked a renewed search for institutions that could capture some of the huge profits from overseas expansion—a search that ultimately yielded the first true company-states.

The Institutional Logic of the Company-States

Geopolitical competition played a major role in driving England and the Netherlands to develop company-states. The immense commercial opportunities arising from rising European appetites for spices further reinforced these pressures. Ever since the Portuguese Estado da India had muscled its way into the Indian Ocean region at the end of the fifteenth century, European rulers and merchants had been aware of the great commercial opportunities to be had from trade in Asian luxury goods. Of these, the fine spices offered especially enticing prospects. Valued for their reputedly medicinal and aphrodisiac as well as culinary qualities, spices such as clove, pepper, nutmeg, and cinnamon were worth literally more than their weight in gold in European markets.[53] As low volume/high value commodities, spice cargoes could yield investment returns far superior to any available alternatives. Exotic objects of conspicuous consumption, for which there were no readily available substitute goods, these spices enjoyed inelastic and rising demand in Europe from the sixteenth through eighteenth centuries.[54] That

51. Kyriazis et al. 2018: 346.
52. Kyriazis et al. 2018: 346.
53. Chaudhuri 1985: 21.
54. Chaudhuri 1985: 21.

such spices could be cultivated in only a very limited number of environments placed a natural ceiling on supply, further sustaining high prices.[55] Finally, the success with which the Portuguese had used naval power to capture a large part of the Europe-Asia spice trade further fueled the temptations of other powers to follow Portugal's example, and carve out their own militarized trading monopolies in Asia.

As they enviously surveyed the Iberians' successes in Asia and sought to emulate them, English and Dutch elites confronted a range of formidable challenges that they eventually resolved through the invention of the company-state.

In planning to enter the maritime spice trade, the English and Dutch first had to face the daunting costs associated this endeavor. These costs began with the considerable outlay required to fund, man, provision, and equip the ships needed for commerce in Asia. Even for a one-off trip, such costs were high. An organized trading presence held out the prospect of lowering transaction and coordination costs.[56] But the infrastructure necessary to support such a project entailed substantial expenditures that England and the United Provinces could ill afford.[57]

Second, insecurity compounded the costs and risks associated with trade. Economic historian Frederic Lane calculated that protection costs constituted the single highest impost associated with trade in the medieval and early modern eras.[58] The absence of a common diplomatic or legal order across Eurasia contributed to this pervasive insecurity. Portugal's unilateral militarization of the Indian Ocean further exacerbated this challenge.

Third, commercial expansion into Asia involved great uncertainties due to Europeans' profound ignorance of Asian cultures, languages, political systems, diplomatic norms, and even geography. Successful commercial penetration in Asia demanded an institutional presence that could accumulate and internalize the

---

55. Chaudhuri 1985: 21.

56. Carlos and Nicholas 1988: 407; see also North 1990. However, for a more critical view on the efficiency of company-state monopolies over more open trading arrangements, see Jones and Ville 1996.

57. Carlos and Nicholas 1988: 411.

58. Lane 1958: 410–11.

intelligence its agents gathered, lest hard-won knowledge and experience be lost at the conclusion of every trading mission. This again counseled in favor of a permanent presence.

Finally, the vast distances separating Europe from Asia, and the considerable time (up to eighteen months) entailed in relaying messages to and from Europe, greatly impeded efforts to coordinate large-scale trade on a transcontinental scale. Commercial agents in preindustrial long-distance trade always had significant de facto autonomy from their masters at home. This raised the danger of official trading operations being undermined by principal-agent problems, in that agents faced powerful temptations to conduct their own private trade at the expense of their employers' (the principals') business.[59] Left unchecked, such principal-agent problems could corrode or even cripple long-term profitability.

The combination of financial expense, commercial and physical risk, uncertainty, and principal-agent problems together presented forbidding entry costs. Existing methods of conducting long-distance trade in maritime Asia also carried disadvantages.

For centuries, African and Asian merchants had conducted commerce in maritime Asia through far-flung resident trading diasporas. These networks relied upon the trust and reciprocal accountability inherent in extended kinship networks to mitigate principal-agent problems.[60] Trading diasporas had long enjoyed extensive rights of residence and self-government in Indian Ocean port cities. Host rulers extended their hospitality and protection in exchange for the enhanced customs revenues generated by foreign trade.[61] For the Dutch and English, however, it was impossible to merely copy this model of the trading diaspora. Cultural and linguistic barriers hindered European entry into these foreign trading systems. More directly, Portuguese violence in the Indian Ocean precluded peaceful commerce. This made trade and war inseparable, necessitating an institutional form that took account of this grim reality.

59. On principal-agent challenges as a problem even company-states struggled to surmount, see Jones and Ville 1996: 903–8; Adams 1996.

60. Curtin 1984: 146; see also Tilly 2005: 8.

61. Fisch 1992: 23.

A second alternative was *laissez-faire* trading, where English and Dutch sovereigns would simply give free rein to their merchants to independently mount their own trading missions to Asia. But such a model had important shortcomings.[62] Merchants were prone to inefficiently disperse their capital across a range of competing enterprises, as happened with private Dutch expeditions immediately before the formation of the VOC.[63] This would jeopardize the financial viability of these trading missions, and with it the customs revenues that both the Dutch and English sovereigns sought to secure. A *laissez-faire* model also raised the risk that the collective goods and infrastructure necessary to support trade with Asia would be undersupplied. The forts, factories, and embassy missions needed to secure and maintain access to Asian markets were expensive.[64] In the absence of direct state sponsorship, any commercial actor prepared to build this infrastructure would need a guaranteed return on this investment. This counseled in favor of a monopolistic solution.[65]

The Estado da India offered a final potential model for emulation. As Europe's first armed trading monopoly in Asia, it had established the great advantages that could be won from an organization that combined the prerogatives of trade, war-making, and diplomacy. The statist hierarchy the Portuguese built in Asia—with the viceroy in Goa as key intermediary between Lisbon and its outposts—demonstrated the viability of organizing a long-term trading monopoly over transcontinental distances.

Against these advantages, however, the Portuguese model also had weaknesses. The Estado da India was hostage to the creditworthiness of its royal proprietors. This creditworthiness deteriorated significantly in the late sixteenth century, owing to Philip II's expensive and ultimately unsuccessful efforts to establish European hegemony.[66] The result was that the Estado da India was starved of the capital necessary to sustain its position in Asia—especially

62. Wallerstein 1980: 47.
63. Boxer 1965: 22–23.
64. Carlos and Nicholas 1988: 401.
65. Jones and Ville 1996: 900.
66. On the Habsburgs' notoriously parlous finances, see generally Drelichman and Voth 2014.

when confronted with Dutch and English competition from the early 1600s. As a direct appendage of Iberian monarchs, the Estado da India also suffered from its sponsors' inattention, relative to more pressing challenges to their power in Europe and the Americas, and dreams of conquest in North Africa.[67]

These problems were to a certain degree idiosyncratic, but there were also some intrinsic weaknesses of the statist model. Most importantly, as a state monopoly, the Estado da India suffered mightily from principal-agent problems. The Crown's fierce protection of its monopoly encouraged endemic corruption among its agents, who were typically on short, fixed term, and non-renewable appointments, and thus faced strong incentives to steal and exploit all available commercial opportunities for personal advantage while they could.[68] This meant that the Portuguese were hemorrhaging revenue even prior to Dutch and English entry into the Asian trade.[69]

In the late sixteenth century, no single existing institution met all of the challenges involved in transcontinental commerce and conquest. But Europeans were familiar with a range of useful precedents. Consistent with European understandings of sovereignty as divisible and capable of delegation, royal charters provided rulers a means to stretch quintessentially sovereign powers—such as the prerogatives of law-making, diplomacy, and war—over long distances.[70] The chartered company-states would thus come to form an early modern iteration of a long-established practice, whereby "[t]he exercise of sovereignty was extended by dividing it." Rulers provisionally assigned privileges to non-state sovereigns in exchange for a portion of the tribute gained from expansion.[71]

The "trading post empires" of Venice and Genoa—and their more recent Portuguese incarnation in the Estado da India—provided another point of reference for the English and the Dutch.[72] These empires demonstrated that rulers could reconcile the imperatives

---

67. Winius 1971; Disney 2009; Subrahmanyam 2012.
68. Winius 1971: 169; Steensgaard 1973b: 67.
69. Steensgaard 1973b: 67.
70. Hsueh 2010: 21.
71. Halliday 2013: 269.
72. On "trading-post empires," see Curtin 1984: 128.

of trade and conquest by using naval supremacy to establish and maintain networks of entrepôts.[73] Late medieval regulated companies lastly provided a precedent for coordinating long-distance trade through commercial monopoly, as with the Company of Merchant Adventurers in the cloth trade referred to earlier.[74]

The medieval innovation of the corporation lastly provided a critical piece of intellectual and legal infrastructure from which company-states could be fashioned. The idea of the corporation was an essential prerequisite to the development of the limited liability joint-stock company, of which the company-states were the crucial early instances. In enabling shareholders to pool capital and risk, limited liability joint-stock companies enabled the English and the Dutch to mobilize and organize the capital from their merchant elites necessary to sponsor overseas commerce, and later conquest.[75]

The first company-states thus synthesized existing practices with new innovations to create an institution well suited for overseas commerce and conquest. Company-states' charters (renegotiated at regular intervals) endowed them with privileges from the sponsoring sovereigns.[76] These charters also conferred commercial monopolies. Monopoly aimed to secure the company-states' profitability, with the promise of profits from exclusive trading privileges offsetting the heavy costs of maintaining the infrastructure on which trade depended.[77]

Company-states would prove well adapted to addressing the challenges of managing protection costs and pooling and mobilizing patient capital. They managed protection costs by maintaining their own armed forces at land and sea, and exercised the prerogatives of war and treaty-making with non-Christian powers. Company-states employed violence defensively, to protect their ships, forts, and factories from local and European rivals, and to fend off interlopers that sought to undercut the company-states'

73. Curtin 1984: 128.
74. Sutton 2002: 32.
75. See, for example, Kyriazis and Metaxas 2011: 365.
76. Stern 2011: 10.
77. Kyriazis and Metaxas 2011: 365.

trading monopolies.[78] But they also used violence offensively, both to break the existing Portuguese maritime protection racket, and in seizing key ports, outposts, and centers of spice cultivation.[79]

The security of returns guaranteed by government-backed monopoly encouraged investors. This provided the necessary "patient" capital to finance company-states' operations.[80] The joint-stock structure meanwhile enabled investors to limit their liability in proportion to the assets invested, while providing them with a passive means of participating in and profiting from the company-states' success. Finally, the separation of ownership and management that the company-states pioneered enabled managers to concentrate on long-term growth rather than short-term profitability and dividend payments, providing a competitive advantage over unincorporated merchant adventurers.[81]

Company-states did not emerge all at once as fully formed institutions. Rather, they evolved through a process of haphazard improvisation and experimentation. It was well into the 1600s before the Dutch, and even more so the English, East India Companies achieved their mature form, combining all the signature strengths of the company-state. Moreover, we must note that the very first English joint-stock foreign trading companies of the sixteenth century had been failures, and provided little reason to anticipate their successors' later triumphs.

The first joint-stock companies—the Muscovy Company and the Levant Company—were founded in England in 1553 and 1581 respectively, and shared many of the same investors and directors.[82] The Muscovy Company aimed to discover a Northeast Passage to Asia and manage England's trade with Russia.[83] Together with the EIC and the Virginia Company, it jointly funded Henry Hudson's early exploration of the bay that later came to bear his name.[84] The Levant Company was granted a monopoly on England's trade with

78. See, for example, Stern 2011: 63.

79. Nijman 1994: 221.

80. Kyriazis and Metaxas 2011: 365.

81. Nijman 1994: 219.

82. Mather 2009: 37. In 1640 the Levant, Muscovy, and East India Companies had the same man as governor, Henry Garway (Wagner 2018: 35).

83. Butman and Targett 2018: 56–57.

84. Bown 2009: 65.

the Ottoman Empire, including caravans coming overland from the East, and it was responsible for the upkeep of the English embassy to the Sultan.[85] It was pressure from merchants of the Levant Company in late 1600 spooked by the early Dutch missions to the Indian Ocean that was the proximate driver behind the issuance of the EIC charter.[86]

Why did these companies abandon their joint-stock form? Pressure from those merchants left out of the initial share issuance for inclusion was seen as more easily accommodated with a regulated company structure. Neither company had the need for the large fixed investments that were required by the company-states (particularly fortified factories), and hence they had less need to pool their capital via joint-stock arrangements.[87] As a result, both lost their joint-stock character in becoming regulated companies with individual merchants bearing unlimited liability.[88] Importantly, neither the Muscovy nor the Levant Company had ever enjoyed the sovereign prerogatives that distinguished the company-states, especially those of war and peace.

The Company-States' Early Successes in Asia

Between them, the English and Dutch East India Companies were the most important vehicles for Western expansion in Asia, and the inspiration for the company-state's spread into the Americas and Atlantic Africa. The EIC was established in 1600, two years earlier than the VOC, but the latter initially overshadowed its English rival. The VOC was better capitalized, initially had a broader suite of sovereign powers, and pioneered company-states' mobilization of large-scale military violence for commercial ends.[89] Having won its empire in Asia earlier, the VOC also suffered from the fundamental trade-off between power and profit maximization earlier than the EIC, prefiguring in its decline the English East India

85. Devecka 2015.
86. Mather 2009: 40–41.
87. Davies 1957: 34.
88. Mather 2009: 60; Wagner 2018: 71.
89. The VOC's starting capital was roughly ten times that of the EIC. See Nijman 1994: 218.

Company's later fate. For these reasons, we begin our analysis with an examination of the VOC's development, before then turning our attention to the EIC.

THE DUTCH EAST INDIA COMPANY

Established in March 1602, the VOC emerged in the context of the United Provinces' ongoing war for independence from the Habsburgs. From the late sixteenth century, the Dutch had been waging large-scale naval warfare against Habsburg colonial interests in the Americas, and to a lesser extent Asia.[90] At the same time, increasing numbers of Dutch merchants had begun to intrude on Portugal's monopoly on the Asia-Europe trade. Between 1595 and 1602, approximately fifty ships leaving from Amsterdam alone successfully undercut the Estado da India, returning to Europe laden with Asian luxury goods.[91] Dutch success in turn spurred England to action, prompting Elizabeth I to issue the EIC's inaugural charter in 1600.

The EIC's origins and evolution will be explored separately below. For now, it is enough to note that the EIC's invention prompted the Dutch to rethink their established practice of pooling capital and naval resources on an ad hoc basis to finance one-off expeditions. This practice was in any case already proving problematic, with a surfeit of competing expeditions cutting into the profitability of each.[92] The newly-formed EIC threatened to further aggravate the problem. Accordingly, the Dutch States-General decided in 1602 to consolidate their Asian trading activities by establishing their own chartered company-state—the *Vereenigde Oost-Indische Compagnie*, United East India Company.

Though the VOC emerged in conscious imitation of the EIC, in practice it can lay claim to being Europe's first true company-state. At the top were the *Heeren XVII* (Gentlemen 17), a management committee drawn from merchant oligarchs originating from the Netherlands' constituent provinces.[93] The *Heeren XVII*

90. Peifer 2013: 87.
91. Gelderblom and Jonker 2004: 650.
92. Gelderblom et al. 2013: 1054.
93. Sgourev and van Lent 2015: 936.

determined the company's overall commercial and political strategy, with responsibility for financing and coordinating individual voyages left to local company directors prior to the VOC's full transition to a limited liability joint-stock company in 1623. Following the VOC's entry into Asia, it soon established Batavia (now Jakarta) as its regional hub.[94] There, a governor-general assumed overall responsibility for advancing the VOC's Asian interests, in consultation with a local governing committee (the twelve-man Council of the Indies).[95] In theory, the governor-general remained beholden to the instructions of the Amsterdam-based *Heeren XVII*. In practice, however, governors-general enjoyed extensive discretion, often pursuing aggressive strategies of territorial expansion in defiance of their distant nominal superiors.[96] As one governor-general wrote to the directors "The Gentlemen in the Fatherland decide things as they see fit, but we do things here as we best understand and decide them."[97]

Tracy notes that "In the Eastern Seas, no European enterprise was more willing to resort to war to gain its objectives than the VOC."[98] In conscious imitation of the Estado da India's seaborne protection racket, the VOC established its own system of compulsory passes to control shipping in the Indian Ocean, even while the company's propagandists (most notably Hugo Grotius) hypocritically condemned the Portuguese for infringing on the freedom of the seas.[99] From the early 1600s, the VOC captured Portuguese ports and forts at key chokepoints on the Indian Ocean littoral. The Spice Islands, Malacca, and Ceylon fell to the VOC, which also established outposts on the Cape of Good Hope and on the coasts of east and west India. Further afield, the VOC also briefly held Taiwan, and even managed to negotiate a permanent presence in Nagasaki, later the sole Japanese concession to Western traders

94. Nijman 1994: 219.
95. Sgourev and van Lent 2015: 936.
96. Sgourev and van Lent 2015: 936.
97. Quoted in Adams 1996: 17.
98. Tracy 1991: 2; see also Nierstrasz 2012: 44.
99. Nijman 1994: 221.

prior to the arrival of Commodore Perry's "black fleet" in Tokyo harbor in 1853.[100]

The VOC's motives for coercion were mainly commercial in character, a fact reflected in the diversity of its victims. Besides the Portuguese, the VOC also clashed with their English counterparts. In Ambon in 1623, the VOC waterboarded and then decapitated ten EIC employees (alongside nine Japanese and one Portuguese), before impaling the English captain's head on a spike, part of a ruthless strategy to win exclusive control over the Spice Islands.[101] The VOC was even more bloodthirsty in its treatment of local populations. Thus, from 1621, the VOC (using a combination of Dutch troops and Japanese mercenaries) almost completely exterminated the indigenous population of the Banda Islands, before resettling the islands with enslaved laborers from elsewhere throughout the Indonesian archipelago to work the VOC's nutmeg plantations.[102]

The VOC's appetite for violence marked the most conspicuous exercise of its sovereign powers, and reflected a mind-set in which war-making and profit-making were inextricably entwined. Indeed, this nexus between the company's military and commercial activities was so tightly integrated to prompt Jan Pieterzoon Coen, one of the VOC's earliest governors-general, to write to his superiors in Amsterdam: "Your Honours should know by experience that trade in Asia must be driven and maintained under the protection and favour of your Honours' own weapons, and that the weapons must be paid for by the profits from the trade; so that we cannot carry on trade without war nor war without trade."[103]

Besides the VOC's emphasis on war, its prerogatives extended to encompass the full range of other activities that we now ascribe to sovereign states. In the absence of the Dutch state, the VOC had the responsibility for conducting cross-cultural diplomacy and engaging in negotiations with local Asian rulers for commercial privileges.[104] Within its own extensive network of settlements,

---

100. Nijman 1994: 217.

101. Clulow 2007: 21.

102. On the VOC's willingness to massacre entire communities that resisted its monopolistic practices, see Burbank and Cooper 2010: 159–60.

103. Boxer 1965: 96.

104. Blussé 2014; Andrade 2018; van Meersbergen 2019.

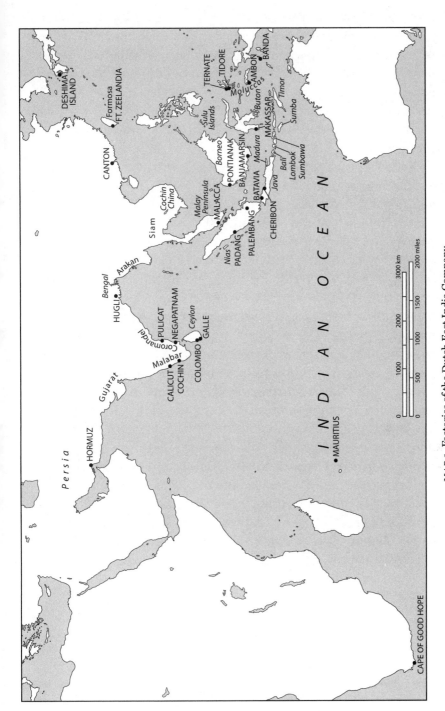

MAP 1. Factories of the Dutch East India Company

forts, and factories, the VOC also administered civil and criminal justice, and coined its own currency.[105] By 1608, the VOC already maintained forty ships and 5,000 men under arms in Asia.[106] This figure rose to 150 ships and 15,000 men by 1644, and to 200 ships and 30,000 men by 1700.[107] Although the VOC's military capabilities paled in comparison with Asia's leading empires, they were sufficient to command the high seas in Asia, and to overawe the VOC's European rivals.

Endowed with sovereign prerogatives, the VOC was nevertheless far more than just the Dutch state's instrument in Asia. For the duration of its existence, profit remained the VOC's primary driver, and the interests of the company's shareholders consistently took priority over all other considerations, including the strategic interests of the Dutch state.[108] Thus, following the Portuguese crown's separation from the Habsburg monarchy in 1640, the United Provinces' strategic interests counseled for a rapprochement with Portugal to allow the Dutch to focus their energies on prosecuting their war of independence from Spain. But as this alignment sat uneasily with the VOC's commercial rivalry with the Estado da India, the company consistently conspired to undermine Dutch diplomatic efforts in this direction, to free the VOC to continue its dismemberment of the Portuguese presence in Asia.[109] Likewise, the VOC's massacre of EIC employees in Ambon inflamed Anglo-Dutch relations at a time when both states' strategic interests in Europe were strongly aligned. Thereafter, the VOC resisted a legal settlement of the Ambon incident for decades and the payment of compensation to the VOC's English victims.[110] This inflamed Anglo-Dutch relations and fed popular English hostility to the Dutch, preventing a reconciliation between two Protestant maritime states that were otherwise natural allies.[111]

105. Ward 2009: 53.

106. Boxer 1965: 69.

107. Boxer 1965: 69.

108. Nijman 1994: 221.

109. Nijman 1994: 222.

110. Clulow 2007: 21.

111. Indeed, at one point in 1624, the Privy Council prevailed upon the EIC to cease publishing accounts of the massacre, for fear of inciting anti-Dutch riots in London. See E. Smith 2018: 619.

Tensions between the United Provinces and the VOC were real, and attest to the fact that the VOC was an entity distinct from the Dutch state itself, with its own constitution and interests.[112] But these tensions should not overshadow the larger story of the VOC's immense success in Asia for at least the first century following its establishment. As both an engine of commerce and conquest, the VOC won out over its European rivals in maritime Asia. The VOC's successes in relation to its Western rivals and Asian hosts testify to the company-state's dynamism as an institutional form.

Turning first to the VOC's success over its European rivals, the VOC shared with its principal Western competitors the advantage of being able to internalize protection costs through the maintenance of its own extensive military establishment.[113] Where the VOC enjoyed a distinct advantage over the Portuguese was in the depth of its pockets, and the larger military forces the VOC was ultimately able to mobilize. Though smaller and better-armed Dutch ships enjoyed some marginal technological advantages over their Portuguese rivals,[114] it was the VOC's superior capacity to finance its military forces that helped it to prevail.

At the peak of its power, the VOC spent somewhere between a fifth and a third of its budget on military expenditures.[115] That it could reliably sustain such expenditures for a protracted length of time gave it great advantages over the Estado da India, an entirely state-based enterprise that had to compete for scarce crown revenues with a range of other Portuguese concerns, most importantly preserving independence from Spain after 1640, but also fighting to protect its possessions in Brazil and Africa.[116] By contrast, the VOC could concentrate its attention and resources exclusively on expansion in Asia.[117]

The second key strength of the company-states was their unmatched capacity to mobilize large sums of patient capital. The separation of ownership from management, possession of

---

112. Weststeijn 2014; Clulow 2014.
113. Pearson 1990: 86.
114. Glete 2000: 171.
115. Mostert 2007: 11.
116. Winius 1971: 117; Cook 1994: 144.
117. Burbank and Cooper 2010: 159.

an independent legal personality, and limited liability structure enabled the company-states to raise large sums of capital that could be continuously re-invested.[118] The VOC's state-backed monopoly on the Europe-Asia trade gave capital-holders the confidence they needed to invest large sums of money into the VOC.[119]

Finally, the VOC flourished as a result of the existence of tight inter-locking ties linking the United Provinces' political and commercial elites. That Dutch political and commercial elites were bound by close familial and patrimonial connections (and were indeed often indistinguishable from one another) provided a strong identity of interest between them.[120] Conversely, the Estado da India remained explicitly subordinate to the interests of the Portuguese monarchy, rather than embodying a shared interest between the monarch and the commercial class.[121]

Besides its institutional advantages relative to its European rivals, the VOC also enjoyed immense success due to its capacity to negotiate access into a wide variety of Asian host polities. For insinuation rather than conquest predominated as the VOC's typical mode of expansion. Here, the VOC and its fellow company-states benefited from Eurasia-wide customs of commercial extraterritoriality.[122] These customs made it possible for the VOC to secure a presence on the littoral periphery of Asia, and establish their network of forts and factories.[123]

Company-states' very existence as products of rulers' charters presupposed an idea of sovereignty as divisible, territorially non-exclusive, and capable of being shared and delegated among multiple actors.[124] Just as they negotiated sovereign prerogatives from their sponsoring states back in Europe, the company-states likewise proved capable of negotiating sovereignty deals with host polities

118. Kyriazis and Metaxas 2011: 365.

119. Undoubtedly, investor confidence was also strengthened by the incredibly close relationship between the United Provinces' political elite and the dominant patrician oligarchs running the VOC, who were frequently one and the same. See Pearson 1990: 85.

120. See generally Adams 1994.

121. Disney 1977.

122. Fisch 1992: 23.

123. Ward 2009: 10.

124. See generally Weststeijn 2014.

in Asia.[125] What is most notable about these deals is their variability, and the company-states' chameleon-like ability to adapt to the demands and opportunities that diverse local contexts presented.

This was clear not just in the commercial and political bargains the VOC and other company-states struck, but also in the legitimation strategies they adopted to win local acceptance. As they spread throughout Asia, VOC employees familiarized themselves with indigenous vocabularies of rule in order to help slot themselves into local hierarchies. Driven by profit, and unencumbered by the hubris that came with direct possession of a royal title, the VOC could happily submit to a foreign monarch such as the Mughal Emperor without fear of embarrassment or loss of prestige.[126] Likewise, in contrast to the Iberian monarchies, the VOC was not hostage to any expectation that it proselytize in the course of expansion. On the contrary, VOC officials trampled a crucifix on the insistence of their Japanese hosts to symbolize their submission, and so secure exclusive trading privileges with the Tokugawa Shogunate, and likewise were willing to kowtow to the Chinese emperor.[127] Indigenous traditions of authority varied yet again in the Indonesian archipelago. There, long-standing traditions of foreign rule by "stranger kings" eased initial local acceptance of the VOC's suzerainty in some polities, the VOC passing as a fictive "grandfather" and paternal patron to local intermediaries.[128]

Notwithstanding its great successes, it is important to acknowledge that the VOC was hardly immune to the challenges of long-distance commerce and conquest, of which the most notable was the principal-agent problem. Like the Estado da India, the VOC struggled to monitor and discipline its far-off and poorly paid agents, and suffered from a host of problems, ranging from endemic corruption through to large-scale desertion, that corroded its performance over time.[129] The VOC's seventeenth-century domination of the Europe-Asia maritime trade made the VOC so profitable that

125. Blussé 2014; Clulow 2014; van Meersbergen 2019; Matsukata 2018; van Ittersum 2018.

126. van Meersbergen 2016: 71.

127. Clulow 2014: 17.

128. Kian 2008; see also Henley 2004: 85–144.

129. Burbank and Cooper 2010: 161.

its directors could temporarily ignore their agents' internal corruption as a second-order nuisance.[130] By contrast, the quickening pace of commercial and military competition in the eighteenth century forced efforts to address this challenge.[131]

Thus, under Governor-General Willem von Imhoff (1742–1750), the VOC permitted its employees to engage in private trade in areas where the Company was already unprofitable, or where it could not effectively enforce its monopoly.[132] These tentative efforts at liberalization (inspired by the more liberal policies of the EIC) aimed to retain employees' loyalty by granting them some scope for legitimate personal enrichment alongside their duties to the company.[133] Ultimately, these reforms failed to arrest the VOC's falling profitability,[134] with the VOC's decline being driven by broader contextual factors (discussed in chapter 3).[135]

THE ENGLISH EAST INDIA COMPANY

The VOC's early triumphs overshadowed the EIC. Though founded earlier than its aggressive sibling, the EIC substantially lagged the VOC in capitalization and militarization, and also in the accumulation and exercise of sovereign powers.[136] Forced out of the Spice Islands in the 1620s, the EIC was compelled to diversify its trading operations from fine spices, to encompass textiles, tea, and eventually opium.[137] The EIC was ultimately the vanguard of European colonial expansion in Asia in the eighteenth and nineteenth centuries, as well as the eventual focal point for criticisms that led to the company-state's wider delegitimation as an institutional form. The EIC also proved better at managing principal-agent problems than the VOC, enabling it to align the interests of the Company and

130. Burbank and Cooper 2010: 161.
131. Nierstrasz 2012
132. Sgourev and van Lent 2015: 944.
133. Sgourev and van Lent 2015: 950.
134. On the broad range of reforms that the VOC pursued in the eighteenth century to mitigate principal-agent problems, see generally Nierstrasz 2012; Wezel and Ruef 2017.
135. Sgourev and van Lent 2015: 951.
136. Nijman 1994: 218.
137. Kyriazis and Metaxas 2011: 370.

employees more closely in a way that helped ensure its commercial dominance in maritime Asia by the mid-eighteenth century.[138]

In 1600, Elizabeth I granted a royal charter to the EIC endowing it with a monopoly on England's trade with the East.[139] Initially limited to a fifteen-year term, the EIC's monopoly was later made permanent, subject to review and renewal of its charter every twenty years.[140] The geographic scope of the EIC's monopoly was immense, encompassing the Indian and Pacific Oceans, and even extending to possession of a colony (St. Helena) in the Atlantic.[141] Having been forced out of the Spice Islands by the 1620s, the EIC refocused the bulk of its commercial activities on South Asia.[142] There, the EIC gradually built up a profitable presence under the protection of successive Mughal Emperors in northern India, and in partnership with petty local rulers (*nayaks*) in the south. From the EIC's establishment of its first fortified settlement in Madras in 1644, the Company progressively established a network of forts and factories stretching across the Indian Ocean littoral. In 1661, the EIC gained control of Bombay from Portugal via the English Crown, following the marriage of Charles II of England to Catherine of Braganza.[143] The company's establishment of a factory at Calcutta in 1690 further consolidated the EIC's presence in India, with Madras, Bombay, and Calcutta becoming the company's three principal headquarters (or presidencies).[144] Despite this expanding geographical reach, the EIC's territorial holdings in India and its accompanying armed forces were minimal before the 1740s.[145]

The EIC's transformation into a large-scale empire, and its pernicious reputational consequences for the company-state as an institutional form, await consideration in chapter 3. For now, we confine ourselves to a consideration of both the key commonalities the EIC shared with its more successful Dutch rival, as well as the main differences that distinguished the two.

138. See generally Erikson 2014.
139. Stern 2011: 8.
140. Stern 2011: 10.
141. Stern 2011: 21–22.
142. Kyriazis and Metaxas 2011: 370.
143. Stern 2011: 22.
144. Barrow 2017: 15.
145. Lawson 1993: 66.

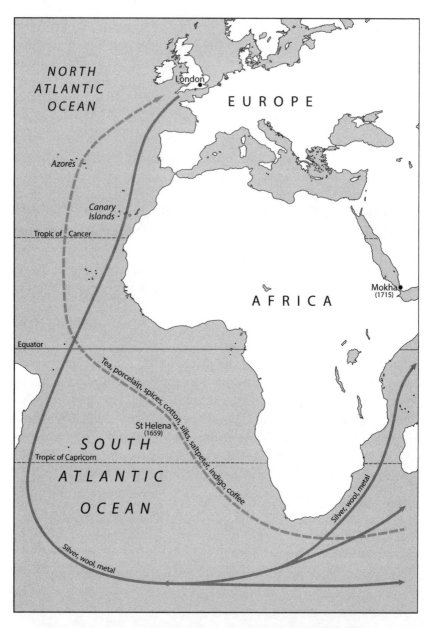

MAP 2. Trade Routes and Factories of the English East India Company

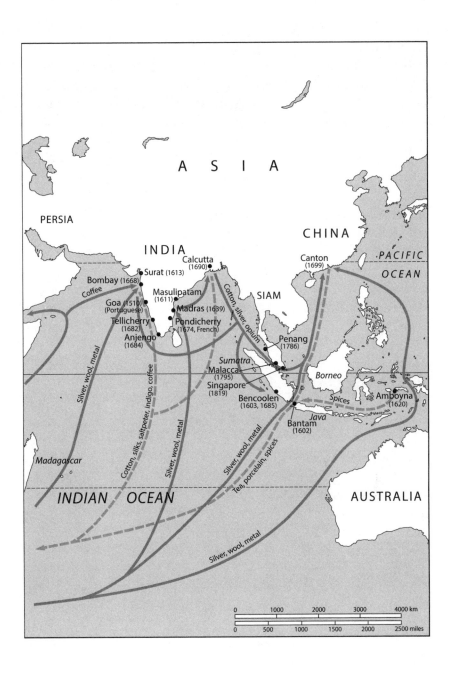

PERSIA

ASIA

INDIA

CHINA

PACIFIC
OCEAN

Calcutta
(1690)

Canton
(1699)

Surat (1613)

Bombay (1668)

Coffee

Masulipatam
(1611)

SIAM

Cotton, silver, opium

Goa (1510)
(Portuguese)

Madras (1639)

Tellicherry
(1682)

Pondicherry
(1674, French)

Penang
(1786)

Anjengo
(1684)

Sumatra

Silver, wool, metal

Malacca
(1795)

Borneo

Cotton, silks, saltpeter, indigo, coffee

Singapore
(1819)

Bencoolen
(1603, 1685)

Spices

Amboyna
(1620)

Silver, wool, metal

Java

Bantam
(1602)

Silver, wool, metal

Madagascar

Tea, porcelain, spices

INDIAN   OCEAN

AUSTRALIA

Silver, wool, metal

0   1000   2000   3000   4000 km

0   500   1000   1500   2000   2500 miles

The EIC's initial business model was built on arbitrage, and depended on securing and enforcing monopolistic trading privileges. Given the complete absence of the English state in Asia, it was left to the Company to serve as the Crown's alter ego, playing the roles of cross-cultural diplomat and (very occasionally) conqueror as well as merchant. The EIC's sovereign privileges included the rights to administer civil and criminal justice within its territories, with a mark of its sovereignty being that litigants and defendants had no right of appeal to the Crown's courts back in England.[146] Alongside possession of these sovereign privileges, the EIC—like the VOC—remained a distinct actor from the English state, with its commercial and strategic interests in Asia likewise sometimes bringing it into disagreement and conflict with the Crown.[147]

The EIC also possessed the generic institutional advantages of the company-state previously described with reference to the VOC. Like the VOC, the EIC competed successfully in the East on the basis of its abilities to internalize protection costs, and to pool and mobilize long-term capital. The EIC also profited from a similar ability to adapt to indigenous hierarchies in host polities. EIC officials proved no less adept than their Dutch counterparts in pursuing strategies to ingratiate themselves with indigenous hosts, whether as loyal vassals to the Mughal Emperor, or on the basis of more equal alliances with local rulers in south India and Southeast Asia.[148] Indeed, a brief contrast between EIC modes of diplomatic engagement with the Mughal India versus south and southeast Asian rulers powerfully dramatizes the EIC's diplomatic dexterity, and its ability to adapt itself to the diverse legitimation requirements it encountered in different Asian polities.

The Mughal Empire initially presented a forbidding challenge for the EIC in the early years of its commercial activities in India. Commercial access depended on the EIC's ritual incorporation as a participant in the Mughal court, and more specifically demanded recognition as a vassal to the Emperor.[149] Complicating matters further, by the time that the EIC arrived in India, the Portuguese

146. Stern 2011: 28–29.
147. Pearson 1990: 91–92.
148. Stern 2008: 282.
149. Roper 2017: 93–94.

were already ensconced at the Mughal court. As EIC employees tried to ingratiate themselves with the Mughals, the Portuguese made much of the ambiguity inherent in the EIC's character as a company-state, and sought to convince the Mughal Emperor that extending privileges to the EIC—as mere merchants—would detract from the imperial dignity.[150] In response, the EIC in 1615 solicited and financed the deployment of a royal ambassador, Sir Thomas Roe, to serve as a sovereign mask for the EIC at the court of the Mughal Emperor Jahangir.[151]

Despite decrying the Mughal Empire as an "overgrowne Eliphant,"[152] Roe nevertheless pragmatically accommodated Mughal demands for submission to advance the EIC's commercial interests. To take one example, Roe willingly submitted to the *khil'at* ritual, despite his initial misgivings, entailing the Emperor's conferral of special robes, reputedly suffused with the Emperor's charisma, to be worn by his loyal vassals.[153] In Roe's instance, participation in the ritual symbolically communicated the subordination of Crown and Company to the Emperor, and marked the EIC's incorporation into the Mughal Empire.[154]

For Roe, playing along with Jahangir's conceits of universal kingship was the price he had to pay to win the EIC commercial access to the Mughal Empire. Given that the EIC rather than the Crown had underwritten the cost of Roe's embassy, and that Roe himself had vested interests in the mission's success, he could reconcile himself to any collateral damage done to the English Crown's dignity in the course of negotiations. By the time Roe departed India in 1619, he had moreover achieved the EIC's main objectives, primarily winning rights of trade and residency in the key entrepôt of Surat, including the right to live in company factories "according to their owne [English] religion and lawes" without the interference of either the Mughals or European rivals.[155] So successfully did Roe discharge his mission that the EIC dispensed with

---

150. Roper 2017: 93–94.
151. Roper 2017: 93–94.
152. Subrahmanyam 2002: 71.
153. Truschke 2016: 89.
154. Truschke 2016: 89.
155. Roper 2017: 94.

deploying another Crown ambassador to the Mughal Empire for over a century thereafter. Forbidden themselves from building fortified settlements, EIC employees subsequently thrived under the Mughal Emperor's protection, and established an expanding network of commercial and political partnerships with local patrons. Having essentially temporarily borrowed the gravitas of the English Crown to win initial entry into the Mughal court, the EIC subsequently had no shame in ingratiating itself as a humble vassal with successive Mughal Emperors to preserve its privileges. This included participation in courtly rituals of obeisance, as well as the liberal invocation of Persianate forms of honorific address ("Emperor of ye Earth and ye Age," "The Divine Shadow of ye holy Prophet Mahomet") and self-deprecation ("ye least of your servants," "kissing ye Floor . . . w[i]th lipps of Respect and obsequiousness . . .") to keep the Emperor's favor.[156]

Where obsequiousness and ritual obeisance paid (quite literally) in their interactions with the Mughal Emperor, the EIC took a very different approach when dealing with local potentates in south India and Southeast Asia. By the time the EIC began to encroach on these regions, neither hosted rulers with the same universal pretensions as the Mughal Emperor. Instead, the EIC adapted to these very different host polities by calibrating its diplomatic strategies accordingly. Thus, in Madraspatnam (the future site of the Madras Presidency), company factors negotiated with the local ruler (*nayaka*) on more or less equal terms.[157] Indeed, in this instance the EIC ended up being "duped" into building up costly fortifications from the company's coffers—fortifications that helped lure commerce to the area, thus enriching the local king.[158] The EIC assumed these costs despite an apparent earlier agreement to share them with its indigenous partner, to the Company Directors' evident frustration.[159] Elsewhere, power relations between the EIC and local intermediaries were even more imbalanced, this time in the Company's favor. Thus, in Bencoolen (on the west coast of Sumatra) as early as 1685, the EIC went so far as to assume status

156. van Meersbergen 2019: 892.
157. Vigneswaran 2013: 109–11.
158. Vigneswaran 2013: 109–11.
159. Vigneswaran 2013: 109–11.

as the local raja, extending its "protection" to local communities who ironically sought outside help to protect them from the depredations of the VOC.[160] This process of empire by invitation fit a broader pattern within parts of the Indonesian archipelago, where, as with the VOC's experience, the existence of "stranger king" customs permitted foreign rule, often as a means of mitigating internecine local conflict.[161] Having themselves emerged from a milieu where sovereignty was divisible and territorially non-exclusive, company-states like the EIC could play the role of supplicant, partner, or suzerain as circumstances demanded, again aiding their spread throughout Asia.

Despite the broad similarities uniting the EIC with its more vigorous Dutch sibling, the EIC was a distant second to the VOC in the European competition for commercial and strategic dominance in seventeenth century maritime Asia. The EIC was less capitalized and less militarized than its Dutch rival.[162] Whereas the VOC had 30,000 men under arms by 1700,[163] the EIC directly employed no more than approximately 1,500 soldiers throughout all of its Indian forts and factories as late as the mid-eighteenth century.[164] The resulting lack of military capabilities necessarily curtailed the EIC's ability to either coerce locals into submission, or to mount a robust and consistent defense against the Dutch and other European rivals.

Company-states also continuously confronted the tension between maximizing power and profit. In its early decades, the EIC's London-based directors proved more successful in constraining their more bellicose employees than the Dutch. Whereas the VOC's agents made early and enthusiastic use of its war-making powers to expand in Asia, the EIC generally preferred to shelter under the protection of local rulers wherever possible to keep the overheads associated with military expenditure in check. This predisposition was reinforced following a disastrous and costly war with the Mughals from 1686 to 1690, which confirmed the EIC's

160. Veevers 2013: 688–89.
161. Henley 2004.
162. Nijman 1994: 218.
163. Boxer 1965: 69.
164. Lawson 1993: 66.

inability to impose its demands on powerful hosts through force of arms.[165]

The EIC also suffered from a more precarious position politically at home. Almost from the outset, the VOC enjoyed the steadfast support of the United Provinces' political establishment.[166] By contrast, the EIC's trading privileges provoked widespread resentment in England from the moment they were granted. In its early decades, the EIC endured the indignity of the Crown granting charters to competing entities, which the EIC was then forced to buy out.[167] As the EIC was the product of royal charter, it also inevitably became embroiled in the struggle for supremacy between Parliament and Crown from the mid-1600s.[168]

Offsetting these disadvantages, the EIC proved better able to manage principal-agent challenges than its Dutch rival. The EIC afforded its employees far greater latitude to engage in private trade alongside their company duties than did the VOC, which only grudgingly and belatedly tolerated such behavior from the mid-eighteenth century, when the VOC was already in relative decline.[169] Both companies suffered from endemic corruption—as indeed did every trading entity operative in maritime Asia during this time. But the EIC's relatively greater willingness to countenance its employees' private trading activities ameliorated this problem.[170] Additionally, private trading also generated positive externalities from which the Company itself benefited, yielding the information from which new trading routes and markets could be created.[171] Partially as a result of this tolerance of its employees' private trading activities, and the catalytic effects on market creation, the EIC's trade in Asia surged sevenfold between 1725 and 1760, eventually positioning it to subsequently challenge the Dutch for supremacy in maritime Asia.[172]

165. Barrow 2017: 17–18.
166. Pearson 1990: 85.
167. T. Roy 2012: 106–7.
168. Erikson 2014: 32.
169. See generally Adams 1996.
170. See generally Erikson 2014.
171. Wezel and Ruef 2017: 1,012.
172. Sgourev and van Lent 2015: 936. Tolerance for private trade was not the only solution to principal-agent problems facing company-states. Elsewhere, for example, the

The above comparison illustrates the bounded variation that characterized the company-states following their emergence at the start of the 1600s. Company-states shared generic properties that favored them over the statist Estado da India in the competition for Asian commodities and outposts in the seventeenth century. But much like sovereign states, company-states varied in their internal organization and comparative advantages, and also in their relative success. The VOC clearly stood as the world's pre-eminent company-state during the seventeenth century, both in terms of profitability and power.

While not an engine of monopoly and conquest on the scale of the VOC, in its first century the EIC did manage to carve out a profitable niche for itself. Following the disastrous war against the Mughals, and the buy-out of a rival English East India Company that had briefly emerged in the 1690s, the EIC's political and financial position stabilized. This allowed it to flourish as a medium for the Asia-Europe trade, as well as an active intermediary in intra-Asian commerce, but also as an increasingly important financier at home.[173] By the early 1700s, the EIC controlled an expansive network of forts, factories, and victualling stations across the breadth of the Indian Ocean littoral, and had diversified its trading activities to offset Dutch dominance over the Spice Islands.[174] The EIC had also managed to keep its military expenditures lower than the Dutch and Portuguese. Following the Mughal Emperor Aurangzeb's death in 1707, insecurity and disorder on the Indian subcontinent forced a departure from this policy, with the EIC eventually displacing the Mughals as India's dominant power. But prior to this time, EIC officials were generally happy to chart a less bellicose course than the VOC, remaining "newtors . . . endeavouring

---

Hudson's Bay Company employed a range of alternative policies (paying high salaries to managers and requiring high bonds from them to discourage private trading, extensive systems of employee monitoring, sustained attempts to cultivate a familial esprit de corps among HBC employees) that proved similarly effective in aligning the interests of principals and agents, without recourse to tolerating private trade. See generally Carlos and Nicholas 1990.

173. Bowen 2006: 30.
174. Smith 2013: 151.

to doe our business, with a great deal of submission and not much charge."[175]

Explaining the Company-States' Success in Maritime Asia

While individual company-states varied significantly in the success they enjoyed, the great profits and power that the Dutch and English East India Companies won in Asia vindicated the company-state as a powerful new instrument of European expansion. That the company-state was subsequently widely copied is further a testament to its early success (as discussed in chapter 2).

Indeed, inspired by the tremendous success of the Dutch and English East India Companies in Asia, rival European states quickly took notice, establishing their own embryonic company-states in response. The mixed record of these imitators nevertheless underscores that even in Asia—the arena where company-states experienced their earliest and greatest triumphs—failure and bankruptcy were more common than success. The reasons for these failures were manifold. In the case of the short-lived Portuguese East India Company (1628–1633), the same principal-agent problems and corruption that had bedeviled the Estado da India also crippled its company-state counterpart, and for similar reasons. For the Portuguese, and later also for the French as well, the company-state model of divisible and delegated sovereignty was a poor fit for rulers that remained wedded to highly centralized conceptions of monarchical power. In both the Portuguese and French cases, the king remained a key shareholder in his company-state progeny. Portugal's king invested 80 percent of the capital of the Portuguese company, with the bulk of remaining funds likewise drawn from government sources such as local municipalities.[176] The French king similarly contributed one-fifth of the capital to the French Company, as well as deciding on dividends and essentially forcing other shareholders to contribute more capital as required.[177] Both

175. Company official, quoted in Bassett 1998: 10.
176. Harris 2018: 110–111.
177. Harris 2018: 111.

thus remained de facto instruments of the monarchy, incapable of leveraging the productive tension between power and profit that underwrote the Dutch and English East India Companies' success.

Other European states, from Sweden and Denmark through to Brandenburg and the Republic of Genoa, also pursued power and profit in Asia with their own company-states. Some of these company-states managed a modest commercial success. To take one example, the Swedish East India Company (established 1731) made a steady profit by concentrating on the export of Chinese tea from Canton.[178] The Swedish company tried to avoid the EIC and the VOC by keeping a low profile.[179] Notably, these smaller company-states were also often founded by interlopers from elsewhere seeking to circumvent the trade monopolies of their home states. Thus, the Swedish company was founded by a Scotsman, while the Danish East India Company was likewise founded by Dutch immigrants.[180] These companies were an attempt to escape the stranglehold of the EIC and the VOC respectively through the establishment of rival trading concerns in outside jurisdictions, but without replicating the latter's full panoply of functions and powers.[181] Conversely, in instances when gadflies such as the Genoese company-state did genuinely threaten to encroach on the larger company-states' interests, the latter did not hesitate to use violence to coerce upstart rivals out of the market.[182] For company-states as for sovereign states, then, size generally mattered. For first mover company-states the VOC and the EIC, their greater capitalization and correspondingly greater military capabilities presented formidable barriers to entry for smaller polities that belatedly spawned company-state imitators in the hopes of emulating Dutch and English success.

As it turned out, no company-states, either in maritime Asia or ultimately anywhere in the world, subsequently enjoyed the same level of success as the VOC and the EIC. Why? How did the company-state's institutional advantages mesh so productively with the environmental context of maritime Asia?

178. Müller 2003: 31–32.
179. Müller 2003: 32.
180. Harris 2018: 111.
181. Harris 2018: 111.
182. Subrahmanyam 1988: 581.

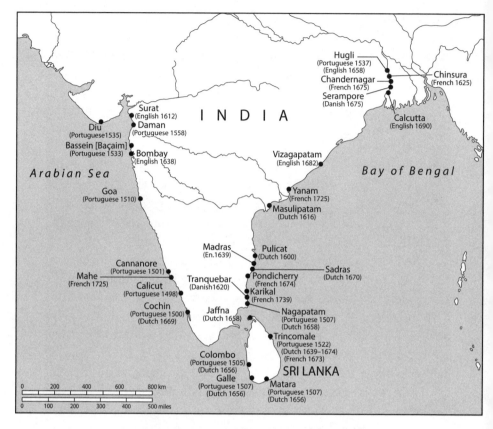

MAP 3. European Settlements in India, 1501–1739

In making sense of the company-states' success in the East, we must revisit some of their innate institutional strengths. Most fundamentally, company-states were hybrid creatures, combining sovereign prerogatives with the pursuit of profit. This dual mandate compelled company directors to manage a delicate balancing act between power and profit. Too great an emphasis on the former would see military overheads skyrocket, endangering the company's long-term profitability and therefore its existence as a viable commercial entity. Too great an emphasis on the latter, meanwhile, would endanger the company's ability to fend off armed European rivals, truculent local rulers, and private interlopers determined to undercut the company's monopoly. This would likewise threaten the company's profitability, and even its physical existence.

Notwithstanding the tensions that came with its dual mandate, the company-state's hybrid structure was valuable first because it made sovereignty stretchable over long distances.[183] This enabled the company-states to engage in the kinds of activities—diplomacy, war-making, and the administration of local civil and criminal justice—that stable commerce demanded, but that distant European rulers were as yet generally incapable of providing.[184] As we have seen, states *could* try to directly undertake these activities themselves, as evidenced in the activities of the Portuguese Estado da India. But the company-states' superiority came from their ability to not only match their statist opponents in internalizing protection costs, but also in their greater ability to mobilize patient capital and mitigate the principal-agent problems inherent in long-distance commerce and conquest.[185]

Lastly, as we have seen, the company-states' adaptability to a diverse array of local environments strongly favored them as vehicles of commerce and diplomacy. Having evolved out of European traditions of heteronomy and divisible sovereignty, company-states were constitutionally well-equipped to negotiate arrangements in which they shared sovereign prerogatives with or subordinated themselves to local host rulers.[186] This flexibility enabled them to play the role of vassals, suzerains, or partners in rule, as local conditions in host polities demanded.

At the time of the birth of the first company-states in the 1600s, Europeans had already been undertaking transcontinental trade and conquest for over a century. But the arrival of the company-state introduced a powerful new means for Europeans to further extend their strategic and commercial reach globally. Company-states offered Europeans a vehicle for expansion that cost rulers of home states nothing, while simultaneously providing a more reliable means of coordinating and controlling far-flung agents of empire than more conventional Iberian models of sovereign state–led colonization allowed. As chartered entities rather than

183. Halliday 2013: 269.

184. Stern 2011: 13.

185. Pearson 1990: 84.

186. Stern 2011: 13; Pettigrew 2015: 501; Pettigrew and Veevers 2019: 20; Nierstrasz 2019: 321.

direct extensions of their home states, company-states were more-over freed from having to uphold the dignity of sponsoring mon-archs and estates. This meant that they could play whatever role they needed to in non-European host polities to maximize their opportunities for power and profit. Company-states were thus constituted through a customized cluster of bargains, which their agents struck with different local rulers at the various nodes of the company-states' non-contiguous networks of forts and factories. A precociously modern bureaucratic chain-of-command oversaw these composite arrangements. The overriding imperative of the profit motive, hard budgets, and answerability to company share-holders helped to hold company-states together, preserving their overall coherence and unity of purpose.

Europeans were far from alone in embarking on large-scale proj-ects of imperial expansion in the early modern period. Indeed, in terms of the size of territories conquered, they were overshadowed by empire-builders such as the Ottomans, Mughals, and the Man-chus.[187] Rather than size, it was the transoceanic character of Euro-pean expansion that made it distinctive. Whereas Asian empires expanded territorially, Europeans were virtually alone in expanding via the high seas, and through coastal and island networks scattered through Asia, Africa, and the Americas.[188] The Iberian monarchies had established an early precedent for centralized and sovereign-state led overseas expansion—though in practice even then they often relied on delegating most of the costs and responsibilities of conquest to motley bands of adventurers.[189] But it was with the advent of the company-state that Europeans contrived an institu-tion capable of financing, coordinating, establishing, and managing militarized commercial monopolies on a transoceanic scale. This was an accomplishment all the more extraordinary for developing without the benefit of industrial-era technologies of communica-tion and transportation.

It was the interaction of these advantages with the congenial environment of early modern maritime Asia that catapulted the

187. On the success of non-European imperial expansion at this time, see generally Barkey 2008; Perdue 2005; and Richards 1993.

188. On non-European exceptions to this general rule, see Prange 2013.

189. Sharman 2019: 40–41.

company-states to success. Company-states first flourished in part due to a serendipitous compatibility between the contrasting preferences of the company-states and Asia's major terrestrial powers. Both Mughal India and Ming (later Qing) China were confirmed continental powers. With the exception of the Chinese fifteenth-century forays into the Indian Ocean, neither Indian nor Chinese rulers saw much value in investing the resources necessary to develop blue water naval capabilities.[190] Instead, both powers sought wealth and power principally on land, taxing agricultural production as their primary income source, with the customs from maritime commerce providing merely supplementary revenues.[191] By contrast, the company-states were maritime enterprises to their core, and relied on their niche military advantage in blue water naval power to muscle their way into Asian commerce.[192] These contrasting but compatible preferences made it possible for the company-states to negotiate a *modus vivendi* with Asia's most powerful terrestrial polities.[193] Elsewhere, where smaller Asian polities lacked either significant terrestrial or naval military capabilities, the company-states could dictate the terms of trade from the barrel of a gun. But most often company-states accommodated themselves to powerful Asian rulers, to the mutual enrichment of both.

Across the Indian Ocean littoral, many polities were segmentary states, understood as polities "in which the spheres of ritual suzerainty and political sovereignty do not coincide. The former extends widely towards a flexible, changing periphery. The latter is confined to the central, core domain."[194] Within such political systems, it was relatively easy for company sovereigns to work with local intermediaries to graft themselves onto existing hierarchies. The existence of "quasi-commensurable political imaginations" linking European company sovereigns and Asian host polities further aided this process.[195] Specifically, both European infiltrators and Asian hosts conceptualized political authority in explicitly

190. Richards 1993; Po 2018.
191. K. Roy 2012: 112.
192. Burbank and Cooper 2010: 162.
193. Phillips and Sharman 2015; Sharman 2019.
194. Southall 1988: 52.
195. Biedermann 2009: 266–67.

patriarchal and paternalistic terms. While their idioms of legitimation were distinct, these partial parallels enabled company sovereigns to position themselves either as dutiful "sons" or benevolent "fathers," easing their acceptance into host polities.[196]

Finally, in addition to the company-states' institutional advantages, and the congruences with host polities, the sheer distance from Europe also contributed to the company-states' successes in the East. Especially when contrasted to company-states' experiences in the Atlantic world, company-states operating in the Asian theater were at far less risk of being chain-ganged into the geopolitical conflicts of their state sponsors, with all of the ruinous financial consequences this co-optation entailed. Distance provided company-states the buffer necessary to focus on their own interests, even in cases where these interests conflicted with those of their sponsoring states. It also raised formidable barriers of entry for European competitors keen to undercut the companies' monopolies. While a perpetual small-scale nuisance, private interlopers struggled to compete with the company-states in Asia, given the higher costs and risks associated with trade so far from Europe.

Even within maritime Asia, however, there were important variations in the fortunes of the company-states. They found it easier to insinuate themselves into host polities across the Indian Ocean littoral than they did in Northeast Asia. The Chinese Empire and Japanese Shogunate were much less segmented polities than those of South Asia, and so they were far less willing to grant substantial powers of self-government to foreign merchant diasporas. Thus, in both the Qing Empire and Tokugawa Japan, Europeans were strictly confined to tiny toeholds (e.g., the VOC's strict seclusion on the island of Deshima in Nagasaki), and were kept as much as possible at arm's length from contact with local intermediaries.[197] That the company-states gained more comprehensive traction in the Indian Ocean littoral than in Northeast Asia highlights the critical importance of favorable local contexts in nourishing the company-states' success.

196. van Goor 1985: 196.

197. On the Dutch in Japan, see generally Clulow 2014. On the VOC's often fraught relationship with China, see, for example, Andrade 2004.

Serendipitously, much of seventeenth-century Asia presented political conditions that helped the companies manage the balancing act between commercial and military imperatives. In South Asia, the Mughal Empire provided conditions in which the East India Companies could thrive under the Emperor's protection. Likewise, following the Ming-Qing transition, the Manchus provided a stable political order that left some space for Europeans to trade on the Qing Empire's maritime fringe. In Southeast Asia, by contrast, many local polities were weak and therefore vulnerable to coercion. This obtained especially for the Spice Islands, which possessed lootable assets not found elsewhere. These contrasting extremes of power—either overwhelming strength or enticing vulnerability—fitted well with the company-states' demands to maximize profit while keeping military expenditures low.

By the eighteenth century, however, this happy alignment between the company-state's characteristics and imperatives and local conditions in maritime Asia would begin to fray. The Mughal Empire's slow motion implosion, and the growth of powerful new indigenous polities in its place, would eventually lead the EIC to embark on large-scale militarization and territorial expansion. This transformation would progressively undermine its very identity as a hybrid entity pursuing commercial and political goals. More generally, the intensification and intrusion of European inter-state rivalries into Asia from the mid-eighteenth century would upset company-states' balancing of power and profit. Whereas maritime Asia in the seventeenth century was the scene of the company-states' greatest triumphs, by the late eighteenth century it would be the setting for their most consequential and transformative scandals. But before this reversal of fortune, the company-state form proliferated, carrying European arms and influence from West Africa to Brazil and New York. The company-states' spread, and their critical role in knitting together an increasingly coherent and integrated Atlantic international system, forms the subject of chapter 2.

CHAPTER TWO

Company-States in the Atlantic World

ONE OF THE MOST NOTABLE aspects of the company-state was the extent to which this form was copied. Many early modern European rulers had ambitions to exploit the new overseas geopolitical opportunities, but few had the resources to do this directly. Especially given the intellectually permissive context for delegating sovereign powers and prerogatives, chartering companies seemed like an obvious way to square the circle between expansive goals and inadequate means. Having covered the origins of the first company-states and their spectacular success in the East, we now turn our attention to the Atlantic world, West Africa and the Americas. The generic company-state model, copied and reproduced from the European ventures in Asia, was fundamental to the construction of the Atlantic international system of trade, war, and diplomacy. In the Atlantic as in the East, company-states were once again at the vanguard of European expansion, and served to knit together political and economic relations in a way that came to constitute the first global international system.

Three companies were particularly important. The first of these, the Dutch West India Company (WIC), was active in Brazil, West Africa, the Caribbean, and North America from 1621. The second and third examples are the Royal African and Hudson's Bay Companies, founded in England in 1672 and 1670, respectively, and coming to hold possessions along the West African coast and present-day Canada. Between them, these three companies fought and traded from the Arctic Circle to the Amazon to Angola, contested Iberian and French positions in the New World as well as feuding with each other, and came to dominate the trans-Atlantic slave trade. The chapter also briefly considers other chartered companies whose ephemeral existence nevertheless often left enduring legacies for the shape of European colonialism, local polities, and these companies' home states.

In surveying the histories of these company-states, the first priority is to show how these hybrid actors were a modular institutional form. The replication and diffusion of the company-state form in the West reflected knowledge transfer in the deliberate emulation of an earlier institutional model.[1] The company-state was a generic institutional solution to a common geopolitical problem faced by European rulers. For example, if the WIC was based on the Dutch East India Company, it was itself the direct inspiration for the Swedish West India Company, and stimulated numerous suggestions in the English Parliament for an equivalent Atlantic company.[2] Some of the Danish company-states' charters were copied word-for-word from those of the Dutch companies.[3]

Second, we establish that it is impossible to properly understand the development of the Atlantic international system without properly acknowledging the central role of the company-states. This extends to both Europeans' relations with indigenous American and African polities, and intra-European struggles to exploit these new domains. It was a recurring feature of company-states' charters that their sovereign powers, especially war and diplomacy, were most extensive in relation to non-European powers. This feature both reflected and entrenched the dichotomy discussed by Keene about the distinct framing and conduct of international relations in Europe, versus relations in the wider world.[4] Scholars have spent much more time examining the first than the second, to the point where in some treatments relations between European states become the totality of international politics. It is one of the commonalities of early modern and nineteenth-century chartered companies that states were willing to delegate relations with

1. Klein 1981: 27; Steensgaard 1981: 260.
2. Bick 2012: 16.
3. Subrahmanyam 1989.
4. Keene 2002.

non-Western polities to company-states, but sought to keep more control of relations with other European powers.

Finally, we also seek to explain the varying performance of the company-states in the West compared with the East, and the contrasting patterns of success and failure within the Atlantic region. Our comparative treatment responds to the tendency in both Dutch and British historiography to write the history of European expansion in each region in isolation from the other.[5] Why did the company-states of the greater Atlantic never establish the kind of corporate imperium as their English and Dutch East India counterparts? Just as there are many reasons why modern corporations succeed and fail (quality of management, strength of competitors, technological change, general economic conditions, etc.), so too there is no one factor that predicted or determined the fortunes of company-states.

Nevertheless, comparing the two areas suggests that the relatively shorter distances in the Atlantic left company-states more vulnerable to both greater political interference from their home states, and greater competition from other European traders. Company-states depended on their monopoly trade to defray the costs of their military-administrative apparatus. Although these monopolies were nowhere perfect, in the Atlantic the barriers to entry were lower for unincorporated independent traders compared with the Indian Ocean. Furthermore, this fact meant that there tended to be more political pressure at home to dilute or revoke company-states' monopoly privileges, struggles that were particularly debilitating for the Dutch West India and English Royal African Companies. Added to this, European great power competition was notably sharper in the Atlantic. Company-states were more likely to be pressed into service in these struggles, or caught in the cross-fire, leading to higher costs and lower profits.

If there was notable variation in the fortunes of company-states between regions, what about the differential success of those in the same Atlantic theater? While many examples of this type were largely abortive, others like the Dutch West India and English Royal African Companies enjoyed a few decades of success, before

---

5. Stern 2006: 694; Greenwald 2011: 2; Pettigrew 2015: 494; Koekkoek et al. 2017: 83.

succumbing to chronic financial problems. These misfortunes were connected with the particular military character of the WIC, and the problems both companies had in maintaining their monopolies. In these cases and others, company-states became locked into a self-reinforcing cycle of failure. Subordination to the ruler's priorities often came at the expense of commercial success, which led to financial dependence on the government, which meant that political priorities displaced commercial ones even more.

In contrast, uniquely among the company-states, the Hudson's Bay Company (HBC) remains in business today, 350 years after it was initially chartered, even though it shed its sovereign powers after two centuries. Yet despite this longevity, and the vast area that came to fall under its authority, the HBC was a very different creature from the company-states of the East. Working with a much smaller capital base, the HBC consistently eschewed the ambitions of many other companies to conquer and exert authority over native polities, largely absented itself from great power struggles, and instead maintained a single-minded focus on profits from the fur trade. Geographically isolated in what was perceived to be a frozen wasteland, it made no call on government money, and this financial independence was central to its managerial autonomy in avoiding the vicious cycle of political dependence and commercial failure noted above.

The Dutch West India Company

The United Provinces of the Netherlands achieved global commercial and strategic success in the 1600s in large part thanks to the Dutch chartered companies. These broke the Portuguese dominance of the Eastern seas and made a powerful bid for supremacy in the Atlantic. According to Immanuel Wallerstein, a country of only 1.5 million people (compared with 10 million in Spain and Portugal, and 16–20 million in France),[6] engaged in a fierce struggle for national survival, nevertheless became the world's first hegemon.[7] It did so despite its loose confederal government, contradicting

---

6. Adams 1994: 319.
7. Wallerstein 1980; Nijman 1994.

the common presumption that equates modernity and political and military effectiveness with centralization. Wallerstein suggests of the Dutch Republic that "One would be hard pressed to invent a structure seemingly less likely to work efficiently or indeed work at all."[8]

For a moment in the mid-seventeenth century the Dutch West India Company (*Geoctroyeerde Westindische Compagnie*) seemed to have built another corporate empire on both shores of the Atlantic to match that of its sibling in the East Indies.[9] It held outposts and colonies in Brazil, the Caribbean islands, Guiana, the Gold Coast, Angola, the West African islands, and present-day New York.[10] Like its Eastern peer, the Dutch West India Company was crucially shaped by the struggle to preserve the Netherlands' independence from the former Habsburg masters. As with the VOC, those forming the WIC considered that trade and war were not only compatible, but actually complementary.[11] The rulers of the Dutch confederation were keen to take the fight to the Iberians' commerce and possessions in the New World, in particular aiming at the flow of American gold and silver that was so crucial in maintaining the armies of the Spanish king. Given this strategic imperative, and the ready model of the VOC available from 1602, in some ways it is surprising that the WIC was formed as late as 1621. This two decades long gap confirms the extent to which military imperatives were even more important for the WIC than for the VOC.

Discussions about an Atlantic chartered company had begun as early as 1606, with the starting point being a word-for-word adaptation of the VOC charter.[12] Subsequent variations, however, made the military-strategic character of the company even more prominent.[13] First, the charter put more emphasis on the aims of commerce destruction and conquest than had the VOC's, including an explicit commitment to piracy.[14] Second, the States-

---

8. Wallerstein 1980: 62.
9. Emmer and Klooster 1999.
10. Israel 1995: 934.
11. Boxer 1957, 1965; Emmer 2003; Schnurmann 2003.
12. Israel 1995: 326; da Silva 2014: 564; Bick 2012: 9–11.
13. Boxer 1957: 8; 1965: 25; Adams 1994: 336.
14. Rodger 2014: 10.

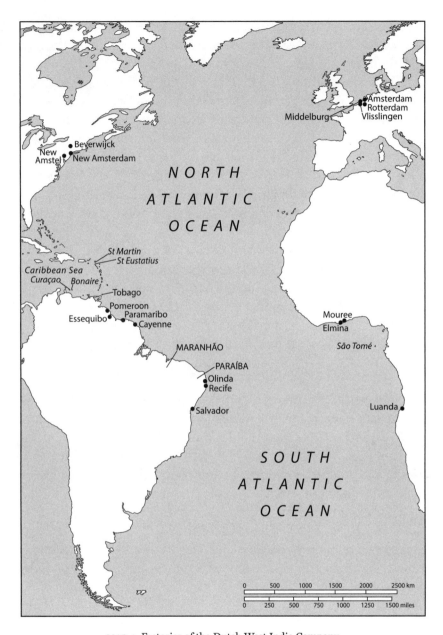

MAP 4. Factories of the Dutch West India Company

General was formally represented on the governing board of the WIC, wielding a tie-breaking vote, and held shares in the company. Third, the States-General committed to pay a direct subsidy, and to supply troops and warships, as long as the WIC paid the maintenance costs. The chartering of the new company was suspended in 1609, however, when the Dutch and Spanish struck a 12-year truce. The fact that the WIC was seen as having no peacetime rationale underlined the extent to which military-strategic concerns outweighed commercial.[15] The social background of the WIC's initial backers, disproportionately those expelled from the Spanish Southern Netherlands, cemented the commitment to war against the Catholic powers.[16]

Nearer the expiration of the truce, shifts in power between Dutch hawks and doves renewed the impetus to open another front against the Habsburgs in the Americas and the Atlantic using the same institutional model as the VOC. Once chartered in 1621 for a term of 24 years, the West India Company set about raising its initial capital of 7.1 million florins, slightly larger than the 6.5 million VOC had begun with, but an order of magnitude greater than the English East India Company, let alone the Royal African or Hudson's Bay Companies fifty years later.[17] Where the VOC had reached its target in a month, however, the newer company took two years. This rather tepid support reflected concerns among investors about the extent to which the new company would pursue piracy and conquest over profits and dividends.[18] These concerns were later shown to be well-founded.[19]

Notwithstanding the differences indicated above, the charter otherwise followed the precedent of the VOC in the suite of legal and sovereign powers conferred, including powers to make war and peace, engage in diplomacy, and carry out administrative and judicial roles in the lands it conquered. "Once again, commerce, capital, and state power worked hand in hand to produce another weapon in the struggle for Dutch independence, profit and influence, and

15. Emmer and Klooster 1999: 62; Schnurmann 2003: 487.
16. Wallerstein 1980: 51.
17. Boxer 1957: 13.
18. Boxer 1957: 12; Bick 2012: 11.
19. Adams 1994: 337; see also Nijman 1994: 226.

once again a company seemed to provide the proper and necessary means."[20] The WIC was granted a monopoly on trade from Newfoundland to the Cape of Good Hope, but also in the Pacific from the west coast of the Americas to New Guinea. Thus trading rights in the whole extra-European world were divided between the two Dutch company-states.[21]

The company was to be run by a board of 19 directors, the *Heeren XIX*. The distribution of directorships among different chambers reflected both the United Provinces' confederal structure, but also the financial and political power of Holland and Amsterdam in particular. The latter received eight votes on the board; Zeeland, four; the Northern Quarter, Maas, and Gronigen, two each; while as noted the representative of the States-General held the nineteenth vote. Although Amsterdam was clearly the most powerful, its dominance was somewhat less pronounced than in the VOC, or for that matter the States-General, where Holland provided over 58 percent of the total revenue.[22] Despite their formal rights, as with the VOC, the WIC often rode roughshod over the wishes of its shareholders, refusing audits and only reluctantly distributing dividends.[23]

THE WEST INDIA COMPANY ON THE OFFENSIVE

Having received its charter and raised the initial share capital, the new company wasted little time in going on the offensive. Though the Spanish were the archenemies of the Dutch, it was Portuguese shipping and possessions that bore the brunt of the WIC's bellicosity, as the company favored its chances against the weaker half of the Iberian union.[24] In line with the strategic plan of its initial "Great Design," in 1623–24 the WIC captured the Portuguese colonial capital of Bahia in Brazil, but were ejected the following year after the States-General mandated that ships destined for Brazil instead blockade the Iberian coast to assist the VOC.[25] Attacks on

20. Schnurmann 2003: 479; see also Israel 1995: 954.
21. Boxer 1957: 8.
22. Adams 1994: 331, 336; Bick 2012: 17.
23. Boxer 1965: 48.
24. Boxer 1965: 26; Emmer 2003: 3.
25. Adams 1994: 339; Odegard 2019: 93.

Puerto Rico and Elmina on the Gold Coast in 1625 were repulsed with heavy losses.

In the Americas the company had more success with their efforts to establish strongholds in New Amsterdam (New York) in 1624, and later in capturing the Caribbean islands of Sint Maarten in 1630, and Curaçao, Aruba, Bonaire, and Sint Eustatius in 1636 (still Dutch possessions to this day). The Company had earlier received its first outposts when the States-General transferred existing forts on the Hudson River and on the Gold Coast to the WIC.[26] In Africa the WIC took the Portuguese outposts of Cape Verde in 1624, and later conquered Arguin, Elmina, and São Tomé from the Portuguese in 1633, 1637, and 1641 respectively, the last mission mounted by Dutch forces from Brazil.[27] In a sign of problems to come, however, the costs of all this military activity substantially exceeded Company revenue.[28]

The West India Company's single biggest coup was to capture the entire Spanish treasure fleet in 1628, at 11 million guilders worth more than the Company's total capital. The haul included an astonishing 177,000 pounds of silver, 2 million hides, and over a thousand pearls.[29] The *Heeren XIX* celebrated with a 75 percent dividend over the next two years. Other WIC naval forces also enjoyed great success in privateering, especially against Portuguese ships bringing sugar back from Brazil. In total the Company took around 600 ships, most of them Portuguese.[30] Boxer puts the value of the ships taken 1623–36 at 7 million guilders, with their cargo at a further 30 million. However even excluding outlays made for the invasion and occupation of Brazil 1630–1652 (discussed below), he puts the WIC's costs over the same period at 45 million.[31]

Like its counterpart in the East, the WIC strongly opposed halting the campaign against Portuguese shipping and possessions after Portugal split from the Spanish monarchy in 1640. Again like the VOC, in defiance of Dutch national interests and orders from the

---

26. Bick 2012: 9.
27. da Silva 2014: 564.
28. Israel 1995: 327.
29. Boxer 1957: 30.
30. Schnurmann 2003: 487.
31. Boxer 1957: 66.

States-General, the WIC swallowed up Portuguese territory after the commencement of the 10-year truce, including lands in Angola, Brazil, and the island of São Tomé.[32] A WIC force from Brazil captured most of the Portuguese settlements in Angola in 1641, aided by allies from the local kingdoms of Kongo and Matamba.[33]

Administratively, by 1642 the WIC had separate regional commands in Angola, Guinea, New Netherlands, Brazil, and Curaçao.[34] The company's African holdings were divided into northern and southern jurisdictions under a "head factor," who was in charge of a hierarchy of factors, subfactors, and assistants, a commander of the garrison, and a chief merchant to manage trade.[35]

Despite its militarism, it is important to stress that the WIC was also genuinely oriented toward making a profit through trade. Its directors were shareholders, as was the States-General. It conducted extensive bilateral trade between the Americas and Europe, and the triangular trade that included Africa also. Although generally seen as a poor relation to the VOC and the trade with Asia, recent scholarship has argued that the Dutch Atlantic trade (both WIC and private trade) was more significant than that to the East.[36] The Dutch Caribbean islands, especially Curaçao, later became important entrepôts mediating trade between the different foreign imperial possessions, often in violation of their respective laws. Along with exporting slaves from West Africa, this last activity was the center of the second WIC's strategy in the Americas after the relaunch of the Company in 1674.[37]

THE WEST INDIA COMPANY IN BRAZIL

If any foreign theater was decisive for the WIC, it was Brazil. The WIC had briefly taken the Portuguese Brazilian capital of Bahia in 1624 before it was retaken by a powerful Spanish-Portuguese fleet the following year. Undeterred, by 1629 the WIC board had

32. Boxer 1957: 160; 1965: 87.
33. Disney 2009: 73–74.
34. Bick 2012: 129.
35. da Silva 2014.
36. Oostindie 2012: 28.
37. Schnurmann 2003.

resolved to make capturing Brazil the Company's main aim. They were attracted by the value of the sugar produced, and their low opinion of Portuguese military prowess, being described by the *Heeren XIX* as "not an enemy to be taken seriously."[38] In 1630 the WIC invasion force of 67 ships and 7,000 men quickly took the then-capital of Pernambuco, the richest area of Brazil. By 1637 after a more difficult period of guerrilla fighting against the Portuguese and their American Indian allies, WIC forces had captured half the districts of Brazil. By 1636 the company had spent 6 million guilders on its Brazilian campaign, and by 1638, with over 5,000 troops in place, Brazil represented more than half of both the Company's revenues and costs.[39]

With the restoration of Portuguese independence in 1640, negotiations brought about a 10-year truce with the Dutch, belatedly including the reluctant WIC and VOC (both companies' share prices fell as a result of the truce).[40] Desperate to stem its financial losses, the WIC then sharply reduced its Brazilian garrison. This reduction proved to be a false economy, however, when Portuguese under Dutch rule in Brazil rebelled in 1645, rapidly taking the countryside (including the sugarcane fields), and forcing the Dutch back into their coastal strongholds. The rebels were surreptitiously supported by the Portuguese colonial authorities in Bahia. The uprising proved a great embarrassment to the Portuguese king, however, who was set on peace with the Dutch so as to save resources to preserve independence from the Spanish. He seemed to regard the loss of Brazil as a price worth paying.[41]

By this stage, however, the WIC was almost broke and completely incapable of salvaging the situation in Brazil without state intervention.[42] In part this parlous situation reflected the fact that by 1648 the provinces were 6.5 million guilders in arrears in the subsidies they had promised to the WIC.[43] Absent financial and military support, company officials warned that all that

38. Boxer 1957: 37, 46.
39. Bick 2012: 196, 234.
40. Boxer 1957: 104.
41. Disney 2009: 226–27.
42. Odegard 2019: 94.
43. Boxer 1957: 217.

would be left of Dutch Brazil would be "the tears of widows, orphans, and other miserable, dejected persons."[44] For their part, the States-General had increasingly lost faith in the commercial and military management abilities of the *Heeren XIX*. Both the WIC and the States-General came to favor a merger with the VOC as a de facto bailout of the former.[45] Asserting its independence, the VOC was understandably unenthusiastic and vetoed the proposal, but it was forced to make a 1.5 million guilder payment in return for its charter renewal, money that was then used to finance a relief mission to Brazil in 1646.[46] This mission enabled the Dutch to hold on, but not to fundamentally improve their position. The resulting stalemate lasted for almost eight more years. Decisive action was vetoed by Amsterdam, whose representatives calculated that their interests were better served by peaceful free trade with the Portuguese than by a WIC victory and a Company monopoly.

Another reason why WIC control was so precarious was because so few Dutch settled the Americas, perhaps a peak of 15,000 including both Brazil and the New Netherlands in North America.[47] In contrast, 200,000 Portuguese had settled in Brazil by 1600, and 250,000 Spanish had migrated to the American mainland and Caribbean.[48] Without any prospect of relief, besieged, and running low on food, supplies, and money, Dutch forces in Brazil surrendered in January 1654. Creditors were only prevented from seizing WIC assets in the Netherlands the following year by order of the States-General.[49]

Even allowing for the fact that Dutch strength was drawn off in the First Anglo-Dutch War from 1652, contemporary observers and even the Portuguese themselves were surprised by their triumph over the WIC in Brazil, a notable contrast with the VOC's decisive victories over the Portuguese Estado da India in Asia.[50] The wider

44. Bick 2012: 76.
45. Adams 1994.
46. Boxer 1957: 187.
47. Emmer and Klooster 1999: 48.
48. Emmer 2003: 2.
49. Boxer 1957: 255.
50. Disney 2009: 229.

significance was that the Brazilian venture had not only taken all the profits from the WIC's other operations, plus the government's subsidies and the de facto transfer from the VOC, but also left the company deeply in debt. The WIC was never a significant military or naval power after this point.[51]

The Luso-Dutch struggle for Brazil briefly stimulated the Portuguese to mimic the company-state form. Such was the effectiveness of WIC and "private" privateers independent of the Company (whose motto was "A turd for trade if there is booty to be had!") during the war that the Portuguese king reluctantly acquiesced to setting up a chartered company.[52] Portuguese shipping losses were such that an escorted convoy system was needed, but the royal treasury was empty, and hence the need for private capital to plug the gap. The solution, more like an extortion racket than a genuine joint-stock company, was to provide former and current Jewish Portuguese merchants immunity from the Inquisition if they invested in the new venture. The 1649 charter of the Brazil Company gave shareholders no control over the running of the company, which issued only one dividend in its existence, and was in practice closely controlled by the king's officials.[53] It was always unpopular with the Church and most of the king's advisors, and with the passing of the crisis, the Brazil Company's monopoly and fiscal privileges were withdrawn, before it was later reabsorbed by the state. The general problem with this and other abortive attempts at Portuguese companies (like that in the East 1628–33) was that the Crown was never willing to surrender enough control to attract private investors, who were rightly concerned about these companies' precarious commercial prospects.[54] Unlike in the Netherlands or England, where the ruling oligarchy was closely merged with capital holders, the Iberians struggled to reconcile the different interests of these distinct groups.

51. Israel 1995: 935.
52. Boxer 1957: 201.
53. Boxer 1957: 209–12.
54. Disney 1977.

THE WEST INDIA COMPANY IN DECLINE

Compounding the WIC's problems in Brazil, in 1648 on the other side of the Atlantic the Portuguese managed to snatch victory from the jaws of defeat when a relief mission from Brazil surprised and routed Dutch Company troops in Luanda, thereby causing the collapse of the WIC's position in Angola.[55] While the WIC's remaining West African possessions were profitable, these profits were not enough to offset the losses incurred in Brazil.

In order to skirt the Company's monopoly, some Dutch investors began to go so far as to put their capital with Danish, Swedish, and Brandenburg company-states that were active competitors of the WIC in Africa.[56] In 1664 Dutch intervention did manage to recapture a string of coastal forts along the West African coast that English forces had taken the year before.[57] Yet here it was ships of the Dutch state rather than the WIC that were the instrument of victory in what became the lead-in to the Second Anglo-Dutch War (it would be over a hundred years later that Dutch state forces would render any such aid to the VOC).[58] Having been captured in 1664, the New Netherlands was formally ceded to England in the 1667 Treaty of Breda. In return the English ceded possession of Surinam to the Dutch, to be governed by the "Society of Surinam," a joint venture of the WIC, Amsterdam, and an aristocratic merchant family until it was nationalized in 1795.[59]

The Company itself had gone broke in 1674, declared "disbanded and destroyed" by the States-General.[60] Though a new company was founded under the same name, this second WIC was missing the same monopoly on trade, but also the sovereign prerogatives inherent to the company-state form, most notably the right to wage war: "The once dreaded war machine had become

---

55. Boxer 1965: 27; Disney 2009: 74.

56. Davies 1957: 11; Emmer and Klooster 1999: 64.

57. Israel 1995: 766.

58. Boxer 1965: 101.

59. Oostindie 2012: 34.

60. Odegard 2019: 88.

a harmless bureaucracy."[61] Shareholders received only 15 percent of the capital they had invested in the original WIC.[62] This second WIC lasted in vestigial form until 1791 before the remaining Dutch possessions passed under direct state rule.

The leading explanation for the failure of the WIC is the discord between Holland and the other provinces, especially Zeeland, that prevented adequate state support for the Company, especially in the pivotal Brazilian theater.[63] Thus Adams states:

> For a decade after 1645, I believe, the company could have won back Brazil if it had received a modicum of the economic and military support that the state was capable of providing. Portugal was a puny sea power compared to the United Provinces, and the Portuguese state was divided over what tack to take with the colonists. The WIC was thwarted not so much by the rebellion as by Amsterdam's and the VOC's refusal to provide the resources to counter it.[64]

Others, however, suggest more deep-seated factors were decisive, ranging from the persistent hostility of private Dutch traders, to the mercantilist policies of other Europeans, to the fact that European state rivalry was much more pronounced in the Atlantic than in the East.[65] As with the French and short-lived Iberian companies, the WIC came to experience a self-reinforcing dynamic of indebtedness, lack of commercial success, and dependence on the state.[66] Because the state was keeping the company afloat, national interests began to take precedence over commercial ones; because commercial concerns were displaced, the company became even more indebted, and hence even more dependent on the state. The shorter distances involved relative to the VOC accentuated the government's ability to influence the WIC.[67] This relative proximity and hence vulnerability to government interference helps to explain the more general success

---

61. Emmer and Klooster 1999: 60.
62. Odegard 2019: 97.
63. Boxer 1965: 50.
64. Adams 1994: 340.
65. Emmer and Klooster 1999; Nijman 1994: 226.
66. Howard 1976: 52; Blussé and Gaastra 1981: 8; Pearson 1990: 95–96; Israel 1995: 327.
67. Boxer 1965: 100.

of the Eastern chartered companies relative to their Atlantic counterparts.[68]

The Royal African Company

The English Royal African Company (RAC) was formed by England's restoration monarchy in 1672. It succeeded the Company of Royal Adventurers Trading into Africa, formed in 1660 with a re-issued charter in January 1663 under the leadership of Prince Rupert (of the Hudson's Bay Company's Rupert's Land fame).[69] The first royally-endorsed English slaving mission from West Africa to the Caribbean by Sir John Hawkins had taken place as early as 1562, and looser English merchant partnerships had been formed to exploit the trade with the area around Senegal from 1588.[70]

The earlier 1663 English African Company had played a pivotal role in the outbreak of the Second Anglo-Dutch War 1665–67. An English admiral acting for the Company of Royal Adventurers Trading into Africa had attacked Dutch WIC possessions in West Africa, thereby helping to spark the wider war.[71] The dispute arose because the WIC considered that a 1661 treaty with Portugal meant that they had inherited the monopoly on European trade with the Gold Coast. Acting in defense of their purported monopoly rights, the Dutch company sabotaged the trading expeditions of its English rival as well as the Danish African Company, in part to punish African rulers who had driven the WIC out of several of their forts.[72]

In response, and excited by reports of a "mountain of gold" in the Gambia, in late 1663 King Charles II sent a squadron of five Royal Navy ships under the command of Robert Holmes to protect the interests of the English company against the WIC, with the king taking the opportunity to increase his own shareholding in anticipation of future success.[73] Later accused of exceeding his orders, Holmes's mission had been highly successful in capturing WIC

---

68. Steensgaard 1981: 252.
69. Scott 1903: 242; Zook 1919: 13.
70. Davies 1957: 39; Carlos et al. 1998: 322.
71. Zook 1919: iii.
72. Zook 1919: 18.
73. Zook 1919: 18, 36.

ships and forts, including the WIC African headquarters of Cape Coast Castle, but also those of other European nations. However, the expedition precipitated Dutch retaliation in 1664–65, which undid all of the English successes bar the last. Samuel Pepys opined at the time that England had been "beaten to dirt . . . to the utter ruine of our Royall Company."[74] What had started as a dispute over monopoly trading rights between companies very quickly escalated to become a war between states. Here it is notable that like the WIC, the English state was much more closely involved in militarily supporting and directing its African chartered company than the English East India Company, when equivalent involvement came only from the mid-1700s.[75]

The resulting struggle wrecked the finances of the earlier English company, which in any case Davies dismisses as "more reminiscent of an aristocratic treasure-hunt than of an organized business."[76] In November 1665 Charles II instructed that all revenue from the Company's voyages should be directed to paying interest on the swelling debt.[77] With no hope of recovery, the company was wound up in 1671, clearing the way for a relaunch of the new Royal African Company with fresh capital in the following year, though some of the debts of the old company were assigned to the new one.[78]

By issuing the charter of a new Royal Africa Company in 1672 in the form of a joint-stock company-state, Charles II "wished to use a monopoly company to supplant the Dutch competition in the Atlantic trades, develop trade with the cash-rich Spanish Americas, and secure and expand English interests in Africa by establishing plantations there, thus supplying gold for the mother country as well as enslaved Africans for England's Caribbean plantations."[79] Added to this was a desire to secure sources of revenue for the monarch independent of Parliament. As with the Hudson's Bay Company, the RAC instantiated a vision "of overseas empire based

74. Davies 1957: 61.
75. Marshall 2005.
76. Davies 1957: 41.
77. Scott 1903: 242.
78. Bertrand 2011: 1.
79. Pettigrew 2013: 22.

upon . . . monopoly trading companies that expressed both the desire to extend state power overseas and the widespread belief in the importance of regulated overseas markets."[80]

As with the other company-states, the charter imbued the Royal African Company with the same fundamentally hybrid public/private character. The Company was again invested with prerogatives of war and peace in relation to non-Christian powers, once again demonstrating the different treatment of European and non-European polities.[81] It could hold any land within this area not already belonging to Christian princes, and was required to present any member of the royal family landing in Africa with two elephant's teeth (i.e., tusks). The new company was granted a monopoly (for a thousand years) on the trade between England and the whole of Atlantic Africa from Morocco to the Cape of Good Hope.[82] The main African goods to be traded were gold (still rumored to be in great quantities along the Gambia River), ivory, redwood dye, and pepper (malagueta), but it was the slave trade that came to dominate. The early efforts at trade, and again those in the 1720s, were bilateral between England and Africa. However the company came to depend on the "triangular trade," whereby goods from Europe (especially textiles) were traded for slaves captured by local African rulers, with the slaves then transported and exchanged with plantation owners in the Caribbean for sugar, which was then sold back in Europe.

Initial capital of £111,000 for the Royal African Company was raised from 200 noble and merchant investors, some Dutch, with this number of shareholders staying largely constant in the following decades.[83] This sum made the RAC the second most valuable of the English chartered companies at the time, behind the East India Company, but far ahead of the Hudson's Bay Company (this disparity in share value lasted into the 1690s).[84] The most influential of the RAC's backers was the Duke of York, brother of Charles II, later to take the throne as James II, who was both the first

80. Pettigrew 2013: 24.
81. Scott 1903: 245.
82. Pettigrew 2013: 4.
83. Norton 2015: 47.
84. Carlos et al. 1998: 323.

Company governor and the largest shareholder.[85] As the governor was largely a figurehead, the task of running the company was left to the subgovernor, deputy governor, and a board of 24 comprising the Court of Assistants, each elected from the shareholders on an annual basis. These then formed specialized committees (e.g., accounts, shipping, correspondence).[86] Though the lags in communicating with agents in the field were not as long as to the East, they were still substantial. Because of the winds and currents, letters from West Africa to England generally went via the Caribbean, taking about five months. A response to a specific query would take at least six months, and letters were often lost.[87]

As noted, as with nearly all of the chartered companies, a combination of commercial and imperial intentions lay behind the formation of the new company. Daniel Defoe, one of the company's strongest public advocates, reasoned that "Trade is carried meerly by Force, and you carry on your commerce as Princes make Treaties, Sword in Hand."[88] Yet compared to the Dutch West India Company, the English company was far less warlike. It tried to avoid conflict with both European rivals and the African polities on which it relied for the supply of slaves and other commodities, although at various points the RAC lost forts to the French (in Gambia in 1695 and thereafter in the 1720s) and Portuguese (in Angola in 1724), as well as suffering from attacks by European pirates.[89] The Company also suffered gravely during the wars with France around the turn of the eighteenth century, especially thanks to the actions of French privateers. Of the 183 Company ships sent from England 1688–1712, 45 were taken by the French and another 12 wrecked.[90] Asserting its sovereign independence, in 1705 the RAC reached a separate peace with its French equivalent, despite the ongoing war between their two home states, defending the decision via the argument that company-states "are impowered to make Treaties of Peace and Commerce (and War too upon occasion) . . .

85. Pettigrew and Van Cleve 2014: 618.
86. Davies 1957; Carlos 1994; Norton 2015.
87. Rönnbäck 2016: 1152–53.
88. Keirn 1988: 245.
89. Bertrand 2011: 11.
90. Davies 1957: 206.

as they find the same suit best with their respective Circumstances at the time, without regard to Peace or War in *Europe*."[91]

The Royal African Company came to maintain around a dozen fortified outposts and small military garrisons up and down the African Atlantic coast, the largest of which (numbering around a hundred) inhabited its African headquarters of Cape Coast Castle.[92] Company outposts along over 3,000 kilometers of coast in the Gambia, Sierra Leone, and Serbro had a factor and 10–20 men, with even smaller stations having 1–5 men.[93] Some of these outposts sheltered small settlements of free Africans who grew both food and commercial crops like indigo and cotton to sell to RAC staff.[94] The company also had its own ships. Its main priority was to exclude interloping private traders with naval patrols to forcibly defend the company's monopoly, sometimes conducted jointly with Royal Navy ships.[95] To this end, the Company had its own vice-admiralty courts, with no right of appeal to the English legal system.[96] It became a crucial player in the trans-Atlantic slave trade, as the RAC shipped more slaves than any other single European concern, around 188,000 individuals.[97] With a brief exception in the 1720s, the RAC did not aim at colonization or territorial expansion.

CHALLENGES TO THE ROYAL AFRICAN COMPANY

The RAC was a success in terms of establishing England's first outposts in West Africa, including the coasts of present-day Ghana, Gambia, and Sierra Leone. At its peak, the share price quadrupled from its initial offering.[98] But the RAC lived a precarious financial existence, lurching from one crisis to another in keeping competitors, lenders, and shareholders at bay. Even in the good times, such as the decade leading up to the Dutch invasion of

91. Pettigrew and Veevers 2019: 25, original emphasis.
92. Pettigrew 2013: 2.
93. Carlos 1994: 319; Wagner 2018: 87.
94. Bertrand 2011: 14.
95. Pettigrew 2013: 30.
96. Pettigrew 2015: 497.
97. Pettigrew 2013: 11; Mitchell 2013b: 422.
98. Scott 1903: 246.

England in 1688, there were suspicions that profits were at least as much the product of sharp accounting practices as genuine commercial success.[99] Rather than foreign military or merchant rivals being the only threat, it was at least as much the RAC's difficulties in managing relations with its English competitors, its customers among the plantation owners of the West Indies (who bought on credit), and Company employees, that were the greatest recurring problems.[100] Added to this were the difficulties that came after the regime change of 1688 because of having been closely associated with the deposed Stuart monarchy.[101] Although there was not the same tension between war and trade that was so debilitating for the WIC, the Royal African Company still faced a difficult balancing act in reconciling political purpose with profits.[102]

As with its Dutch Atlantic counterpart, but unlike the chartered companies of the East, the Royal African Company was constantly threatened by private traders, not only in a direct commercial sense of eroding the RAC's monopoly trade, but perhaps even more so politically.[103] These private traders agitated in Parliament and the press for the repeal of the Company's monopoly. In this cause free-traders were often supported by West Indian plantation owners, unhappy with the supply and price of slaves.[104] The debate hinged upon whether the country's intertwined commercial and political national interests were best advanced through a continuing policy of monopoly, or free trade.[105]

While the Stuarts were in power this opposition had little effect; indeed, the Royal Navy helped check interlopers by seizing their ships off the coast of Africa.[106] After the Dutch invasion of 1688, however, the company was shorn of its most important source of political support, and left open to the criticism of its opponents. Though at first there was no formal repeal of the monopoly, in practice the RAC lost the legal right to enforce it by seizing interlopers'

---

99. Davies 1957: 79; Zahedieh 2010: 876; Norton 2015: 48; Wagner 2018: 40.
100. Davies 1957; Pettigrew and Van Cleve 2014: 634; Norton 2015: 49–50.
101. Carlos and Kruse 1996: 312.
102. Pettigrew 2013: 4–5; Norton 2015.
103. Carlos and Kruse 1996.
104. Norton 2015.
105. Pettigrew 2013.
106. Carlos and Kruse 1996: 305.

ships. A later compromise arrangement, the Ten Per Cent Act of 1697, saw private traders contributing this portion of their profits as duty to the Company, money which was to be devoted to the upkeep of the RAC forts. The RAC and its supporters argued that private traders, who conducted all their business from their ships, were free-riding on the costs of maintaining these forts, said to be an important national strategic asset.[107] But there were always problems with collecting the tax. The Company's monopoly was later broken altogether when parliamentary opponents managed to block efforts at renewing the RAC's charter before it expired in 1712. By this point the Company's share of the slave trade had crashed, and it was struggling to pay its bills.

An apparent savior appeared on the scene in 1720 in the form of James Brydges, first Duke of Chandos, whose fortune was originally built on embezzlement during his time as army paymaster.[108] The Duke hoped to revive the company with bold changes in its finances and strategy. First he led a re-issuance of shares to restore the RAC's financial position. The Duke then sidelined the Court of Assistants in setting up a parallel secret management committee. This group sought to shift trading away from slaving and the triangular trade, and toward bilateral trade based on African commodities, especially gold, but also indigo, ginger, and other horticultural goods (believed at the time to cure gout and gangrene). These new goods were to be secured by a program of territorial expansion and settlement.[109] By 1726, however, this strategy had completely failed, generating enormous losses. Chandos ruefully concluded "Ever since I have had the misfortune to know any thing of the Company, disappointments, vexations and loss have been all the fruits we have reapt from our care and application."[110]

With its private sector options exhausted, in 1730 Parliament voted an annual subsidy of £10,000 for the maintenance of the Company forts.[111] But after accusations of embezzlement, this lifeline

---

107. D. Smith 2018: 97; Jones and Ville 1996: 910 suggest that the forts were more useful for political protection at home than military protection in Africa.

108. Mitchell 2013a: 547.

109. Mitchell 2013a: 557.

110. Pettigrew 2013: 172.

111. Mitchell 2013a: 576.

was forfeited in 1746, leading to the bankruptcy of the Royal African Company in 1752. Adam Smith saw this outcome as a decisive repudiation of charter company monopolies.[112] A new African Company of Merchants was created, but rather like the second Dutch West India Company, this company was much more a creature of Parliament than the RAC. It depended on public funds for the maintenance of its African outposts, answered directly to the British government, and has been described as "essentially a non-profit organization."[113]

WHY DID THE ROYAL AFRICAN COMPANY FAIL?

Some company-states are written about in terms of their success, stereotypically the English and Dutch East India Companies, while others are examined as tales of failure. The Royal African Company is one of the latter. What, then, explains its failure?

A common view blames the corruption and inefficiency of Company officials in Africa,[114] the kind of principal-agent problem often said to represent a major challenge for all the company-states, given the huge distances between European headquarters and those trading across the seas.[115] The kind of private trade among company employees held by Emily Erikson to be crucial to the success of the EIC was banned by the RAC in 1680, with the Company performing thorough searches of inbound and outbound ships for contraband. In this respect, the RAC adopted the same policy as the Hudson's Bay Company (and the VOC for most of its existence). Unlike its North American counterpart, however, the RAC suffered a very high turnover of staff.[116]

All Europeans in West Africa faced a staggeringly high death toll from diseases: "Overall, of every ten Europeans sent to Africa by the [Royal African] company, six died in the first year, two more

---

112. Carlos and Kruse 1996: 291.

113. Wagner 2018: 22.

114. Davies 1957; Wilson 1965.

115. Willan 1956; Davies 1957; Rich 1960a; Chaudhuri 1978; Glamann 1981; Carlos and Nicholas 1990, 1993; Adams 1996; Erikson and Bearman 2006. Adam Smith was an early critic along these lines.

116. Carlos 1994: 331.

between their second and seventh year, and only one returned to Britain."[117] Even those who survived the tropical conditions seldom renewed their three-year contracts, perhaps because, in contrast to the HBC, the African Company almost never paid bonuses.[118] The main tool to keep Company staff on the straight and narrow was a bond of 6–10 times annual salary, guaranteed by friends or family, money which was supposed to be forfeited in the event the individual was dismissed from Company service.[119]

As well as or instead of problems with staff integrity, others point to the cost of the forts (mandated as the responsibility of the Company in the RAC charter), especially relative to private traders working from their ships without such fixed overheads, as symptomatic of the incompatibility of pursing political-strategic and commercial imperatives.[120] These forts had taken a third of the Company's initial capital, and then cost £20,000 per annum in upkeep.[121] Certainly the RAC struggled to compete against private traders, and so the loss of its monopoly, first de facto then de jure, was crucial. The success of supposedly primitive merchant partnerships lacking the joint-stock form, limited liability, separation of ownership from management, and legal personality is something of a cautionary lesson about assuming that modern institutional forms will always outcompete older rivals.[122] Unlike the HBC, where thanks to ice there was only seaborne access for as little as a couple of months a year, or the Eastern companies at a far greater distance, given the lower barriers to entry, the RAC and other Atlantic chartered companies faced constant competition from domestic and foreign private traders.[123]

This in turn raises the political question of why the Company could not defend its monopoly prerogative in Parliament. Carlos and Kruse see this defeat as essentially bad luck, as the Company's political, and therefore commercial, fortunes were derailed by

117. Headrick 2010: 146–47.
118. Carlos 1991: 146.
119. Carlos 1994: 323.
120. Carlos and Kruse 1996: 291–92; Norton 2015: 51, 68.
121. Zahedieh 2010: 874.
122. Steensgaard 1973; North 1990.
123. Carlos 1991: 143, 149; Norton 2015: 71; Wagner 2018: 43.

backing the losing Stuarts in the 1688 Revolution.[124] Davies also agrees the revolution was crucial, yet as discussed below, the Hudson's Bay Company was just as compromised in this regard, but survived.[125] Pettigrew sees a much more finely balanced political and ideological struggle over the legitimacy of the RAC's monopoly claim after 1688.[126] Proponents of free trade (in slaves) could better align themselves with the prevailing intellectual currents of the day compared with what was increasingly seen as backward and anachronistic monopoly practices.

Company-States and African Polities

A central purpose of this book is to examine the role played by the company-states in building the first global international system. One important aspect of this process was the relations that developed between Western polities, including the company-states, and non-Western rulers. It is a recurring feature of the company-state charters that their sovereign prerogatives were largely (though not exclusively) aimed at non-Western polities. In this way, the charters reflected and entrenched the divide between what Europeans saw as two very different kinds of international relations.[127] The first was between states within European international society, the family of Christian, civilized nations, while the second was with alien, extra-European polities. Company-states were one of the main institutional innovations to deal with the new demands of this second sort of international relations in both the early modern period and the nineteenth century.[128] Because those who study international politics have overwhelmingly concentrated on state-to-state relations, in the jargon those between "like units," the crucial aspect of cross-cultural relations has often been neglected. Hence the importance of interactions with African polities.

The history of Atlantic Africa prior to the nineteenth century is often framed through the tropes of the "new imperialism" of the late

124. Carlos and Kruse 1996.
125. Davies 1957: 103; Wagner 2014; Zahedieh 2010.
126. Pettigrew 2015, 2018.
127. Gong 1984; Keene 2002.
128. Stern 2008: 270; 2015: 35.

1800s.[129] In particular there is a default presumption of Western military and technological superiority during the early modern era, European domination of Africans in the slave trade, and a credulity and lack of commercial sophistication among the Africans. These conclusions are at best incomplete, but usually just wrong. These myths persist in part because histories of the RAC (and the Dutch WIC in Africa) devote surprisingly little attention to relations with Africans, instead tending to concentrate on company structure and strategy, political debates in the home state, or relations with other European actors.[130]

Thornton in particular has noted the ethnocentric and anachronistic way in which the effectiveness of African armies against European foes in the early modern era has been ignored.[131] He notes that from the end of the fifteenth century "Europeans did attempt conquest in Africa . . . or at least tried to use military force to advance their interests," efforts that "produced no real results."[132] Although disease was part of the reason for this lack of success, as both Europeans and their pack animals died in droves, Western technology did not confer any particular advantage.[133] African armies routinely employed guns from the 1600s onward.[134] Davies argues that the Africans could have driven the Europeans out at any stage, choosing not to because local polities benefited from the trading relationship.[135] A Company employee observed "a factor once settled ashoare is absolutely under the command of the king of the country where he lives, and liable for the least displeasure to loose [sic] all the goods he hath in his possession with danger also of his life."[136] Davies is similarly dismissive of European forts: "numerous . . . examples are recorded of African successes against European forts . . . the defence of the Gold Coast settlements against native attack depended less on fortification and more on diplomacy and the dissentions amongst the African peoples of the

129. Thornton 1999; Quirk and Richardson 2014.
130. For a list of exceptions, see Bertrand 2011: 8–9.
131. Thornton 1999: 8.
132. Thornton 2011: 168.
133. Sharman 2019.
134. Vandervort 1998: 24–27.
135. Davies 1957: 6.
136. Davies 1957: 29.

region."[137] Even in the 1720s the attempts of the Royal African Company to seize and secure inland gold mines foundered in the face of "the irrefutable power of the African states."[138] Thus the RAC was expelled from its fort at Whydah by Dahomey in 1727.[139]

One of the powerful African intermediaries indispensable to the Europeans trading in Africa to have received some coverage is John Cabess (or Kabes) at the Gold Coast trading settlement of Komenda, the site of forts held by the RAC and WIC, and very close to both the English headquarters at Cape Coast Castle as well as WIC-held Elmina. Cabess began as a subordinate ruler in the West African kingdom of Eguafo, but thanks to his trading and diplomatic success became both a local ruler in his own right, while also receiving regular payments from the RAC. The Royal African Company depended on Cabess for labor and supplies in building their fort at Komenda in the 1690s. One RAC official noted the need to "appease" Cabess, as without his help "nothing can be done."[140] Cabess was "adept at extorting payments and bonuses at critical times in the progress of construction, fully realizing . . . the heavy dependence of the English on both his resources and his good will."[141] He had a veto over the RAC local commander, forcing the removal of three in the period 1687–1714.[142] His support of other African allies in clashes with the WIC led to sharp Dutch defeats in 1695 and 1697.[143] Beyond their relations with Cabess, the English also had to pay and acknowledge the suzerainty of the Eguafo ruler (who was similarly recognized by the WIC).[144] The Europeans' position in the region "approximated more to that of tenants than sovereigns."[145] It is worth remembering that the company outposts generally had tiny garrisons, and thus were very vulnerable; for example the nearby RAC fort at Sekondi was destroyed

---

137. Davies 1957: 263.
138. Pettigrew 2013: 172.
139. Bertrand 2011: 13.
140. Henige 1977: 8.
141. Henige 1977: 9.
142. Henige 1977: 14.
143. Law 2007: 147, 152.
144. Law 2007.
145. Davies 1957: 281.

by African forces in 1694.[146] Only 480 RAC soldiers were sent to the Gold Coast in total 1694–1713, of whom around 60 percent died of disease in their first year.[147]

The English and Dutch companies sought to improve their position in the Gold Coast through intriguing in local succession disputes, though Africans often proved to be the more adept schemers. For example, after the RAC had connived in the murder of the king of Eguafo at Cape Coast Castle as part of a long-running conspiracy to put their candidate on the throne, the new king then transferred his loyalties to the WIC, who had offered better financial terms.[148] RAC officials complained that even John Cabess had become "very much Dutchified,"[149] and that when it came to the intervention of both European companies in local African politics "nothing has been done to less purpose on either side."[150]

Africans were equally adept in their trade with Europeans: "African sellers of commodities and enslaved labourers insisted on receiving valuable, high-quality merchandise in exchange and frequently rejected goods that did not measure up."[151] In particular, the success of European textiles was dependent on anticipating and reacting to the changing vagaries of West African fashion tastes.[152] Neither side had much regard for commercial integrity of the other, seeing them as "without exception, crafty, villainous and fraudulent."[153] When it came to the slave trade, Europeans in general and the RAC and WIC in particular had little control over supply. The unfortunate captives were brought to European forts or ships by African intermediaries in greater or lesser numbers depending on the pattern of local wars and famines.[154]

Given the nature and patterns of interactions between Europeans and Africans, the central point here is to underline the distinction whereby European expansion by company-states can by no

146. Law 2007: 160.
147. Carlos 1994: 319.
148. Law 2007: 167.
149. Law 2007: 166.
150. Davies 1957: 369.
151. Mitchell 2013b: 422.
152. Mitchell 2012.
153. Davies 1957: 286–87.
154. Carlos 1994: 317.

means be read as meaning European domination or imperialism.[155] Like their counterparts in Asia, the company-states in Atlantic Africa were generally working from a position of inferiority, dependence, and vulnerability vis-à-vis local polities and traders. More generally, Davies notes that "Between 1620 and the end of the century every nation concerned in the African trade experimented with companies. These corporations were very different from one another in many respects, but in each instance the outcome was the same: failure. By 1700 the chartered company, though not yet eliminated from the African trade, was discredited and doomed."[156]

The Hudson's Bay Company

The Hudson's Bay Company (HBC, or to give the company its full title, "Governor and Company of Adventurers of England Trading into Hudson's Bay") was typical in its institutional form as a company-state, but exceptional in its longevity, with a continuous institutional existence down to the present day. The coverage of the HBC here deals with its origins and rise in the 1600s and 1700s, while the story of how the company lost its sovereign privileges in the nineteenth century and became a "normal" corporation is held over until chapter 3. Like the Royal African Company, the HBC was a product of Restoration England. Some of the same prominent aristocrats were early backers of both, especially Prince Rupert. The same early modern mercantilist mind-set that motivated the formation of the RAC was just as important for the Hudson's Bay Company.[157] The 7,000-word charter issued 2 May 1670 thus "differed hardly at all from those of many similar royal grants."[158] It proclaimed the Company as "absolute and true lords and proprietors" of all the lands of the rivers and streams that drained into the Hudson's Bay, something like 3.8 million square kilometers, covering much of present-day Canada and some of the northern United States, a huge domain that was more than doubled in size to cover

155. Marshall 2005.
156. Davies 1957: 17.
157. Carlos and Lewis 2010: 38; D. Smith 2018: 72.
158. Newman 1998: 77.

a quarter of North America in the nineteenth century.[159] The Company was empowered to build forts, administer civil and criminal justice, conduct diplomacy, and make war on non-Christian powers as "one Body Corporate and Politique, in Deed and in Name, really and fully forever," as the 1670 charter put it.[160] In thus substantiating one of our main claims about the generic nature of the company-state form, Stern underlines that "The Atlantic and East India companies came from the same stock; they were both corporate bodies politic, founded in charters, letters, patents, and instruments of incorporation but functioning as political authorities and communities in their own right."[161]

Just as the search for the spices of the Indies had stimulated voyages to the East, so too exploration of the Hudson's Bay and its surrounds had been prompted by the search for a Northwest Passage to the Pacific and Asia.[162] But it was the fur trade that was at the heart of the HBC. Somewhat ironically in light of its long and impassioned defense of monopoly trade, the Company got its start with the help of French defectors frustrated by commercial restrictions imposed by the governor of New France in Montreal.[163]

In now familiar style, the company was set up as a joint-stock, limited liability entity with legal personality. It was to be run by a board of seven (the Court of Assistants, later the Committee), and a governor (none of whom visited North America until the 1930s), initially Prince Rupert, as well as a deputy.[164] The initial capital contributed by the original 18 shareholders, £10,500, was tiny compared to the other company-states examined here, perhaps a tenth of the RAC capitalization and a twenty-fifth of the EIC.[165] The governor and board in London determined the goods to be traded in North America, and handled fur sales in England. The Company's agents in the field traded with local groups for fur pelts, as it was

159. Galbraith 1949: 458.

160. Rich 1960a: 53–55.

161. Stern 2006: 702; see also Cavanagh 2011, 2017; Erikson and Assenova 2015; Pettigrew 2015.

162. D. Smith 2018: 78.

163. Rich 1960a.

164. Carlos and Nicholas 1993.

165. Carlos et al. 1998: 323.

the American Indians who did the actual trapping and skinning of the animals. Just as the slave trade was crucially shaped by African suppliers' taste in fashion and the spice trade by culinary tastes, so too the fur trade was largely driven by the status of felt hats made from beaver pelts among European customers. A single hat could cost two to three months' average wages.[166]

The HBC set up half a dozen factories on the bay, with no permanent inland presence until a century later.[167] In the 1670s the HBC had only around 60 staff in North America, rising to 200 in the early 1700s and 530 in 1799, though once again, most of the actual work of the fur trade was done by non-employee Native Americans.[168] The severe northern climate meant that the bay was only navigable for as little as two or three months a year, making for an annual shipment of correspondence, trading goods to, and furs from Rupert's Land.[169] The Company banned private trade by its staff (very much against the precedent of the EIC, but following the example of the RAC), searching ships and intercepting correspondence to ensure compliance.[170]

For most of its history the Company remained adamantly opposed to settlement in its vast domains. English or other European settlers were seen as undermining the fur monopoly, causing problems with the Native Americans, and creating political headaches with their demands for representative government.[171] Well into the nineteenth century, the Company maintained that most of Canada and the Oregon territories were not suited for settlement or agriculture.[172] As discussed in chapter 3, this opposition to settlement had the effect of endangering British and later Canadian claims in North America.

In England, the HBC managed to keep a much lower political profile than either the Indian or African chartered companies.[173] Despite its close links with the Stuart monarchy, the Company kept

166. Carlos and Lewis 2010: 23, 35.
167. Carlos and Lewis 2010: 7.
168. Rich 1960a: 119; Newman 1998: 129, 157.
169. Carlos 1991: 143.
170. Carlos and Nicholas 1990, 1993.
171. Galbraith 1957: 215–16; Rich 1961: 681.
172. Galbraith 1957: 333; Bown 2009: 235.
173. Williams 1970: 153; Wagner 2014: 183.

its rights substantively intact after 1688. The HBC and its supporters also subsequently managed to hold out against the rising tide of anti-monopoly opinion, perhaps because it handled a much smaller proportion of overall foreign trade than the RAC and EIC.[174] The Company was thus independent in law and practice: "it was up to the HBC to establish itself in Rupert's Land, defend its establishments, make alliances with locals, and challenge any intruder that entered its jurisdiction."[175]

If the Dutch WIC was the most pugnacious of the early modern company-states, the HBC was one of the least. The era of military competition between French and British involving the HBC lasted only until the Treaty of Utrecht in 1713. Even though France and Britain fought over North America for another 50 years after this point, the HBC was able to opt out of the struggle. The earlier fighting between the French and the HBC was essentially small-scale, nothing like that of the Luso-Dutch conflicts in Brazil and Africa. In 1686 a French *Compagnie du Nord* convinced the French authorities in Montreal to mount an expedition against the HBC forts. At a time of peace between England and France, around 100 French and Mohawks trekked overland and captured three of the four HBC posts extant at the time, generally encountering only token resistance.[176] The outbreak of general war between England and France 1689–97 led to further fighting, with several forts changing hands, and a naval clash between French and Royal Navy ships in Hudson's Bay in 1697.[177] The French got much the better of the fighting against the HBC, which usually surrendered quickly. The Company was left with just one outpost.[178]

The period until the settlement of 1713 that granted British, and hence the HBC, sovereignty over the Hudson's Bay were lean times for the Company.[179] The share price was reduced by half, and at one point share trading was halted. But as Newman notes, "It is somehow typical of both the Company's unwarlike character and its

174. Williams 1970: 149–50.
175. Cavanagh 2011: 28.
176. Rich 1960a: 214–18.
177. Rich 1960a: 254–55.
178. Smandych and Linden 1996: 47.
179. Rich 1960a: 58.

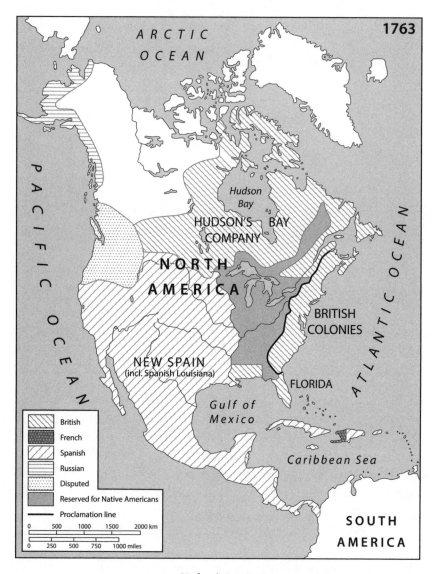

MAP 5. Hudson's Bay Company

enduring diplomatic shrewdness that even though the English lost every important battle, when all the fighting and all the negotiating were done, the Hudson's Bay Company reigned supreme over the territory of its choice."[180] The HBC sent observers to the peace

180. Newman 1998: 111.

negotiations, but the French government refused to deal with either the HBC or the VOC in the treaty, insisting all claims come from states.[181] In stark contrast to the EIC's heavy involvement in the South Asian aspects of the Seven Years' War, the HBC was missing in action 1756–1763. The only exception after this point was in 1782 with the French capture of Prince of Wales Fort, in true Company style surrendered without a shot being fired, and then recovered by diplomacy the following year.

THE HUDSON'S BAY COMPANY
AND THE AMERICAN INDIANS

What of relations between this company-state and the local American Indian polities?[182] Trade with the Indians was often an annual affair, with great trading ceremonies as the year's pelts were brought to the outposts for exchange. The commercial success of the HBC may in large part have been due to their unknowing integration within centuries-old Native American trade networks.[183] If the HBC had their monopoly selling to England, so too for long periods the Cree had a near monopoly in supplying furs to the Hudson's Bay outposts and on-selling the Company's European trade goods, with later competition from the Assiniboine, Ojibwa, and Chipewyan.[184] Each party thought little of the commercial acumen of the other.[185] The Cree and later other groups traded many of the HBC goods they gained to other Americans for a huge mark-up.[186] Other groups such as the Tsimshian west of the Rockies successfully manipulated the HBC to situate its trading posts such

181. Rich 1960a: 425, 419.

182. We have mainly opted for *American Indian* as the least problematic term, mainly because it is a better fit with historical usage than *First Nations* or *Native American*. *First Nation* has relatively recently become the preferred contemporary Canadian term, but aside from excluding some groups (e.g., Inuit), it tends to ahistorically project a modern geographic and linguistic conception of current-day Canada back in time. *American Indian* may also be the preferred term in the United States, e.g., the National Museum of the American Indian, not the National Museum of the Native American.

183. Newman 1998: 167.

184. Rich 1960b: 37; Carlos and Lewis 2001: 1,042; Bown 2009: 202.

185. Newman 1998: 168.

186. Newman 1998: 167–68.

that the Tsimshian could regulate other tribes' access to the flow of European goods.[187] In large part as a result of this trade, local Americans in the 1700s probably had a higher standard of living than the European working class of the time.[188] Like their European counterparts experiencing a "consumer revolution" at the same time, Indians increased their expenditure on luxury goods such as tobacco, textiles, and alcohol.[189] As HBC factories were male-only, many HBC servants took Indian wives, though this practice was increasingly frowned upon in the nineteenth century.

Commerce was in part ritual. As with the trade in Atlantic Africa, the locals largely set the terms of trade. In line with the gift-giving ethic of Native American societies, "The company directors became aware, as had the French traders earlier, that if they were to attract significant numbers of Indians to its posts, it would be essential to conduct trade in a way that mirrored this native practice."[190] The HBC waited in their factories for Indian trading parties to come to them to exchange furs. As such, there was no way the HBC could obtain the furs by force; instead the Company was dependent on the locals, as contemporaries recognized.[191] For most of the period, and despite its charter monopoly, the HBC faced fierce competition for Indian trade from first the French and then the North West Company. In accordance with this advantageous position, Indian traders were demanding consumers: "In a world where neither side could coerce the other, Natives' preferences were paramount."[192] Thus "The fur trade of the Hudson Bay was, in fact, a vibrant set of relations between two equal partners."[193] Rich goes further in maintaining that "The Indians held the whip hand" in trade.[194]

Although there were occasional minor clashes, there were no wars between the Company and native polities, and in general relations were much more harmonious than those with the private traders. Given the huge imbalance in numbers, and the American

187. Marsden and Galois 1995: 179.
188. Carlos and Lewis 2010: 13.
189. Carlos and Lewis 2001: 1,038.
190. Carlos and Lewis 2010: 53–54.
191. Smith 2018: 76.
192. Carlos and Lewis 2002: 285.
193. Carlos and Lewis 2010: 68.
194. Rich 1960b: 43.

natives' mastery of guns and horses, the HBC would have been wiped out in any significant military confrontation (Company "forts" were usually at best rough stockades).[195] In their struggles around the turn of the seventeenth century, both the Company and their French opponents were heavily dependent on various Indian groups for intelligence and military support.[196] Rather than the standard European divide-and-rule tactics so common elsewhere, the Company sought to prevent conflict between local polities, which was viewed as bad for business. West of the Rockies in the nineteenth century, the Company occasionally undertook punitive missions against Indian villages to avenge the death of individual traders. Such missions had very mixed results, however, and were generally seen as an expensive and risky diversion of labor most profitably used on other tasks.[197] The Company made no effort to convert the Indians, and was hostile to others trying to do so. Excepting only the small encampments around its forts (numbering perhaps in the low hundreds) it made no effort to exert authority over the locals.[198] The Indians' position certainly worsened as the nineteenth century went on, but this was more a result of disease and unfavorable demographic trends than the actions of the HBC.

Thus rather like the company-states in West Africa, for most of its corporate reign the HBC remained on the periphery of native polities that were culturally and economically independent, and militarily superior. As such, to preserve their commercial and physical viability the Europeans had to adapt to the non-Europeans at least as much as the other way around.

ASSESSING THE HUDSON'S BAY COMPANY

An overall discussion of the fate of the HBC is held over until chapter 3, but it may be helpful to engage in a preliminary comparison. The Hudson's Bay Company was a much more modest enterprise than the English and Dutch East India Companies.

195. Steele 1994.
196. Cavanagh 2011: 32.
197. Galbraith 1957: 125; Rich 1961: 602; Dean 1997.
198. Easley 2008: 74; Cavanagh 2011: 37–40.

While this is often regarded as an astute focus on commerce and profit, the lack of military capability meant that the company came within a whisker of complete destruction at the hands of the French in the 1690s, almost went broke as a result shortly afterward, and was lucky to have its terrible performance on the battlefield reversed in the later treaty negotiations. After 1713, the HBC had the singular advantage of being insulated from military competition with both Western and non-Western rivals. Because of the long winter freeze, the HBC was also relatively free of interference from the government in London. Its small size in terms of capital, staff, and the absolute value of trade, and the absence of heavily populated possessions like Bengal or Java, all meant it could generally avoid political controversy.[199] Crucially, the Hudson's Bay Company never needed financial support from the government.[200] This not only removed a potential source of friction, but posed a consistent defense against would-be reformers: without the HBC monopoly, who would pay for the forts and outposts seen as crucial for anchoring British claims on huge swathes of North America? The answer could only be the public purse, and both the government and parliament shied away from this commitment, leaving the HBC monopoly intact.[201]

The Diffusion of the Company-State Form

It is important to briefly examine other more ephemeral company-states. First, it further reinforces the idea of a generic company-state form that was copied by different rulers facing equivalent challenges of overseas expansion and hence cross-cultural relations. Unlike sovereign states at the time, company-states could be summoned into existence overnight by royal or legislative fiat. Second, the failures help put the successes in context, and perhaps give greater purchase in answering questions as to why company-states experienced such different fortunes. Third, even short-lived companies often formed the basis of lasting state colonization, for

---

199. Vanek 2015: 399
200. On this basis even Adam Smith wrote in favor of the Company (Wagner 2012: 10).
201. Williams 1970: 162; Peters 2010: 188; Wagner 2014: 202; Vanek 2015: 401.

example the English Virginia and the various French companies. Finally, even when abortive company-states left little mark abroad, they sometimes had crucial consequences for the sponsoring state, the Scottish Darien Company being a classic instance.

As has been noted in passing, the Swedes, Danes, and Brandenburgers also formed chartered companies devoted to exploiting Atlantic and Eastern trade modeled on their more famous English and Dutch equivalents. Contemporaries well understood this dynamic; speaking of the EIC a parliamentarian observed in 1730 that "the advantages of this trade as now carried on by the company are so many and so great, that we see other nations begin to envy us, the [Holy Roman] Emperor, Denmark and Sweden are attempting to imitate us by erecting companies."[202] After several abortive attempts from 1621, in 1731 the Swedish monarch chartered an East India Company to trade with China.[203] An example of the direct transfer of what had now become a generic institution, the Swedish East India Company was co-founded by a Scottish veteran of both the English EIC and the Habsburg Ostend Company, Colin Campbell.[204] The company also included other former employees and investors of the Ostend Company.[205]

Feldbæk suggests that there were up to 20 Danish companies chartered in the period 1616–1843.[206] Once again, the emulation and direct knowledge transfer was obvious:

> Holland provided the prototype for the founding of the Danish East India Company in 1616. Dutch promoters were behind the application of Copenhagen merchants to Christian IV for the establishment of the Company, and the Company's organization was a close imitation of the Dutch East India Company's charter of 1602—several articles being direct translations of the Dutch original.[207]

202. Wagner 2018: 179.
203. Sundmark 2015; Hellman 2019.
204. Benner 2003: 328; Müller 2003: 32.
205. Koninckx 1978: 41.
206. Feldbæk 1986: 204.
207. Feldbæk 1986: 206.

Subrahmanyam confirms that "The Dutch model seems heavily to have influenced this Company . . . the nine directors who managed the affair were even given the Dutch title of *bewindhebbers*."[208]

The French were equally keen emulators, Colbert in particular being attracted by the notion of company-states, if not the associated delegation of authority and property rights that came with this model.[209] Again working explicitly from the model of the VOC,[210] he formed a variety of French East and West India companies, with other companies for the Baltic and the Levant: "These companies Colbert quite openly described as armies, brought into being to wage war specifically on the Dutch . . . And perhaps it was because they were so explicitly instruments of state power, because they were so obsessively controlled from the center, that they failed to flourish anything like as successfully as did their Dutch and British rivals."[211] In this regard, the French experience parallels that of the Portuguese Brazil Company and others trapped in a cycle of state dependence in a more prolonged fashion: "From 1642 until 1731, the [French East India] Company, in its myriad forms, was locked in a perpetual cycle of borrowing, bankruptcy, liquidation, and reorganization."[212] Just as the Dutch formed the WIC to challenge the Spanish, so too the French formed their East India Company to challenge the Dutch.[213] Despite its tribulations and uncertainties, in 1720 the French *Compagnie des Indes* held possessions from the Mississippi Valley to Senegal to Yemen to the Bay of Bengal.[214] After another state bailout it was capable of mounting a strong challenge to the EIC in South Asia in the 1740s. The charters of the French companies in turn provided the direct model for the later Russian-American Company (discussed in chapter 3).

In 1695 yet another company-state appeared on the scene with the formation of the Company of Scotland Trading into Africa and the Indies. It has become more commonly known as the Darien

208. Subrahmanyam 1989: 43.

209. Heijmans 2019.

210. Gottmann 2013: 539; Berg et al. 2015: 127; Hodges 2019: 290.

211. Howard 1976: 52; see also Davies 1957: 19; Prakash 1998: 79; Berg et al. 2015: 127–28.

212. Greenwald 2011: 17; see also Davies 1957: 20–21.

213. Margerison 2006: 27.

214. Greenwald 2011: ii.

Company after Darien, Panama, the location of the Company's disastrously unsuccessful attempt at colonization centered on a "New Edinburgh." The company was once more directly modeled on the English and Dutch chartered companies.[215] Endowed with the power to "plant Collonies, build Cityes and Touns or Forts," the Company was granted a global monopoly on trade into Scotland for 31 years. By founding a settlement on the Isthmus of Panama, the plan was to trade into both the Atlantic and the Pacific.

Two successive expeditions in 1698 and 1699 turned out to be death traps, however. Eleven of the 14 ships involved were lost, and almost 70 percent of the 2,000 people who embarked from Scotland perished through disease, starvation, shipwreck, and military losses to the Spanish.[216] The latter were very conscious of the corporate nature of their opponents: the Spanish commander reasoned in surrender negotiations that his Scottish counterpart was not a soldier serving his king but a "member of a trading company and as such he need not comply with the formalities that war and honour would normally demand."[217]

Although the expeditions to Darien achieved nothing in Central America, the collapse of the Company, which had lost every penny of a massive £400,000 initial share offering, four times more than the Scottish government's annual revenue, helped to wreck Scotland's finances and precipitate the union with England in 1707 (the two countries having been ruled by the same monarch in a personal union from 1603).[218] The most important sweetener for the Scottish supporters of the Union was an English bailout of Darien shareholders.

The Iberian Alternative

If so many early modern rulers sought to extend their influence across the oceans through the expedient of chartered companies, why did two of the most successful European empire-builders, Spain and Portugal, never really adopt this strategy? While both

215. Watt 2007: 23; Paul 2009: 3.
216. Watt 2007: 192–93.
217. McKendrick 2016: 208.
218. Watt 2007: xvii, 63; Paul 2009: 2.

monarchies (ruled by a single king in a personal union 1580–1640) largely avoided company-states, the extent to which they neverthe-less sought to delegate the risks of intercontinental exploration, commerce, and colonization bespeaks the limitations faced by all rulers at the time. From Christopher Columbus and the even earlier Portuguese expeditions along the Atlantic coast of Africa, to the conquistadors and donatory captains of Brazil, the Iberian kings authorized various groups of adventurers to go forth and conquer in their name.[219] In return, these adventurers got to keep most of what they found.

Yet despite occasional abortive attempts to emulate the company-state form (e.g., the Brazil Company discussed briefly earlier in the chapter), the Iberians were never willing to delegate enough formal or practical autonomy to these companies to attract sufficient private investment to make them viable. As Cavanagh puts it, in "massive contrast" to the English and Dutch, "Iberian expansion into the New World was principally facilitated by short-term, individual contracts."[220] All chartered companies faced a bal-ancing act between satisfying the political priorities of the states that first authorized them on the one hand, and the demands of profit and commercial viability, on the other. Reflecting this atti-tude of distrust for private agents, after a few decades powers that the Iberian kings delegated to the initial wave of adventurers were subsequently reclaimed by the state as new possessions were sub-ordinated into imperial chain-of-command arrangements from Madrid and Lisbon.

Comparing the Atlantic Company-States and Assessing Cross-Cultural Relations

The knitting together of an international system from Europe to Atlantic Africa and Rupert's Land in the early modern period cer-tainly cannot be equated with any process of Westernization, colo-nization, or the diffusion of the sovereign state as an institution. While from the latter 1400s the Portuguese had largely had West

219. Kamen 2002; Restall 2003; Disney 2009; Sánchez 2016.
220. Cavanagh 2016: 503; see also Pereira 2019: 307.

African trade to themselves after seeing off an early Spanish challenge at the Battle of Guinea in 1478, chartered companies from the Netherlands and England became powerful rivals in the 1600s, while French, Brandenburg, Danish, and Swedish company-states were also active in the region. Although the resource scarcity, new geopolitical opportunities, and permissive ideational context discussed in chapter 1 were important, these company-states arose as copies of a generic form transferred from one country to the next, with the charters closely following earlier precedents of the VOC and EIC, sometimes word-for-word. The direct influence of these earlier precedents is especially obvious with regard to their hybrid character as profit-seeking, privately-owned joint-stock companies that were also authorized to go to war, engage in diplomacy, and conquer and administer territory outside Christendom. These company-states made a series of overlapping sovereignty claims along the length of Atlantic Africa, in the Caribbean, and deep into North America, bound up with monopoly trading rights that they sought to coercively enforce against their own nationals and foreigners alike. There was nothing like a border between different European concerns, however, with outposts sometimes interspersed amongst each other.

For all their institutional similarities, however, the varying fortunes of different company-states across and within regions are at least as striking. At the broadest level, none of the Atlantic company-states ever came close to matching the success of the EIC or VOC, a puzzle even to contemporary observers like Adam Smith.[221] This inferior performance seems to have reflected the disadvantage of relative proximity to Europe, which entailed both greater commercial competition, and greater exposure to military struggles of the great powers.[222] These factors in turn led to domestic attacks on monopoly trading rights, and pressure to subordinate profit-seeking to rulers' strategic aims. The Hudson's Bay Company is something of the exception that proves the rule: insulated from domestic competitors by the frozen sea, from the early eighteenth century the HBC also managed to absent itself from

221. Stern 2015: 26.
222. Norton 2015: 71.

successive Anglo-French wars.[223] More generally, it is notable that the company-state form was consistently used for long-distance trade, even though most trade of the day took place locally.[224]

Moving beyond the comparison of different European actors, what of Atlantic company-states' relations with Africans and Americans? First it should be clear that these were nothing like the stereotypes of the conquistadors or the Berlin Conference, of Europeans sweeping all before them and then dividing up imperial possessions. The company-states had no substantive political authority over local populations anywhere in Africa or the Americas, the brief experience of Dutch Brazil notwithstanding. Europeans realized that they could not conquer in Africa or North America; indeed, oftentimes they were not even secure in their fortified outposts. For the company-states and the other Europeans, their toeholds were generally held on the sufferance of local rulers.[225] Commercial exchanges generally favored Africans and American Indians at least as much as Europeans. European company-states and private merchants alike were dependent on local traders and rulers as both the suppliers of key commodities like furs, slaves, gold, and ivory, but also as discerning and assertive consumers of European goods. Europeans had to adapt to local African and American systems of commerce, credit, and culture more than vice versa.[226] Diplomatically, both European and non-European actors sought to play off their rivals within and across this divide. International relations in West Africa and much of North America in the 1600s was thus a highly plural international system composed of various African and American polities and European company-states and sovereign states interacting on a basis of rough equality.

223. Wagner 2018: 78.
224. Davies 1957: 33.
225. Vandervort 1998: 26; Chase 2003: 203.
226. Carlos and Lewis 2010; Quirk and Richardson 2014.

CHAPTER THREE

The Fall of the Company-States

AROUND 1750, COMPANY-STATES remained the pre-eminent vehicles for European expansion in much of the world, despite their increasingly mixed record of commercial and political success. But by the mid-nineteenth century, the great company-states had either disappeared entirely (the Dutch East India Company), were teetering on the brink of abolition (the English East India Company), or were about to surrender their sovereign powers, becoming exclusively private commercial entities (the Hudson's Bay Company). By this time European publics increasingly regarded company-states not just as redundant, but also mildly scandalous relics of a bygone age. How can we explain this transition? Whereas histories of the chartered companies tend to take a single instance and concentrate on its golden age, this chapter is a comparative study of the failure of company-states.[1]

We argue that the company-states' decline reflects the combined effects of intensifying geopolitical competition, ideological delegitimation, and functional redundancy. Company-states always had to reconcile the imperatives of power and profit-seeking. In Asia in particular, conducive local circumstances helped the company-states to thrive during the seventeenth century. This generally contrasted with the less hospitable and more sharply competitive

---

1. The lack of comparative studies of company-states is regularly bemoaned as a major failing of current scholarship in the field. See Stern 2009: 1,150; Nierstrasz 2015: 4; Clulow and Mostert 2018: 16; Pettigrew and Veevers 2019: 11; Nierstrasz 2019: 317.

environment of the Atlantic international system, where companies were more often roped into their sponsoring states' conflicts, usually at the expense of their profits, autonomy, and even their very existence.

From the mid-eighteenth century, the accelerating globalization of European inter-state rivalries steadily undermined the company-states' ability to reconcile power and profit. Failure to adapt to intensifying military competition risked jeopardizing companies' existing territorial holdings and local monopolies. Increased expenditure on security and territorial expansion often cost the companies more than they could sustain.

In some instances—most notably the VOC—failure to adapt to a more competitive environment propelled company-states to military defeat, bankruptcy, and eventual nationalization. For the VOC, this result reflected unfavorable long-term trade trends, but more importantly military challenges from French and British states far more powerful than the Portuguese Estado da India. In others, such as the HBC, geopolitical pressures to protect sovereign territorial claims through settler colonialism clashed with the Company's commercial interests, and its limited inclination and ability to govern sizable European settlements. Company directors were pressured by state authorities to sell back their charter privileges, ending the HBC's hybrid character.

In the case of the EIC, it was the Company's unparalleled success in reinventing itself as a large-scale territorial power that paradoxically doomed it. Its very success in carving out a huge empire in South Asia spurred renewed scrutiny from the British Parliament, and prompted debate on what the Company's expansion meant for both ideas of sovereignty and the public/private divide. By the late eighteenth century, British thinkers were already challenging mercantilist ideas and beginning to articulate a new science—political economy—that posited an increasingly sharp distinction between the public realm of political power and the private realm of the market. As new distinctions between the public and the private took shape, the EIC's continued possession of sovereign prerogatives appeared strange, even dangerous.

Reinforcing these pressures, by the early nineteenth century, company-states were becoming increasingly redundant. They had enjoyed their heyday at a time when European rulers' weakness heavily constrained state-led and financed inter-continental expansion. At that time, company-states played a critical pioneering role as cross-cultural mediators in negotiating access to markets in Africa, the Americas, and Asia, and in closing the knowledge gap (cultural, linguistic, and diplomatic) that had impeded long-distance commerce. By the early nineteenth century, however, the company-states' very success in helping to knit together an increasingly globalized economy facilitated their undoing. Where once companies had been indispensable substitutes for sovereign state power, by the 1800s, this was no longer the case. The Dutch, Canadian, and British governments took over the apparatus of rule set up by the chartered hybrid actors to exercise direct public sovereignty.

We begin by revisiting the perennial balancing act companies had to strike between the imperatives of corporate sovereignty and commercial viability. This tension lay at the heart of the company-states' early success. But it proved ever harder to reconcile with the globalization and intensification of European inter-state rivalries from the mid-eighteenth century. We sketch the broad interaction between the company-states' Janus-faced character and these escalating military pressures, before then moving for the remainder of the chapter to consider three key cases that illustrate the diverse ways this interaction helped drive the company-states' decline.

The Dutch and English East India and the Hudson's Bay Companies responded to rising geopolitical pressures in different ways that nevertheless culminated in their transformation or abolition. Following its incredible successes in the seventeenth century, the VOC slowly declined over the eighteenth century, being effectively bankrupt by the time it was nationalized in 1795. The relative decline of the spice trade, escalating costs of rule, and increased military competition fatally sapped the Company's profitability. The tensions between its dual mandates proved impossible to manage in the more competitive eighteenth-century geopolitical environment as France and especially Britain deployed state armies and navies to the East.

In contrast, the HBC never harbored great aspirations for conquest and rule, but rather sought to maintain a low profile. This entailed both adroit efforts to sidestep controversies in Britain concerning its chartered privileges, as well as a generally pacific posture in both its dealings with indigenous polities and its relations with Western rivals. Increasing geopolitical threats from the United States in the nineteenth century unsettled this model, however, creating new pressures for Britain to consolidate its holdings in North America via colonization. The HBC eventually was forced to sell off its chartered privileges, with the Company's lands transferred to the new Dominion of Canada.

The EIC proved the most successful of all company-states in adapting to the rigors of military competition. Militarily insignificant as late as the 1750s, by the close of the Napoleonic Wars the EIC dominated the Indian subcontinent, disposed of an army of over 250,000 troops, and ruled many more subjects than the British Crown itself. But success came at a steep price. The EIC's vast conquests greatly strained its coffers, with revenues from land taxes in newly conquered territories failing to cover the costs of rule and administration. Even more important, the consternation in Britain that the EIC's expanded dominions evoked eventually saw it widely delegitimized, and its operations subject to increased parliamentary surveillance and control. Though the Company's abolition came only following the Indian "Mutiny" (1857–59), in the preceding decades it steadily surrendered its hybrid character, shorn of both its commercial privileges, and also its ability to operate as a sovereign entity beyond the bounds of direct parliamentary control.

Taken together, the VOC, HBC, and EIC illustrate diverse trajectories of company-state decline. The VOC was unable to manage the tensions of its dual imperatives in a more competitive geopolitical environment, suffering military defeat and commercial ruin. The HBC went entirely private, relinquishing sovereign power through the sale of its political and commercial privileges back to its sponsoring state. Victorious on the battlefield, the EIC finally succumbed to attacks on its legitimacy spawned by its success, the specter of a company-run subcontinental empire inspiring parliamentary intervention and the EIC's slow-motion nationalization as an appendage of the British state.

Despite these differences, by the mid-nineteenth century these companies' evolution exemplified a broader shift away from the company-state as a preferred vehicle for long-distance commerce and conquest. In particular, the EIC's abolition in 1858, and the 1869 Deed of Surrender marking the HBC's sell-off of its sovereign privileges, together seemed to portend the company-state's disappearance from the international system. That this development coincided with multilateral efforts to ban mercenarism and privateering moreover suggests a momentous historical turning point, in which Western states had resolved to decisively banish private international violence.[2] Yet as chapter 4 will demonstrate, within two decades, company-states had been resurrected, spearheading renewed colonial expansion from sub-Saharan Africa to the South Pacific. Consequently, this chapter concludes with a brief appraisal of the normative state of play in an increasingly European-dominated international system in the mid-nineteenth century.

The Profit-Power Balancing Act and the Existential Challenges of Company-States

Company-states differed from sovereign states because of their dual pursuit of profit and power. Company-states existed to make money, and more specifically to exploit the lucrative opportunities for long-distance monopoly trade in commodities like spices, furs, and slaves that developed during the early modern period. Europeans' ignorance about the outside world hindered attempts at long-distance commerce, as did insecurity stemming from endemic banditry, piracy, and inter-state competition. The absence of shared norms or diplomatic practices to facilitate global commerce further complicated European long-distance commercial expansion. For these reasons, company-states also came equipped with a broad palette of sovereign prerogatives deemed necessary to secure access to competitive and often violently contested markets.

Company-states' hybrid identity was their signature strength in the right contexts. As limited liability joint-stock corporations, it

2. Thomson 1994; Percy 2007.

was easier for them to mobilize large amounts of long-term capital to fund costly expansion compared with merchant partnerships where capital was pooled and then divided after each individual expedition.[3] The company-states' longer time-horizons helped create a willingness to innovate managerial practices to address principal-agent problems. Alongside these advantages, the company-states' possession of war-making powers enabled them to defend their assets from predators, but also to force their way into markets and sometimes violently assert monopolistic or monopsonistic control within them.

But while the company-states' duality was in some circumstances a source of strength, it could also be their Achilles' heel. Profit maximization and power maximization were not always—or even usually—aligned. In the volatile conditions of the early modern world, an exclusive focus on profit was risky: pacifism would likely invite predation, and with it the swift destruction of assets and commercial viability. Company-states that lost sight of their commercial motives, however, risked jeopardizing their very existence through excessive military spending and conquests. Soldiers and sailors had to be trained, fed, quartered, and equipped with the materiel necessary for them to be effective in battle, all of which cost a great deal of money. Naval warfare was always risky, putting in harm's way ships that were extremely expensive to replace. Territorial conquest often came at a high cost to company-states' balance sheets.

In an international environment where long-distance trade and war remained closely entwined, company-states could not afford to ignore either. Yet too much emphasis on one or the other risked institutional viability. Getting this balancing act right was always challenging, all the more so in environments such as the Atlantic international system, where sponsoring rulers' strategic rivalries tended to compromise company-states' autonomy. But from the mid-eighteenth century, the globalization of European inter-state rivalries exacerbated this tension. The result of these changed conditions in each of the three cases discussed below was that corporate empires were nationalized by the state.

3. Steensgaard 1973; North 1990.

The Dutch East India Company

It is difficult and in some sense arbitrary to pick the peak of the VOC's power, but there is no doubt that by the mid-1600s the VOC had conclusively eclipsed the Portuguese in the East. The Dutch company had ejected the Portuguese from a string of their key outposts, from Japan to Malacca to the Spice Islands to the shores of India. By largely excluding their English chartered company rival from current-day Indonesia, the VOC had taken control over the spice trade. A spectacular commercial success, it was also the most powerful European military force in the region with the strongest navy in the Indian Ocean (although it was no match for the various Asian great powers on land). The Company's peak profit was achieved in 1672.[4] Largely a maritime network, by the later 1600s the VOC had also begun acquiring political control over more substantial territories in Java and Ceylon, a trend that continued the following century. At this time it was regarded by itself and even its rivals as the most successful example of the company-state form.[5] Subsequent economic historians like Steensgaard and North have portrayed the VOC as the epitome of institutional modernity, efficiency, and effectiveness.[6]

The eighteenth century, however, saw the decline and fall of the Company, ending amid bankruptcy and dissolution. What explains this profound reversal of fortune? There is a variety of explanations, spanning economic and political accounts that complement or contradict each other to varying degrees. Some scholars have argued that internal institutional dysfunction sapped the Company's commercial viability, or that the Company failed to adapt to changing patterns of trade in the eighteenth century. More political explanations suggest that the VOC sacrificed profits for the burdens of rule, or that the Company's decline was a reflection of broader power dynamics, especially the rise of British naval power at the expense of the Dutch, both in Europe and in the East.

4. Blussé and Gaastra 1981: 8.
5. Boxer 1965: 67, 277; Erikson and Bearman 2006: 200.
6. Steensgaard 1973; North 1990.

The relative decline of the spice trade and increasing costs of territorial rule gradually sapped the Company's profitability, but the proximate cause of its end was declining military competitiveness culminating in catastrophic military defeats in the 1780s and 1790s. In keeping with our main thesis, "The VOC and WIC may have been devoted chiefly to trade, but profits on the scale they sought were not to be had, in Europe or the Indies, without military and territorial power."[7] Though the Netherlands retained their East Indies possessions after the Napoleonic Wars, from that point sovereign prerogatives were monopolized by the public authorities.

CORRUPTION AND PRINCIPAL-AGENT PROBLEMS

The first explanation for the decline of the VOC, favored by contemporary wags but also historians much later was that the VOC was a case of *"Vergaan Onder Corruptie"* ("Collapsed Under Corruption").[8] As discussed earlier, one of the main challenges for any European entity conducting trade over vast distances was ensuring that employees across the ocean (the agents) were following the orders and advancing the interests of managers and shareholders in Europe (the principals), rather than feathering their own nests. The months-long communication lag in each direction precluded any close control, or even supervision. Many scholars have seen this problem of aligning incentives between directors and servants as the single greatest problem confronting company-states.[9] For those favoring a principal-agent explanation of decline, the main challenge is to explain why the VOC was able to manage agents successfully in the 1600s, but not as the 1700s went on.[10]

The major, but by no means the only, form of abuse of company interests among the VOC staff was "private trade," i.e., individuals transporting goods on Company ships to be sold for personal profit. Erikson argues that the fact that EIC staff were allowed to engage

---

7. Israel 1995: 951.

8. Boxer 1965: 205; see also Braudel 1984; Gaastra 1981.

9. Davies 1957; Carlos and Nicholas 1990, 1993; Adams 1996; Erikson and Bearman 2006; Erikson 2014; Norton 2015; Sgourev and van Lent 2015.

10. Nierstrasz 2012: 6, 152.

in private trade, whereas private trade was forbidden to their VOC counterparts, was the single most important factor in explaining the contrasting performance of the two companies in the 1700s.[11] According to this logic, EIC staff had a superior personal incentive that their VOC counterparts lacked in making sure that ships followed the most profitable routes and traded in the most profitable commodities. Because principals' and agents' incentives were poorly aligned in the VOC, its operation became less and less efficient. For Adams, "Dutch decline was imminent when alternative opportunities for private gain, available via the ascending English East India Company, allowed Dutch colonial servants to evade their own patrimonial chain and encouraged its organizational breakdown."[12] These servants did so first by using English entrepôts to evade the VOC prohibitions on servants' private trade, and then by using EIC bills of exchange to repatriate the resulting illicit gains to Europe.[13] This may go some way to answering the question of why VOC "corruption" seemed to be more damaging in the eighteenth century than in the seventeenth.

MALADAPTION AND CHANGING TRADE PATTERNS

The second major trend said to explain the decline of the VOC, both absolutely but especially relative to its English rival, is changes in trade patterns in the 1700s.[14] The importance of the spice trade waned relative to that in textiles and tea, which became consumer staples. Although the absolute value of spices shipped by the VOC remained the same, the proportion of spices in total cargos by value went from 60 percent in the mid-1600s, to less than a third by 1700.[15] It is argued that the VOC's very success in monopolizing the trade in nutmeg, cloves, and mace from the Southeast Asian islands, and later cinnamon from Ceylon, made it unwilling or unable to adapt to the more competitive trade in new commodities.[16] This

11. Erikson 2014.
12. Adams 1996: 12.
13. Adams 1996: 23.
14. Israel 1995: 940, 998.
15. Goodman 2010: 66; see also Gaastra 2003: 129; Nierstrasz 2012: 78.
16. Scammell 1989: 22; Adams 1994: 343; Berg et al. 2015: 132.

conservatism may have been exacerbated by the familial or patrimonial basis of the Dutch elite.[17] Conversely, the initial failure of
the EIC, whereby it was muscled out of the Spice Islands by the
Dutch company, is said to have been a blessing in disguise, as it was
better situated to capitalize on new opportunities and changes in
consumer tastes. Commodities like tea, textiles, and coffee could
not be monopolized in the same way as the VOC had done with the
spice trade, either because they were too widely produced, or in the
case of tea, because the Chinese at Canton held the whip hand.[18]

Declining commercial performance immediately endangered
the other bases of company-state power. For all their sovereign prerogatives, the company-states did in the end face hard budget constraints; they could and did go broke. Aside from the direct need
for commercial viability to satisfy shareholders and directors, companies' militaries had to be paid out of their revenues. In line with
Coen's aphorism about the intimate connection between trade and
war, failing commercial performance and military atrophy could
create a vicious cycle of negative mutual reinforcement. The Dutch
West India Company's experience in Brazil discussed in chapter 2
is a stark illustration of this predicament whereby financial problems sapped military strength, which then worsened the Company's
finances still further.

Erikson's argument forms something of a link or hinge between
the internal institutional account of the VOC's decline outlined
above, based on the principal-agent problem, and this one emphasizing failing commercial performance, especially relative to the
EIC.[19] She holds that the internal institutional failure to align
incentives within the VOC explains why it was comparatively slow
to adapt to new trading conditions, and hence was outcompeted.
Aside from the shift away from spices as the dominant commodity
in the Europe-Asia trade, the intra-Asian trade was also changing
in the 1700s. In part these changes reflected the decline of empires
like the Mughals and the Safavids, in part increased competition
from other Europeans, especially with the rise of the British in

17. Adams 2005.
18. Nierstrasz 2015.
19. Erikson and Bearman 2006: 204–5; Erikson 2014: 52–53; see also Devecka
2015: 91.

the second half of the century.[20] The profits from the intra-Asian trade had always been crucial in ameliorating the structural trade deficit that otherwise saw specie drain from Europe to the East. The VOC's hostility to private trade either when carried on by its own staff, or by interlopers (private trade was compared with "a plague in the body of the Company that should not be allowed time to creep deeper into it, but should be suppressed and extirpated with strong remedies") is said to have made it slow to adapt.[21]

Increasing commercial problems were reflected in the growing debts of the VOC in the first few decades of the 1700s. Recognizing this trend as untenable, from the 1740s the *Heeren XVII* resolved to focus on only the most profitable aspects of its business, the Europe-Asia trade in key commodities, while retrenching on more marginal goods, and relaxing its strict prohibition on private trading by VOC servants.[22] In the 1750s the Company progressively abandoned outposts in the Persian Gulf and Southeast Asia.[23] Despite constant tinkering, these reforms ultimately proved unable to restore the VOC's fortunes. In some ways they may have actually exacerbated the problem, as liberalization and retreat simply created more room for the increasingly dominant English traders, both EIC and private, who entered the markets vacated by the Dutch Company.

MISSION CREEP AND OVERSTRETCH

Whether because of mismatched internal institutional incentives, or poor performance in the broader market, the accounts above are largely economic. Yet it is a core thesis of this book that the company-states were more than just businesses. Focusing on their role as sovereigns and powerful actors in the early modern international system, the second set of explanations puts geopolitics to the fore. Here the reasoning is that either the VOC succumbed to some version of mission creep and imperial overstretch, or that

20. Gaastra 2003: 59; Nierstrasz 2012.
21. Weststeijn 2014: 15; see also Berg et al. 2015: 127.
22. Nierstrasz 2012: 73.
23. Gaastra 2003: 59–60.

the general decline of the Dutch relative to Britain and France in Europe and the East was ultimately fatal for the VOC.

The VOC had been a reluctant colonist, making initial exceptions for the very small Spice Islands that were crucial for its monopolies.[24] Ever concerned with controlling expenditure, the *Heeren XVII* saw territorial rule and the associated costs as an expensive distraction from the main mission of making profits. Thus in the 1600s the VOC domains largely took the form of maritime networks.[25] In Java, the heart of the VOC's Eastern realms, from the 1670s, however, the Company was increasingly drawn into loss-making interventions in local politics. Company troops would support one faction in internecine disputes like succession struggles, only to then have to intervene again to enforce the terms of the deal they had struck for committing their support.[26] The failure of local Javanese rulers to make the agreed-upon payments and concessions led to the Company throwing good money after bad in punitive missions, with even the victorious wars being a "financial disaster" for the Company.[27] Similarly, in their possessions in India it is said that the VOC's efforts to entrench its presence through fortification cost more than the profits of the pepper trade these forts were defending.[28] In 1741 the VOC was forced to suppress a major rebellion in Java at the same time as battling against the King of Travancorc in India, a struggle the Company lost.[29] In the 1760s the Company expanded its rule in Ceylon, conquering the whole of the coastline from its forts acquired from the Portuguese in the preceding century, and warring against the King of Kandy in the interior.[30]

Through these struggles the VOC was increasingly "transformed from a merchant enterprise into an empire . . . the cost of maintaining this empire overtook profits . . . the process of territorial settlement took on a life of its own and eventually became a demanding

24. Boxer 1965: 94; Ricklefs 1993: 228–30; Locher-Scholten 1994: 94; Thompson 1999: 165; Kian 2008: 294.

25. Ward 2009.

26. Wills 1993: 99; Kian 2008: 297–98.

27. Ricklefs 1993: 226.

28. Odegard 2014.

29. Koshy 1989.

30. Wickremesekera 2015.

source of expenditure and financial debt."[31] In line with this trajectory, over its existence the VOC dramatically increased its staff roll: "In 1625 the VOC had 2,500 servants settled in the East, by 1700 this had grown to 13,000 and by 1750 increased to 20,000 men" across 30 outposts.[32] By 1780 the VOC had 28,150 employees, not counting the slaves who made up between one- and two-fifths of the population of VOC settlements.[33] (In its lifetime, the Company shipped over a million Europeans to the East on 4,800 ships.[34]) The military-related costs of the VOC now came to between 50 and 70 percent of its total spending, and were used to pay for 10,000 troops in the 1700s.[35] By the time of its dissolution, there were approximately 2.5 million people living under Company suzerainty, mainly in Java.[36] The VOC itself was aware of the risks of territorial expansion and the burdens of rule for its commercial success and longevity, but nevertheless the Company was drawn down this path.[37]

The result of this trend was that in the eighteenth century the VOC's revenues stayed roughly stable, but its expenses steadily increased,[38] of which most were devoted to the imperatives of war and rule. Thus it is said that for all the efforts of its directors in the Netherlands, the Company lost its commercial orientation, and hence ultimately its business viability. Of course the EIC also underwent a transformation from trader to ruler on a far more spectacular scale than the VOC, but the former was able to capture huge new revenue streams of tax from the rich and monetized Bengali economy, whereas the Dutch operated in much smaller areas and extracted tax in labor.[39]

31. Ward 2009: 31.
32. Goodman 2010: 65.
33. Erikson and Assenova 2015: 4; Vink 2003.
34. Nijman 1994: 218.
35. Nijman 1994: 224; Mostert 2007: 19; Goodman 2010: 62. By way of comparison, in 1773 the EIC commanded 54,000 troops (Roy 2011: 208).
36. Vink 2019: 33.
37. Weststeijn 2014: 18, 22.
38. Gaastra 1981: 61–63; 2003: 56, 127.
39. Nierstrasz 2015.

GEOPOLITICS AND PAX BRITANNICA

Though the decline of the VOC was the result of many causes, probably the most important is that in the eighteenth century both the VOC and the Dutch state were simply unable to match the growth in power of France but especially Britain. As the United Provinces fell out of the ranks of great powers, the VOC was progressively overpowered, exacerbating unfavorable trade and revenue trends that fatally undermined its commercial viability.[40] Though violence in the East between Europeans had from the very beginning been linked to enmities at home, from the 1740s this link became much more direct. France and Britain sent increasingly large expeditions to fight in South Asia, rather than just relying on their respective Company armies and local allies as in the past (though such state support was by no means a one-way street: the EIC was forced to make loans and subventions to the Parliament, as well as contributing Company troops for various imperial expeditions).[41] In part as a result, the British won control of South Asia, and their resulting naval and commercial dominance increasingly marginalized the VOC throughout the Indian Ocean.

The culmination of this trend was the Fourth Anglo-Dutch War of 1780–84, sparked by a dispute over the right of Dutch ships to trade with Britain's American and French opponents. Despite facing multiple opponents around the world, British forces nevertheless took all the VOC outposts in India, including its local headquarters of Negapatnam.[42] The Company only managed to hold on in the Cape and Ceylon thanks to French naval assistance. Even worse was the damage to shipping and revenue, as the Dutch Europe-Asia trade was completely blocked. Total financial losses from the war amounted to 60 million guilders, essentially ending the Company's financial independence.[43] The peace treaty of 1784 opened trade in all the VOC's possessions to British merchants, destroying the almost two-century-old spice monopoly.

---

40. Boxer 1965: 105.
41. See Marshall 2005.
42. Israel 1995: 1,096–97.
43. Adams 1994: 347. These losses are put at 43 million by Goodman (2010: 68).

Well before this time, however, the Dutch Republic had let its navy fall into deep disrepair. Naval policy had always been fraught, as the inland provinces had routinely failed to contribute funds to this cause.[44] After 1713 the Dutch had radically cut their naval spending.[45] As a result of this weakness, the meager Dutch state naval forces sent to the East for the first time in the 1780s made little difference. Previously, the Company had been very reluctant to call on state support, seeing this as a threat to its independence.[46] By the time they turned to the state for assistance, the Dutch state had little to give.

Nierstrasz sees a military turning point in a failed VOC effort to prevent the EIC's domination of Bengal in 1759 during the Anglo-French Seven Years' War.[47] At a time when the two countries were at peace and the British were preoccupied with fighting farther south, the VOC conspired with Nawab Mir Jafar to replace the EIC as the dominant traders in Bengal, sending 1,500 European and Malay troops from Batavia. Having caught wind of the Dutch plan, however, the three Royal Navy ships fought and captured the seven vessels of the VOC on 23 November 1759, immediately after they had landed the expedition. The Dutch armed merchant ships were no match for the British ships of the line, a result that demonstrated the crucial shift in the naval balance. Over the following two days EIC forces completely defeated the Dutch Company's expeditionary force at the Battle of Bedara. In the same decade the VOC lost ships and fortresses in India to French forces also.[48]

If by the end of the eighteenth century the VOC had suffered comprehensive military defeat and commercial collapse, the United Provinces were doing little better. Through the 1700s the Netherlands had suffered military, economic, and demographic decline.[49] The country was invaded by Prussia with British encouragement in 1787, before being completely overrun by the French in early 1795. Dutch naval power was finally extinguished by the British in

44. Israel 1995: 1,095.
45. Boxer 1965: 106–8.
46. Nierstrasz 2012: 37.
47. Nierstrasz 2012: 40–42.
48. Nierstrasz: 2012: 37–38.
49. Boxer 1965: 272–88.

1797.[50] The newly installed Dutch Patriot government of the Batavian Republic nationalized the VOC by decree 24 December 1795 (the second WIC had been similarly nationalized in 1792), though the VOC governing institutions and personnel in the East Indies were retained. By the time the charter expired 31 December 1799, the VOC had debts of 119 million guilders.[51] Later during the Napoleonic Wars the British conquered the Cape, Ceylon, and Java. Although the East Indies was returned to the Dutch, at this point it was clear that the Dutch possessions in Asia were in effect maintained at the pleasure of the British.[52] Significantly, though the Dutch were allowed to re-establish their empire in the East Indies, there was no thought of re-establishing a chartered company to run it. Instead, responsibilities for rule and trade were separated in line with new ideas concerning the divide between public and private, and the distinct roles of states and companies.

CONCLUSIONS

Even if the VOC had managed to better align corporate and individual incentives, and been more flexible in adapting to shifting trade patterns, it is difficult to see how these would have offered protection against growing British dominance, at first in South Asia, and then throughout the Indian Ocean region. Though the VOC undoubtedly suffered from the malfeasance of its staff, this had always been the case, and this problem was common not just to other companies, but to the Portuguese as well. As Boxer puts it, even in the heyday of the Dutch Company, "everyone from Governor-General to cabin boy traded on the side and everyone knew it," with complaints about this fact beginning less than a year after the company was first founded.[53] The VOC essentially built this "corruption" into its business by keeping wages low. The longest lived company-state of them all, the Hudson's Bay Company, was stricter than any of its East Indian equivalents in banning private trade by staff. At the time in the later 1700s when the VOC

50. Israel 1995: 1120–27.
51. Gaastra 2003: 170.
52. Oostindie 2012.
53. Boxer 1965: 201.

was allowing its staff more freedom to trade privately, the EIC was cracking down on this practice.[54]

If the VOC ultimately failed to reconcile the demands of trade and rule, of being a company and a state, due to a process of mission creep, once again the same can be said of the EIC. Erikson's argument that the VOC lost ground to the EIC because of the former's excessive militarization seems to rely on the picture of the English Company before the battle of Plassey as a peaceful group of merchants,[55] a picture that Stern has convincingly rebutted.[56] It is also important to realize that without the sustained use of force in the 1600s, the VOC would never have been able to create its spectacularly lucrative monopoly on the spice trade in the first place.[57]

The Hudson's Bay Company

In some sense we cannot speak of the end of the Hudson's Bay Company; uniquely among the companies considered in this book, it lives on today. Yet although it is still very much a going business concern, the HBC is no longer a company-state, having surrendered its charter and its sovereign powers almost exactly 200 years after its founding in 1670. But the fact that this chartered company survived so long, when others had either failed, like the Royal African Company or Dutch companies, or were absorbed into the state apparatus, like the English East India Company, demands explanation. This section analyzes the longevity of the HBC and its eventual transition from a company-state to a "normal" company by looking at a series of near-death experiences.

The first of these has been covered already: the French military predation that reduced the Company's holdings to one outpost during the War of Spanish Succession. Here the HBC's underwhelming military performance was reversed by British diplomatic success when, thanks to adroit HBC lobbying, the terms of the Treaty of Utrecht in 1713 compelled the French to hand back all the Hudson's Bay outposts they had captured. The second instance was a

54. Erikson 2014: 66–67.
55. Bowen 2006; Lawson 1993.
56. Stern 2009, 2011; see also Wellen 2015.
57. Adams 1994; Andrade 2004.

sustained political attack in the mid-eighteenth century aimed at revoking the Company's charter and empowering a rival company. The third was the fierce commercial challenge mounted by the rival fur traders of the North West Company that strained the HBC's finances and led to violent confrontations in the decades around the turn of the nineteenth century. The final episode was that leading up to the Deed of Surrender between the Company, Britain, and the new Dominion of Canada 1869 that saw the end of the HBC as a company-state.

THE DOBBS AFFAIR AND THE
THREAT TO THE CHARTER

After the recovery of its Hudson's Bay forts from the French, the Company showed extraordinary consistency in keeping the lowest possible political profile, and in maintaining its fixation on the bottom line in its fur trading.[58] The HBC took care that its charter was not public, nor were the names of its shareholders or directors. After 1700, shares traded privately.[59] It carefully controlled correspondence from its North American posts back to Europe, censoring letters and journals.[60] Aside from its secrecy, the Company could remain unobtrusive in part because it was small, with much less capital than the Royal African Company, let alone the East India Company (in 1720 the relative figures were £451,350 for the RAC, £3,194,080 for the EIC, but only £103,950 for the HBC).[61] Its presence in North America was correspondingly modest: a couple of ships a year, a handful of outposts on the periphery of the Hudson's Bay, and around a few hundred employees on-site.[62] The Company took pains to stay on good terms with native polities, and from 1713 until the 1780s the HBC avoided clashes with the French also.[63] Thus unlike either of its East India counterparts, or the Dutch West India Company, the HBC resolutely avoided

58. Wagner 2014: 183–85.
59. Davies 1966: 176.
60. Williams 1970: 151–52.
61. Wagner 2014: 183.
62. Williams 1970: 150.
63. Rich 1960a; Cavanagh 2011: 32.

both war and rule. Yet in some ways it was the very modesty of the Company's aims that began to cause problems.

A central rationale for granting the original charter in 1670 was not just to enrich a particular coterie of well-connected private investors, but to foster English wealth and power, ideally by the discovery of a Northwest Passage to the Indies.[64] Arguing from this initial logic, in the 1740s one well-connected agitator, Arthur Dobbs, became a fierce critic of the HBC for failing to discover the fabled passage, and preventing others from doing so through the Company's refusal to share maps and knowledge of the region. Through personal lobbying and pamphleteering, Dobbs also attacked the HBC for failing to promote the kind of inland coloni-zation and settlement that he maintained would boost commerce, strengthen the British position in North America, and displace the French. He attacked the legitimacy of monopolistic chartered com-panies in general, though later also sought a charter for his own rival North Western Company (distinct from the later North West Company), a contradiction the HBC seized on. This campaign against the HBC was supported by merchants from Bristol and Liverpool in particular.[65]

In 1749 these critics jointly engineered a parliamentary commit-tee of enquiry into the HBC, which received petitions and heard testimony from opponents of the Company. Their objections were that the HBC was a small clique that had generated outrageous profits for itself while singularly failing to advance "the public good," i.e., the country's intertwined mercantile and strategic inter-ests, especially vis-à-vis the French.[66] A few years later a polemic along similar lines said that for 80 years the Company had been supine, "asleep at the edge of a frozen sea." In its response to the general parliamentary debate that followed, the HBC argued (accu-rately) that its profits were modest, that there was no passage, and (less accurately) that the climate and conditions of the bay area made settlement and agriculture impossible.[67] Like the nineteenth-century company-states discussed in chapter 4, the HBC worried

64. D. Smith 2018: 72–78.
65. D. Smith 2018: 94.
66. Williams 1970; Peters 2010; D. Smith 2018.
67. Peters 2010; Vanek 2015; D. Smith 2018.

about the presence of Europeans outside of the Company hierarchy who might challenge its commercial and political control.[68] Perhaps presciently, the Company also worried that settlers would upset generally harmonious relations with the Indian polities on which the HBC depended.

Though the Company's opponents muddied the waters by criticizing monopoly charters while also petitioning for one themselves, the debate covered much of the same ground as that over the Royal African Company.[69] Was "the public good" better advanced by monopoly or free trade? Should the aim be arm's-length trade with indigenous polities or extensive settlement? How best should cooperation with native polities best be secured? How best to achieve Britain's strategic goals and protect against European rivals? Though by this time public opinion was firmly set against monopolies as a matter of principle, the HBC won the vote by a two-to-one margin.

The debate came to hinge on the forts around the bay, which were seen as important for the general British presence in the region, in the same way as the RAC's forts in West Africa. Parliament concluded that these forts could only be maintained in one of two ways: through a monopoly company, or through direct subsidies from the government, as parliament was now doing in West Africa. In this respect, the contrast between the African and Hudson's Bay Companies was stark: the former had been in financial disarray for decades and was an expensive ward of the state, whereas the latter was completely self-supporting, with both customers and shareholders generally satisfied. Parliament was reluctant to jeopardize an arrangement that seemed to be working reasonably well and cost it nothing.[70] Even Adam Smith, a fierce critic of monopoly and chartered companies, wrote that given the exceptionally difficult conditions of the far North, the HBC was doing a creditable job, in that the Company could "engross the whole, or almost the whole trade and surplus produce of the miserable though extensive country comprehended within their charter."[71]

68. Galbraith 1957; Royle 2011.
69. D. Smith 2018.
70. Williams 1970: 162–64; Peters 2010: 188; D. Smith 2018: 103–4.
71. Adam Smith, quoted in Rich 1960b: 53.

THE COMMERCIAL CHALLENGE
OF THE NORTH WEST COMPANY

If the challenges of the early and mid-eighteenth century were first military and then political, from the 1780s the third was commercial. This was posed by the North West Company, a rival fur trading concern operating from Montreal, led by Scotsmen, but largely staffed by French Canadians. Unlike the HBC, the North West Company was neither chartered nor a joint-stock company, being a partnership without either legal personality, limited liability, or the sovereign prerogatives of the company-states.[72] To this extent, the "company" label, although conventional, is misleading.

For the first century of its existence, the HBC had eschewed inland expansion, instead waiting for the Cree and later Assiniboine Indians to make their annual trip to the bay outposts, at which point beaver pelts were exchanged for goods from Europe according to a set schedule of prices.[73] The French, however, had long taken the approach of spreading out into the vastness of North America to trade directly with the Indians. This put them at odds with the Iroquois and the Cree, who sought to impose and defend their own monopolies; the Europeans were not the only ones who suppressed competing traders with armed force.[74] Twenty years after the defeat of New France in 1760, the partners of the North West Company exploited the passivity of the HBC in once more pushing inland, taking a much larger share of the trade than their more established rival.[75] The North West Company set up dozens of new outposts beyond Rupert's Land in Indian Territory, ultimately advancing all the way to the Pacific. Its directors were also much closer to the action, remembering that none of the HBC directors had ever set foot in North America at this time. The new company allowed their agents considerable flexibility and initiative, whereas the HBC sought to micromanage trade according to set policies and prices.

72. Davies 1966: 168.
73. Rich 1960a.
74. Rich 1960b: 36–38; Hughes 2016: 50–60.
75. Davies 1966: 169.

Though their primary motive was commercial, the Montreal-based upstarts also sought to protect the claims of the British Crown from the newly independent United States, a point they consistently played up to the authorities.[76] In agitating for their own monopoly charter, the partners contrasted the energy of their North West Company in pushing forward the imperial cause with the lethargy of the HBC. They argued that this failure invalidated the HBC charter; the fact that Parliament had not renewed the charter beyond 1690 certainly raised pointed legal questions.

Competition between fur traders turned violent. From its Alaskan vantage point, the Russian-American Company hypocritically decried "a shocking spectacle of assorted ravages, thievery, murders, and native rebellions inspired by one side against the other."[77] A murder in 1802 showed the legal problems of existing arrangements outside the provinces of Canada and Rupert's Land (where HBC sporadically enforced criminal justice).[78] A Montreal court said it had no jurisdiction over Indian Territory, as specified in the royal proclamation of 1763 at the end of the Seven Years' War, and so the murderer could not be prosecuted under British law.[79] Worried not just about public order but also the legitimacy of its claims to the area vis-à-vis the United States at the time of the Louisiana Purchase, British authorities extended Canadian criminal law over the territory, though in practice this only applied to crimes involving Europeans.[80]

Given its inferior numbers, there was no question of the HBC simply expelling its rivals by force. Though it had begun establishing forts inland from the 1770s, by 1799 the HBC still only had a staff of 500 in North America, compared with almost 2,000 for the North West Company.[81] Nor was there a clear legal path in either British or North American courts to assert the monopoly claimed

76. Hughes 2016: 62–65.
77. Tikhmenev 1978 [1863]: 168.
78. Smandych and Linden 1996.
79. Newman 1998: 322.
80. Hughes 2016: 68.
81. Newman 1998: 253, 271.

by the Company on the basis of the original 1670 charter.[82] Furthermore, any court decision would have to be enforced by the Company itself, rather than the Crown. However the HBC was not without advantages, especially as the competition reached its decisive phase 1810–1821.

The permanent legal personality of the Company meant that it could attract more credit on better terms than the North West partners. The separation of ownership and management allowed the directors, all of whom had other sources of income, to tolerate losses in pursuit of longer-term gain. In contrast, the North West Company's owners directly depended on a continuing flow of profits. The HBC also benefited from its shorter lines of transportation compared to the huge overland distances its competitor had to traverse.[83] The North West traders had to move the pelts overland to Montreal and then to London on American-flagged ships. These distances grew longer as the Nor'Westers progressively exhausted the population of fur animals and moved on to even more remote locations.

In 1811 in an exceptional departure from the Company's distaste for settlements, a major shareholder of the HBC, the Earl of Selkirk, established the Red River settlement in the heart of territory claimed by the North West Company, populated by displaced Scottish Highlanders. This required a treaty with the local Ojibwa and Cree rulers.[84] The resulting tensions saw a North West Company–led attack on the HBC settlers in Red River in 1816 that left 21 of the latter dead. Together with declining profits that caused dissension among its partners, the political fallout of this incident proved fatal for the North West Company. The British government imposed a merger with the HBC in 1821 with the Hudson's Bay men retaining control. An Act of Parliament in the same year reaffirmed the HBC's charter monopoly, and extended it to the Arctic Ocean and the Pacific.[85]

82. McNeil 1999.
83. Carlos and Lewis 2010: 7.
84. McNeil 1999.
85. Rich 1961: 404–5.

THE END OF THE COMPANY-STATE:
SETTLEMENT AND SURRENDER

The belated end of the Hudson's Bay Company as a company-state came with the Deed of Surrender, signed 19 November 1869. In many ways the broad outlines of a deal had been apparent for at least a decade, with only one main sticking point: who would pay to compensate the HBC for the end of its charter privileges? Although it remained profitable, the tide of settlement and worries about irredentism from the United States, meant that even the HBC directors were increasingly reconciled to the end of the charter (as long as the price was right). When approached by the British government in 1856, one spokesman for the Company had offered to sell for £1 million.[86]

The Company's last addition to its territories, Vancouver Island, was only granted in 1849 on the condition that the HBC make it a settler colony.[87] The reasoning behind the decision to entrust this mission to the Company, despite its meager record of colonization over the preceding two centuries, is entirely typical of the whole company-state experience: "London wanted a political and military foothold on the west coast of North America but wanted it on the cheap"; the HBC promised to bear all the expenses.[88] Perhaps predictably, the HBC's efforts to build a settler colony on the island failed, and the HBC's grant to Vancouver Island was withdrawn in 1858.[89]

Concerns in Parliament about the legitimacy of a company exercising sovereign prerogatives, so prominent for the EIC, had never gone away with regard to the HBC.[90] In 1857 Parliament convened a select committee on the Hudson's Bay Company. The clear conclusion was that any lands suitable for settlement should be taken from Company auspices and ceded to the colony of Canada.[91] However, the committee also recommended that lands not suitable for settlement be retained by the HBC, supposedly for the welfare of the Indians and the fur trade alike (though one parliamentarian

---

86. Galbraith 1957: 340.
87. Royle 2011.
88. Perry 2001.
89. Royle 2011.
90. Galbraith 1957: 178; Perry 2015: 159.
91. Great Britain, Parliament, House of Commons 1857: iv.

rhetorically asked "Is it not a known fact that the brown race disappears in proportion to the coming of the white race?").[92] In his testimony to the committee, the HBC governor flatly denied that any of its land was suitable for settlement.[93] The report was notably equivocal on the legal force of the Company charter.[94]

Absent the required capital to buy out the Company from its remaining possessions, the Company lived on for another decade, but the writing was on the wall. The old question of how best to advance imperial interests now argued for settlement rather than a chartered company, and pressure from the Canadians steadily mounted.[95] The British North America Act of 1867 and Rupert's Land Act of 1868 laid the legislative ground for the end of the charter (skepticism about the charter persisted into the final legislation, with reference to the charter rights "thereby granted or purported to be granted to the said Governor and Company" in "the Lands and Territories held or claimed to be held by the said Governor and Company").[96] In 1869 the British government resolved to break the financial deadlock by guaranteeing a £300,000 loan to the government of a newly federated Canada, to be used to compensate the Company for the end of its charter. Under the terms of the agreement the Company also retained one-twentieth of its land in private ownership, a legacy that proved generous enough to secure its finances as the fur trade dwindled.[97] The Company sought to resist the deal, but the combined opposition of the British and Canadian governments made its position untenable.[98]

GEOPOLITICS AND THE HUDSON'S BAY COMPANY

To what degree is the Hudson's Bay Company representative of the company-state form? As observed earlier, its original charter was entirely typical in its combination of private and sovereign powers, not only in relation to the other company-states set up in the

---

92. Great Britain, Parliament, House of Commons 1857: 25.
93. Great Britain, Parliament, House of Commons 1857: 47–53.
94. Great Britain, Parliament, House of Commons 1857: xi.
95. Galbraith 1957: 428.
96. Rich 1961: 881.
97. Galbraith 1951.
98. Newman 1998: 575.

Restoration period, but also with reference to the Dutch and other nations' company-states. Relative to its English East India counterpart and the Dutch VOC and WIC, however, the HBC was notable for its unwarlike disposition. The two Dutch companies maintained fleets of dozens of warships and thousands of troops, while the EIC waged a series of major wars to conquer the whole of South Asia. The HBC military resources were trivial, its battlefield record risible, and its total staff varied between 100 and 1,500 from the seventeenth to the nineteenth centuries. Even as late as 1857, when in theory its writ ran over something like a twelfth of the Earth's land, only 139,000 Indians and 13,000 settlers inhabited its domains, and even these were largely outside the jurisdiction of the Company as such.[99] The HBC had been somewhat significant in the political-economic struggle with the French to 1713, but the Company's geopolitical significance for British North America became much greater in the nineteenth century. Though in some ways it imperiled British claims, nevertheless without the HBC there might not be a Pacific Canada today.[100]

But what, then, was the Company actually surrendering with the Deed of Surrender? First of all was the uncertain legal claims in the royal charter, and its 1821 parliamentary extension, of something that was not quite sovereignty and not quite ownership over the vast territory of Rupert's Land. Secondly, it gave up the right to administer British and Canadian laws in its territories, powers that had been very seldom used in any case.[101] Finally, it gave up its monopoly claim to the fur trade, a right consistently asserted but often challenged.

While the HBC did little to rule, and more to discourage than encourage colonization, its survival depended on the fact that it never took money from the public purse, whereas the only realistic alternatives for asserting any sort of British presence in the region were seen as expensive and uncertain. Because it did so little governing, there was no move to subject it to regular parliamentary control or scrutiny like the EIC, and as there was no parliamentary

99. Great Britain, Parliament, House of Commons 1857: 58, 92.
100. Galbraith 1957: 174.
101. Rich 1961: 428.

renewal of the charter 1690–1821, the HBC was spared the recurrent controversies that these instances occasioned for the other company-states. The HBC might have lived so long because it did so little, threatened so few, and cost outsiders nothing at all.

By the nineteenth century, however, the priority of settlement for economic but even more so geopolitical reasons trumped any respect for the Company's chartered rights. The French threat had long gone, and relations with the Russian-American Company after 1834 were congenial. The new threat was the expanding United States. In the mid-1840s tensions rose between the British Empire and the United States over the border between them in the Pacific Northwest.[102] HBC posts and American settlements were interspersed in the disputed territory.[103] For a time, it seemed like war might break out over the issue. The HBC was an important part of war planning, with the cabinet in London deciding to leave fighting in the Northwest to Company forces, aided by the Royal Navy.[104] Eventually both sides agreed on a border largely following the 49th parallel. The United States had gotten the better of the deal thanks to having more settlers in place, and hence a stronger commitment to the territory.[105] The Company's unwillingness or inability to attract settlers increasingly put British and later Canadian geopolitical interests at a massive disadvantage vis-à-vis the expanding Americans. The HBC again proved this deficiency in Vancouver Island, where Fort Victoria was established to try to preempt American settlement.[106]

The threat from the south only grew more pressing in the following decades. Rather than outright invasion, the worry was more that sheer weight of numbers would be decisive: American settlers would move north, especially from Minnesota, and then call for protection from the US government. The Company would be unable to contest such a claim, and the British government unwilling. At times Britain seemed almost resigned to most of present-day Canada falling to the United States.[107]

102. Fitzmaurice 2014: 203.
103. Keith 2007.
104. Galbraith 1957: 237–40; Rich 1961: 724.
105. Galbraith 1957: 250; Bown 2009: 230.
106. Royle 2011: 6.
107. Galbraith 1957: 410; Rich 1961: 794–95.

Making the issue more acute was the tendency of the US campaigns against the Sioux to spill over the border. Washington demanded that wanted Sioux sheltering in HBC lands be expelled back to the United States, or else US forces would cross the border to apprehend them. The Company requested London send troops; the British government declined. London instructed the Company not to let US forces into its territory; the Company ignored this direction.[108] US forces crossed the border, leading a Montreal newspaper to complain "what can we think of a Government which on the demands of a foreign power strips itself of the highest attribute of sovereignty, abandons the hitherto sacred right of asylum, virtually hauls down the British flag in the Indian territory, and allows the armed forces of another nation to pursue and murder with its connivance."[109] Both the imperial government in London and that of the new federation of Canada became convinced that as a matter of urgency they must end the HBC charter and settle the Company's territories to forestall US expansionism.

Summing up, HBC rule over vast swathes of North America had long ago been stripped of its legitimacy, as even Company directors recognized. It was nevertheless able to fight a long rearguard action thanks to uncertainties about whether settlement was viable in many of its lands, and due to the final sticking point of who would pay to extinguish the Company's claims. Though able to insulate itself from great power rivalry for long stretches, ultimately it was the strategic threat of the United States to British North America and Canada that brought about the end of the HBC as a company-state.

The Paradoxes of Success—The East India Company's Transformation and the Delegitimation of Company-States

From the mid-eighteenth century the EIC was the most militarily and commercially successful company-state, but also the most controversial. While it managed to shelter under the Mughal Emperor's

108. Galbraith 1957: 398; Rich 1961: 857.
109. Galbraith 1957: 399.

protection for the first century of its operations in South Asia, the empire's decline from the early 1700s forced the EIC to reappraise its passive military posture. This region's accelerating political fragmentation posed new security challenges. Further aggravating this instability, the French East India Company's introduction of European-style military innovations from the 1740s sharpened local geopolitical competition. Later, powerful new indigenous polities such as Mysore and the Maratha Confederacy eventually provoked the EIC to a policy of universal conquest throughout the subcontinent.[110]

The EIC's transformation into the "Company Raj" proved a powerful catalyst for the company-states' delegitimation, and so marks a critical inflection point in their history. In making sense of this process, we first present a précis of the EIC's expansion and the resulting tensions it posed for the balancing act between profit and power. We then turn to the shifting political context of late eighteenth-century Britain, taking particular note of the sharpening distinction between public and private spheres that was then beginning to take root. Finally, we consider the often rancorous debates that accompanied the EIC's early expansion, and the permanent changes Parliament imposed on the Company as a result of this contestation.

The EIC's evolution into a territorial empire can be divided into several phases. The first, beginning with the Company's arrival in India in 1612, and extending down to the 1740s, has already been covered in chapter 1. During this time, the EIC abjured large-scale territorial holdings, both because of restrictions imposed by local rulers (most notably the Mughal Emperor), or because the Company directors themselves sought to avoid the expense of conquest and administration. From the 1740s, the EIC began a process of militarization, largely in response to the activities of the French East India Company. A state-owned and directed enterprise, the French Company enjoyed little commercial success, but was the first European company to seek wealth through taxing agriculture extensively

110. For an excellent overview of the EIC's military expansion on the Indian subcontinent, see Roy 2008.

in the territories within its control.[111] The resulting land-hunger brought with it increased military expenditures, especially once the French Company constructed an Indian-manned army trained in Western-style practices of drill, discipline, and infantry-based warfare.[112]

From the 1740s, and culminating in the Seven Years' War, the EIC responded by mimicking French methods in building up its own European-style sepoy army to fend off the French Company.[113] Throughout this second phase of the EIC's evolution, these innovations were ad hoc, defensive and as yet unconnected to any desire for large-scale territorial expansion.[114] The growth of the EIC's military capabilities nevertheless fueled a hunger for greater revenues, to be had through either commerce or conquest. Initially, the EIC focused on the former, aggressively expanding its trading activities inland from the Calcutta Presidency, and making the most of the tax exemptions gifted to it by the distant Mughal Emperor. The EIC's activities—and attempted extension of its tax privileges to include its local intermediaries—eventually brought it into conflict with the governor of Bengal, Siraj ud-Daula, who regarded the Company's policies as undermining his own local state-building efforts.[115] Sharpening conflict between the governor of Bengal and the EIC and its indigenous commercial allies eventually culminated in ud-Daula's ouster, and the EIC's later reluctant assumption of de facto sovereignty over Bengal from 1765.[116]

Relying as much on processes of subversion and infiltration as direct battlefield confrontation, the EIC's takeover of Bengal nevertheless marked a turning point. Henceforth, the EIC was a major territorial power in India, exercising de facto control over some of the subcontinent's richest and most fertile territories.[117] For most of the remainder of the eighteenth century, the EIC refrained from further large-scale conquests, hoping to preserve a balance of power

111. Nierstrasz 2012: 33.
112. Nierstrasz 2012: 33.
113. Lynn 2003: 45.
114. Lynn 2003: 45.
115. Bryant 2013: 171.
116. Marshall 1987: 89.
117. Marshall 1993: 54; 2005: 54.

in India favorable to its commercial and strategic interests. But from the late eighteenth century, under the aggressive leadership of Governor-General Richard Wellesley, the EIC forsook a balance-of-power strategy in favor of paramountcy. This short but intense period in the EIC's evolution saw its defeat of its two most potent Indian rivals—Mysore, in the Fourth Anglo-Mysore War, and the Maratha Confederacy, in the Second and Third Anglo-Maratha Wars.[118] With its indigenous rivals mainly defeated by 1818, the EIC consolidated its vast new empire in the ensuing decades, eventually also crushing the Punjab—India's last powerful state—in 1842.[119] Continuing territorial expansion and dispossession of the descendants of client Indian rulers who died without male heirs followed, contributing to growing Indian disaffection and the eventual "Mutiny" of 1857–59.[120] Faced with the near-loss of its Indian Empire, Britain divested the EIC of its responsibilities in 1858—by which time it had in any case long since ceased to enjoy any practical autonomy independent of the British state.[121] Thus the EIC made a relatively rapid but also largely unplanned transformation into a large-scale territorial empire.

For this study, the Company's territorial expansion is most relevant for the impact it had on the EIC's trade-off between power and profit-seeking, and thus on its overall institutional character. At the most superficial level, one can argue that the EIC's territorial expansion from 1765 testified to both its commercial and geopolitical success. While the company's stocks had fluctuated between £50 to £150 from 1693 to 1720, from 1765 until 1813, the share price ranged between £120 and £250.[122] From an army of merely 3,000 troops in 1757, the EIC expanded its forces to 35,000 by 1779, 70,000 by 1790, and to 153,000 by 1808.[123] This militarization moreover coincided with the growth in the Company's territorial footprint, from its initial outposts in the Presidency towns of Calcutta, Madras, and Bombay, to eventually encompass two-thirds

118. Deshpande 2012: 2,491.
119. Deshpande 2012: 2,495.
120. Darwin 2012: 256.
121. Lawson 1993: 161–62.
122. Robins 2006: 26.
123. Roy 2013: 1,143.

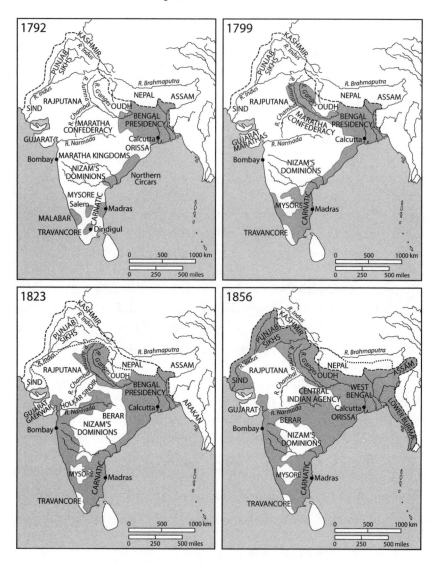

MAP 6. The East India Company's Territorial Spread, 1792–1856

of the Indian subcontinent, with the remainder being composed of client Princely States beholden to the EIC.[124]

At first glance, then, the EIC's conquest of India appears an unqualified success. Further scrutiny nevertheless reveals a tectonic shift in the Company's character that came with large-scale

124. Keay 2000: 396.

conquest—a shift that ultimately left it dangerously exposed to political challenges from its opponents back in Britain. Territorial conquest changed the EIC's primary revenue base, with taxes on agriculture and local commerce outstripping revenue from the EIC's trading activities. Initially, the EIC's business model had followed that of the VOC, resting on the arbitrage opportunities that came with both the intra-Asian "country trade," and the long-distance trade in Asian luxury goods.[125] But following the conquest of Bengal, the EIC gradually exchanged the role of merchant for that of ruler, with a growing proportion of its revenues coming from the taxation of the Indian peasantry.[126] Over time, the costs of maintaining large permanent standing armies in India reinforced this tendency. Company directors did not want to sacrifice profits to support the costs of conquering and keeping Indian territories or administering Indian populations.[127] Consequently, the costs of empire had to be borne overwhelmingly by the EIC's Indian subjects—with sometimes devastating humanitarian consequences.

The increased costs of defense and administration, and the often disastrous impact of the Company's rule on the local population, together sharply increased parliamentary scrutiny of the company's activities. In 1770, following the failure of the monsoon and widespread drought, Bengal was afflicted by a devastating famine that wiped out up to a third of its population.[128] Determined to maintain its tax revenues, the EIC increased its exactions at this time. Unscrupulous Company agents manipulated local rice markets to create their own private fortunes, further aggravating Indian misery.[129] Through a combination of rapacity, neglect, and incompetence, the EIC's activities dramatically worsened the plight of its subjects. Moreover, despite the huge increase in revenues won through conquest, and later violently extracted from starving locals, the Company's financial position worsened. While gross revenues remained high, the EIC still struggled to offset the huge and ongoing costs of maintaining its army and fortifications.

125. Marshall 1998: 488.
126. Marshall 1998: 506.
127. Marshall 1998: 506.
128. Meurer 2012: 221.
129. Dirks 2008: 54.

Indeed, so dire was the EIC's underlying financial position at this time that the Company was forced to petition Parliament for a loan of £1,400,000 in 1772 to keep itself afloat.[130]

Despite the outward appearance of high paper profits and healthy dividends for stockholders, by 1772 no less a personage than the Bengal governor, Warren Hastings, observed of the Company's plight: "The Treasury was empty; the Company was involved in debt; its revenue was declining, and every region of Hindostan groaned under different degrees of oppression, desolation, and insecurity."[131] Having secured an emergency loan from the government, and off the strength of anticipated revenues from its territorial empire, the EIC was able to pay back its debt by 1776.[132] But from then on, its financial relationship with the British government was transformed. Whereas previously the EIC had often lent large sums of money to the government, this relationship was reversed after 1772. From this point, the EIC would regularly seek state financial support, and was moreover compelled to forgive earlier government debts to the Company in exchange for the renewal of its charter in 1793.[133] This change in the EIC's financial relationship to the British state ensured more consistent, careful, and critical parliamentary scrutiny of the Company's activities thereafter—eventually culminating in the delegitimation of the EIC, and by extension company-states more generally.

The role of shifting conceptions of legitimacy played an especially important role in the fate of the EIC. To contextualize this discussion, we must first revisit the context that had made the company-states possible in the first instance. As company-states emerged and evolved over the seventeenth century, they reflected a conception of sovereignty as divisible and capable of delegation to multiple actors, and were predicated on mercantilist ideas that conceived no clear distinction between public and private realms.

By the mid-late eighteenth century, mercantilist thinking continued to hold sway within Britain's political, commercial, and economic establishment. But an embryonic science of political

130. Sivramkrishna 2014: 790.
131. Sivramkrishna 2014: 790.
132. Bowen 2006: 36.
133. Bowen 2006: 36.

economy was also beginning to take shape. Prominent thinkers were beginning to conceive of the economy as centered on an autonomous market composed of rational utility-maximizers, and to denounce the tyranny and corruption they associated with monopolies.[134] Simultaneously, the continued strengthening of government through major conflicts such as the Seven Years' War solidified a more unitary and centralized conception of state sovereignty.[135] Together, these two trends helped sharpen an emerging differentiation between the *public* and the *private* as two distinct and separate social domains. Thus, the *public* increasingly connoted the sphere of collective life associated with the exercise of governmental power.[136] The *private* by contrast captured the realm of family and civil society, as well as that of the market economy.[137] Initially conceived as part of ongoing debates seeking to set the legitimate limits of rulers' power, this new form of thinking also implicitly envisaged boundaries on the exercise of "public" powers by private agents.[138]

The progressive sharpening of a public/private divide in British political thought thus unsettled many of the core assumptions that had first enabled the company-states. The emerging science of political economy did not itself delegitimize the EIC. Rather, it fed into a more general climate of opinion that was increasingly hostile to actors that seemed to transgress the public/private divide. Within this new context, an actor like the EIC was more vulnerable. The EIC had always attracted critics jealous of its commercial privileges, and the Company had had to defend its monopoly throughout its existence. But whereas earlier criticisms of the EIC had targeted its specific privileges, the emergence of a nascent public/private divide held out the possibility of a more total critique

134. See, for example, Grewal 2016. It is nevertheless worth noting that the public/private distinction had earlier antecedents, and only fully crystallized in Anglo-American thought and legal practice over the nineteenth century. See generally Horwitz 1982.

135. On the progressive consolidation of stronger states as a result of "military fiscalism" throughout this period, see generally Bayly 1998: 28–47.

136. On the "sharpening" of the divide between the market and state affairs that developed from this time, see Hill 2006: 637.

137. Grewal 2016: 431.

138. On the critique of "Old Corruption" that began to take purchase from this time, see generally Rubinstein 1983.

of the EIC on the basis of what it was—"a state in disguise of a merchant, a great public office in the disguise of a counting house."[139]

While the rise of the public/private divide provided the permissive context for the EIC's delegitimation, it was the specific challenges and catastrophes attending the first years of its rule in Bengal that gave its enemies back in Britain their opportunity. The Great Bengal Famine dramatized for many the EIC's evident failure to rule justly.[140] For while the EIC did manage to squeeze greater wealth from its conquests relative to its Indian predecessors, this came at an appalling human cost.[141] With varying degrees of cynicism and sincerity, the Company's critics in Britain seized on the EIC's cruelty and incompetence to challenge its right to rule over a population much greater than Britain's own.

The famine not only discredited the Company's bombastic claims to administrative superiority. Additionally, in the greater parliamentary scrutiny and popular interest it attracted, the famine also provoked more general consternation over the great corruption of the Company's agents. Frustration over Company agents' exploitation of the EIC's monopoly privileges to enrich themselves was not new. But the huge reservoirs of wealth that came with the new Indian land revenues provided correspondingly gargantuan opportunities for illicit enrichment. Indeed, in time they helped create a new class of conspicuously rich EIC employees—the so-called nabobs. Prominent Britons quickly denounced the nabobs not only for their ostentation, but also for the perceived threat to British liberty that they potentially posed, if they could leverage their wealth into corresponding political influence in Parliament.[142] With the British government deeply invested—quite literally—in the Company after 1773 through its status as a key creditor, increased scrutiny eventually yielded a succession of scandals over the conduct of EIC officials. Most notoriously, Edmund Burke's impeachment of

---

139. Burke 2003 [1788]: 147.

140. Dirks 2008: 54.

141. It is worth noting that even the EIC at its most rapacious faced significant constraints on its ability to collect the land tax, and that the magnitude of its increased demands relative to its Indian predecessors remains a subject of debate among historians. See Travers 2004: 519–21.

142. Travers 2007: 217.

Warren Hastings provided a focal point for a more general critique of the Company's dominance in India, which yielded permanent changes in its constitution.

Reflecting on the company's ruinous rule in Bengal, Burke decried assigning powers of war and peace—"those great, high prerogatives of sovereignty"—to a "subordinate power" such as the EIC.[143] In a similar vein, another anonymous critic argued that only the king was the "supreme Arbiter, by the British constitution, of all matters of war and peace."[144] The EIC, by contrast, was depicted as "the most complete system ever known of fraud and violence, by uniting, in the same persons, the several functions of Merchant, Soldier, Financier and Judge; depriving, by that union, all those functions of their mutual checks, by which alone they can be made useful to society."[145] This newfound concern at combining commercial and political functions in the one entity likewise found expression in Burke's lamentation that the company had become since its establishment "that thing which was supposed by the Roman law to be so unsuitable—the same power was a trader, the same power was a lord."[146]

The underlying motives driving these critiques were naturally diverse, and ranged from sincere apprehension at the Company's massive accumulation of economic and political power, through to more base jealousies at exclusion from the Company's lucrative privileges. The individual motives nevertheless matter less than the emerging discomfort with company-state arrangements that they generally reflected, and the EIC's increased political vulnerability arising from this discomfort.[147] Even more fundamental were the long-term institutional consequences of these scandals. The more sustained scrutiny that resulted prompted extensive revisions to the Company. Thus in 1773, the Regulating Act mandated that the EIC's board of directors needed the Crown's assent in appointing

143. Burke 2003 [1788]: 146.
144. Anonymous 1772.
145. Anonymous 1772: iv.
146. Burke 2003 [1788]: 147.
147. On rising discomfort at political forms that diverged from the sovereign state and the impact of same on the EIC's legitimacy, see Stern 2008: 283.

the Company Governor-General in India.[148] Simultaneously, the Crown set up its own courts in India, superior to the Company's existing judicial system.[149] Later, in 1784, the India Act established a state Board of Control to supervise the Company board, further subordinating the EIC under the British state's direct surveillance and supervision.[150]

Concurrent to these changes in the EIC's relationship to the British state, critics meanwhile invoked liberal critiques of monopoly to gradually strip away the Company's remaining commercial privileges. In 1813, Parliament revoked the Company's monopoly on trade with India, while its China monopoly was abolished in 1833.[151] Cumulatively, these interventions tore apart the company's original character as a commercial profit-maximizing entity, to the extent that by the time the Government of India Act was passed in 1853, the EIC was reduced to a mere bureaucratic extension of the British state, to rule India only "until Parliament shall otherwise provide."[152] With the end of its rule already in view, it was therefore no surprise when the EIC's authority in India was revoked a mere five years later, following the "Indian Mutiny." The EIC persisted for a short time afterward managing the tea trade on behalf of Britain, only to be formally wound up in 1874.[153] But by then, its existence as a company-state—dedicated to profit and endowed with sovereign prerogatives—was already over.

Finally, beyond questions of legitimacy, a more mundane but no less pivotal factor also contributed to the East India Company's demise—its growing functional redundancy. As metropolitan states' colonial ambitions broadened from the mid-eighteenth century, company-states' existing transoceanic infrastructure proved a tempting target for appropriation. Simultaneously, metropolitan states themselves were in any case independently strengthening their capacities for global expansion, threatening to make the company-states irrelevant. This combination of

148. Lawson 1993: 85.
149. Benton 1999: 568–69.
150. Lawson 1993: 124–25.
151. Lawson 1993: 159.
152. *Government of India Act* 1853.
153. Robins 2006: 26.

creeping appropriation and metropolitan state-strengthening together diminished the need for company-states, accelerating their demise.

The EIC—like its counterpart company-states in Asia and elsewhere—had first arisen when direct connections between Europe and the polities of the wider world were virtually non-existent. A key part of the company-states' raison d'etre was their role as vanguards of European expansion. Company-states laid the foundations for a more durable European overseas presence. They did so by initiating, establishing, and maintaining cross-cultural diplomatic networks, as well as by discovering information about new markets and polities, and thereby closing information asymmetries that had previously inhibited European long-distance commerce and conquest.[154] Company-states like the EIC also laid down the logistical infrastructure necessary for a permanent European transoceanic presence, establishing powerful merchant fleets and the complex networks of forts, ports, and victualling stations necessary to sustain them. Finally, particularly for the EIC from the mid-late eighteenth century, company-states' commercial and diplomatic activities nourished thickening webs of indigenous collaborators—be they soldiers, scribes, spies, or creditors—that could potentially be enlisted for purposes of colonial conquest.[155]

The company-states had played an indispensable role in carving out pathways for European long-distance colonization. But by the mid-late eighteenth century, the reasons for reserving this function as the company-states' distinctive preserve were no longer clear. Instead, geopolitical competition encouraged metropolitan states to eye the company-states' infrastructure as an asset that they could appropriate to advance their own colonial ambitions. From the Seven Years' War onward, metropolitan states acted on this temptation through conscripting company-states' assets into colonial conflicts. In Asia, as previously in the Atlantic, this harmed the company-states financially and encroached on their autonomy. Crucially, it also blurred the lines between company-states and their home-state sponsors, calling into question the continued need for

154. van Meersbergen 2019; Harris 2018: 88.
155. Bayly 1983.

maintaining the company-states as a separate class of institutions. As expanding metropolitan states piggybacked on company-states to extend their global reach, the latter risked being assimilated as administrative subsidiaries of the former.

The specter of incremental nationalization loomed over all company-states. But it had an especially decisive role in hastening the EIC's demise as a company-state. This trend was clear from the Seven Years' War, during which the British state had enlisted Company ships and men to capture Manila from the Spanish in 1762. Subsequently, "[t]he government realised that here was a resource it could use as an extension of British power in the East and which, it also believed, would be at no cost to the Treasury."[156]

This trend continued with the American Revolutionary War, during which the Company was for the first time compelled to pay for royal troops sent out to India.[157] Following Britain's defeat in the Revolutionary War, the metropole's attention swung eastward, where co-opted Company assets again offered a potentially inexpensive platform for British colonial expansion. Here, the British state benefited from the EIC's prior transformation into a heavily militarized "fighting company" after 1756.[158] Specifically, the growing British Empire became "dependent upon the lifeline provided by the Company's commercial system because without the existence of permanently established supply chains over extended lines of transoceanic communication, the Company's forces could not have functioned effectively for any great length of time at all."[159] Critically, just as company forces were dependent on the EIC's logistical infrastructure, so too were the British royal forces stationed in India, by then rapidly emerging as a crucial hub in Britain's expanding imperium.

The EIC's logistics system, fortified through its wars with the French and local Indian polities, thus became a springboard for the British state's colonial expansion. In return for its "generosity" in preserving the EIC's rapidly vanishing monopoly privileges, the

156. Ward 2013: 62.
157. Ward 2013: 62.
158. Bowen 2011: 35.
159. Bowen 2011: 35.

British state moreover pressured the EIC to support the war effort in both the Revolutionary and Napoleonic Wars.[160] This entailed deployment of company troops in attacks on Ceylon (1795, 1803, and 1815), Malacca and the Moluccas (1795), Egypt (1801), Réunion and Mauritius (1810), and Java (1811).[161] Likewise, the EIC was also pressured into aiding the British war effort in other ways, from loans to the leasing of ships, to the direct conversion of East India-men into warships with crews recruited by the EIC.[162]

Alongside this creeping nationalization by a thousand cuts, the EIC also had to contend with a British state that was more expan-sive in the geographic scope of its ambitions, and more institu-tionally capable of realizing them than ever before. From the mid-eighteenth century, for example, the Royal Navy's commission extended "to make discoveries of countries hitherto unknown," pro-viding a warrant for its increasing penetration into the Pacific.[163] Under the pressures of recurrent war with its colonial rivals, Britain moreover undertook a series of far-reaching reforms to strengthen its logistical and administrative ability to coordinate and wage war simultaneously on multiple continents.[164] The establishment of a permanent Secretary of State for War and Colonies in 1794, respon-sible for planning and coordinating expeditionary operations and defending Britain's overseas colonies, marked the capstone of this revolution in state capacity.[165] Fittingly, this office's first occupant, Henry Dundas, also simultaneously served as President of the Board of Control for India, the administration now charged with supreme governmental oversight of the EIC.[166] This combination of roles exemplified the EIC's progressive absorption into the Brit-ish colonial apparatus, and its effective death as an institutional entity separate and distinct from its metropolitan sovereign state sponsor.

160. Ward 2013: 63.
161. Ward 2013: 63.
162. Ward 2013: 63.
163. Williams 1996.
164. Morriss 2011: 77.
165. Morriss: 2011: 30.
166. Morriss 2011: 30.

Conclusion

This chapter has charted the company-states' decline from the mid-eighteenth through to the mid-nineteenth centuries. Their decline reflected a combination of intensifying geopolitical competition, ideological delegitimation, and growing redundancy. Intensifying geopolitical competition sharpened the profit-power tension at the heart of the company-states' constitution. Different company-states pursued diverse strategies of muddling through (the VOC), selling out (the HBC), or leveling up (the EIC) to manage this tension. But the outcomes of each—insolvency and nationalization, full privatization, or delegitimation occasioning creeping nationalization—all meant the end as a distinct institutional form. An increasingly sharp dichotomy reordering social life into distinct *public* and *private* categories significantly corroded support for company-states. And the company-states' very success in laying down the foundations for inter-continental commerce and conquest effectively made them seem obsolete and no longer necessary to many from the mid-late eighteenth century onward.

Zooming out from our individual case studies, more general trends in the nineteenth century advanced the company-states' demise. The spread of revolutionary new communication and transportation and communication technologies like the steamship, the railway, and the telegraph together propelled a profound compression of time-space.[167] This revolutionary increase in interaction capacity further heightened European states' aspirations to assert direct command and control of trans-continental empires. It held out the promise of enabling metropolitan states to effectively disintermediate relations between themselves and their colonial appendages, cutting out hybrid middlemen like company-states.

At an institutional level, meanwhile, this period saw the acceleration of two unfavorable developments for the future of company-states. Within European polities and their colonial extensions, rulers built on earlier administrative innovations, increasingly embracing what Buzan and Lawson have dubbed "rational state-building."[168]

---

167. Buzan and Lawson 2015: 70.
168. Buzan and Lawson 2015: 34–35.

This entailed rulers' increased capacity for direct rule, and a corresponding intolerance for the forms of shared sovereignty and indirect rule that had traditionally defined most early modern states.[169] The mid-nineteenth century also saw a parallel effort to rationalize and standardize relations between as well as within polities.[170] The rise of a supposedly universal system of positivist international law promised to eradicate the diverse patchwork of bespoke arrangements company-states had earlier practiced in building the first global international system. Positivist international law was both Eurocentric and state-centric. In its Eurocentrism, it allowed no meaningful concessions to indigenous customs and conceptions of legitimacy of the kind that had once underpinned company-states' localized bargains.[171] In its state-centrism, positivist international law also increasingly excluded the practices of corporate diplomacy and war-making that defined the company-states.[172]

The mid-nineteenth-century international system reflected the growing consolidation of the public/private divide, and with it, a rising intolerance for practices and actors that seemed to transgress this distinction. In 1856, the Treaty of Paris inaugurated system-wide prohibitions on mercenaries and privateers.[173] The broad acceptance of this treaty among Western states suggested the incremental consolidation of norms prohibiting non-state actors from engaging in international violence. Likewise, the era saw the slow entrenchment of republican and liberal conceptions of legitimacy in the international system's Atlantic core.[174] This sat uneasily with earlier conceptions of sovereignty as a divisible bundle of prerogatives that European rulers were at liberty to assign to favored individuals or entities, such as company-states. Republican and liberal ideals conversely conceived sovereignty as residing (in theory) with a community of equal national citizens, with violence to be exclusively monopolized

---

169. Buzan and Lawson 2015: 34–35.
170. On this point, see generally Rovira 2013.
171. Rovira 2013: 40.
172. Rovira 2013: 96.
173. Thomson 1994: 70.
174. Thomson 1994: 147–48.

by states, and employed solely for the purposes of protecting and advancing the interests of the sovereign nation.[175]

These trends together led to an international environment that was increasingly hostile to company-states. Nevertheless—and this is crucial for understanding how it was possible for would-be imperialists to later resurrect them—there was as yet no explicit norm or prohibition on company-states or on other forms of "private" imperialism by 1860. Whereas before company-states were seen as either unremarkable or essential, by the mid-nineteenth century, the Western world increasingly regarded them as anachronistic relics of a bygone age.

Norms against other forms of private international violence, such as mercenarism and privateering, were only just beginning to be institutionalized. When it came to the specific practice of imperialism spearheaded by company-states, the companies' advocates could still mount plausible arguments in their defense. This is most famously illustrated in John Stuart Mill's spirited if ultimately unsuccessful attempt to defend the EIC's continued suzerainty in India in the wake of the "Mutiny."[176] Mill lost the argument. But the fact that he was still able to even make arguments for the Company's continued supremacy in India demonstrates the contestable nature of the presumption against company-states at this time.

For these reasons, the resurrection of company-states in the late nineteenth century would not entail a simple replication of their earlier form. Certainly, the prime motivation for licensing company-states—colonialism on the cheap—remained constant. But the new generation of company-states that developed from the 1870s would be more strictly surveilled and more carefully superintended by sponsoring governments than before. And when they eventually reneged on their core promise and required financial rescue, the failure of these companies would eventually ensure the company-state's extinction.

---

175. Thomson 1994: 147–48.

176. On Mill's defense of the East India Company as the entity best placed to continue to rule India, see Moore 1983: 510–14.

CHAPTER FOUR

The Resurrection
of the Company-States

BY THE EARLY nineteenth century, the first wave of chartered companies like the Royal African Company, the Dutch West and East India Companies, and the French and Scandinavian company-states had gone broke or been subordinated to their respective governments. Even those that lived on, most notably the Hudson's Bay Company in North America and the still-expanding East India Company, were more subject to state control, and less able to engage in war and diplomacy on their own account. It seemed like these hybrid public/private enterprises were on their way out, shunted aside by increasingly powerful states.

Yet the nineteenth century saw the birth of a new wave of company-states, pressed into service in the vast expansion of European empires, from the Americas, to Africa, to Asia and the South Pacific. Harking back to precedents from an earlier age, the British, Russian, German, Italian, Belgian, and Portuguese governments returned to the company-state model.[1] Hence the first main question of this chapter: why the resurrection of the company-state?

The company-states of the nineteenth century shared close institutional similarities with the earlier generation. But the similarities in form were not matched by their achievements. In practice, none of these new chartered companies enjoyed anything like the political, military, or diplomatic latitude of their predecessors. None built great fleets, mustered formidable armies, or ruled millions of

---

1. Stern 2015: 19; Press 2017: 6–7.

subjects. What governing prerogatives they were granted they commonly shirked, leaving states to step into the breach as imperial
administrators. Even on commercial terms, the nineteenth-century
company-states were disappointing. Although they often produced
crucial legacies in shaping European expansion during the time of
the "new imperialism," these companies generally lived a precarious
financial existence, often kept alive only by public subsidies. Thus
the second major puzzle to be answered: why did the second wave
of company-states do so poorly compared with the first?

Perhaps the most commonsense answer to these related puzzles
is that, while nineteenth-century states wanted extra-European
empires for a mix of strategic, commercial, and prestige concerns,
they also wanted them on the cheap. Like their early modern forerunners, these governments sought to enjoy the benefits of imperial expansion, or at least to avoid the purported geopolitical consequences of missing out, while passing the costs on to somebody
else. In this case, "somebody else" was private capital, tempted by
the prospect of monopoly profits. If, then, the motivations for the
early modern and nineteenth century company-states were broadly
similar, why were the results so different? As demonstrated below,
the new wave of company-states had come into a different world, a
different era, and these different circumstances crucially restricted
their prospects.

In the nineteenth century, European states had come much
closer to monopolizing powers of war, rule, and diplomacy than
their counterparts in the early modern era. Having fought hard to
arrogate these core sovereign prerogatives, they were now more
reluctant to share them. More than just a matter of inclination,
nineteenth-century states had much more ability to actually wield
these powers, including at great distances from the metropole.
While early modern rulers were delegating sovereign powers over
distant lands that they could hardly have exercised even if they
had wanted to, this was much less true of European governments
as the 1800s progressed. In part this was a change of material
capacity, and the transport and communication technologies that
had the effect of shrinking distances. Even more important were
the waxing fiscal, administrative, and military capabilities of the
state.

Like their early modern counterparts, the sovereign powers of the nineteenth century company-states were generally restricted to dealing with non-Western polities, while the home government retained the responsibility of relations with other Western states. This fact once again evidences our key point about the distinction between intra-European relations, on the one hand, and those between Europeans and non-Europeans, on the other, a major theme of this book. But by the 1800s, and especially the end of the century, there were few if any areas of the earth not subject to European claims, meaning that in practice company-states were often marginalized in external relations as imperial claims were settled between Western states. The non-Western polities that chartered companies did engage with were not the great powers of the Mughals or the Chinese of the seventeenth century. Thus by the nineteenth century, increasing Western military and commercial dominance, and the increasing spread of European empires, meant that the cross-cultural relations of the early modern era were giving way to international relations taking place within the same global Eurocentric frame.

But the changing context also related to fundamental shifts in the climate of opinion, and beliefs about legitimate rule. Government leaders, metropolitan and imperial state officials, and settlers of the new extra-European possessions increasingly saw war and rule as inherently public prerogatives of the sovereign state, as we do today. The idea of private wars and diplomacy, commonplace in the 1600s, was now conceived as dangerously archaic and illegitimate, especially if they involved other Western states. Often this mind-set was shared by those in the new company-states themselves, especially as sloughing off the burdens of rule might well make commercial sense from their self-interested corporate point of view. If states were keen to pass the costs of expansion and administration to new chartered companies, for their part these companies were often keen to pass the costs back to the public purse, and get on with making profits (or at least trying to). Each side defined their interests in terms of what the ideas of the day specified as possible and appropriate.[2]

2. Finnemore 1996.

The remainder of the chapter substantiates these claims by looking at second generation company-states hailing from a variety of national contexts across the nineteenth century, active from North America to Africa and the South Pacific. Thus in chronological order we examine the Russian-American Company in Alaska, the British South Africa Company, and the German New Guinea Company, before lastly considering the singularly misnamed Congo Free State.

The Russian-American Company

In the 1600s Russian fur traders had covered the huge expanses of Siberia and reached the Pacific Coast. It was the fur trade that drew Russia into the global economy, with taxes on the trade generating 30 percent of state revenue in the mid-seventeenth century.[3] In the 1700s traders began to venture out across the Bering Sea to the Aleutian Islands and the North American coast as far south as California. Once again supporting our theme that states were quite marginal in pushing forward European expansion, most of this trail-blazing was conducted by freebooters and adventurers. Although the government had sponsored the Bering expedition of 1741 that gave rise to the initial Russian claims on American territory, for the rest of the eighteenth century efforts to traverse the passage to Alaska were largely driven by private merchants.

While fur-trapping in Siberia was centered on the sable, in the North Pacific it was the sea otter that was the prime pelt, worth up to ten times that of beaver.[4] Sea otters were difficult to hunt, however, and prone to overexploitation, given their low rate of reproduction. Exhaustion of stocks around Kamchatka saw almost 20 fur trading firms mounting missions ever farther out into the Kurile and Aleutian Islands, and then to America.[5]

The largest of these enterprises, the Irkutsk-based Shelikhov-Golikov Company, set up the first permanent post on Kodiak Island in 1784, putting down an uprising by locals in the process.[6]

3. Vinkovetsky 2011: 54–55.
4. Gibson 1980: 129.
5. Anichtchenko 2013: 38; Wheeler 1971: 421.
6. Tikhmenev 1978 [1863]: 14; Vinkovetsky 2011: 33.

Shortly afterward, these merchants began lobbying the government of Catherine the Great for a monopoly charter.[7] An appeal to this end in 1788 was pitched in terms of advancing imperial interests in bringing Alaska, California, the Kuriles, and the Aleutians within the empire.[8] While commercial concerns were clearly primary, the Shelikhov-Golikov Company had indeed been working to extend claims of Russian sovereignty.[9] Despite an initially sympathetic hearing from her officials, the Empress vetoed the proposal. Evincing a highly selective commitment to liberal principles (given that autocratic Russia's economy was based on serfdom), she reasoned that "this petition is sheer monopoly and exclusivity of trade, which is contrary to my principles . . . we are in every way of the opinion that trade should be free."[10] The Empress directly disparaged the company-state as an institution, judging that they were "all being ruined and soon the English and Dutch [companies] will be in the same decline that the French now finds itself."[11] The more general problem, which hamstrung proponents of Russian America for decades afterward, was that Russian rulers from Catherine onward were much more concerned with European diplomacy, and then expansion in the Caucasus and later Asia, than with building an empire in the New World.[12]

Undeterred, the Shelikhov-Golikov partnership pushed forward with its plans, unifying various Russian Pacific fur traders to form the United American Company in 1798 and launching an expedition to establish an outpost in Alaska.[13] It renewed the appeal for a charter during the brief reign of Tsar Paul, this time successfully. Once again, for the Russian government the main attraction was that the Company "reduced the costs and risks of practicing colonialism," being "imperialism on the cheap."[14]

The charter for the newly created Russian-American Company (*Rossiyskaya-Amerikanskaya Kompaniya*) was modeled

7. Matthews 2013: 71–73.
8. Grinëv 2015: 13.
9. Tikhmenev 1978 [1863]: 20–24; Wheeler 1987: 44–49.
10. Grinëv 2015: 13–14.
11. Wheeler 1987: 51.
12. Mazour 1936, 1937; Gibson 1978; Smith-Peter 2015.
13. Andrews 1927.
14. Vinkovetsky 2011: 67, 186.

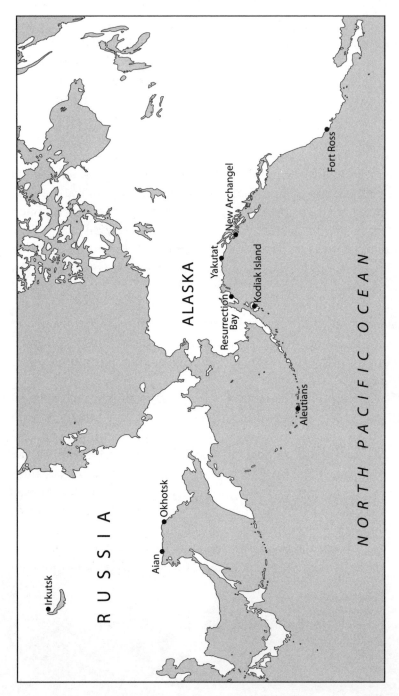

MAP 7. Russian-American Company

on the British East India Company: "Russia looked to its British competitors for models of company governance that might, if suitably modified, provide similar profits without threatening Russian imperial order."[15] It created a new joint-stock entity, Russia's first (the previous fur trading firms had been partnerships), and granted a 20-year monopoly on the fur trade North of the 55th parallel in America, as well as in the Aleutian and Kurile Islands.[16] The new Company had the right to use armed force on land and sea, to issue money, and to make agreements with the natives of the new lands.[17] The Company was bound to pacify the natives, and later developed a significant religious role.[18] The land remained the property of the state rather than the Russian-American Company, however, and the Company had no judicial powers.[19] Aside from the merchant firms that had created the Company, shareholders increasingly included courtiers, senior government officials, and even the Tsar himself, leading to an early relocation of the directors from Irkutsk to St. Petersburg.[20] In a sign of things to come, the new Company had a responsibility to keep the Tsar closely informed of its activities, and the government appointed an inspector (the Correspondent) within the Company to handle political matters.[21]

ESTABLISHING RUSSIAN AMERICA AND
RELATIONS WITH LOCAL POLITIES

Its legal position secured, the new Company soon faced a more practical problem: in 1802 its initial Alaskan outpost had been stormed and destroyed, with 20 Russians and 130 Aleuts massacred by the Tlingit people who had their homes in the area.[22] The Tlingits proved to be tenacious opponents over the years on land and in the coastal waters of Alaska. They attacked the Company headquarters even as late as 1866, the penultimate year of

15. Easley 2008: 78; see also Nichols 1967: 14; Wheeler 1987: 58; Smith-Peter 2015: 2.
16. Vinkovetsky 2011: 8.
17. Tikhmenev 1978 [1863]: 54–55; Bown 2009: 172–73.
18. Nordlander 1995.
19. Morris et al. 2014: 91.
20. Matthews 2013: 131.
21. Mazour 1944.
22. Gibson 1978: 368.

the Company's presence.[23] Vinkovetsky notes "A force of just a few hundred [Tlingit] warriors could be a serious threat to the very existence of Russian America."[24] The Tlingits were greatly strengthened by the habit of American traders to sell muskets and even cannons in return for furs,[25] leading the official Company history to conclude that they "were better armed than the Russians."[26]

Though the Tlingit also came to be important trading partners for the Russians, especially for food and furs, they did so on a basis of equality.[27] Company strategies to institute a system of indirect rule over the Tlingits by anointing pro-Russian "main chiefs" failed, as did their efforts to mimic the native practice of potlatch.[28] The Company record complained "this warlike and completely savage people have blocked all the efforts of the colonial administration to change and develop their moral qualities," and so recommended that the Company should "compromise in some matters when their childlike vanity is affected."[29] Thus the verdict of a government inspector in the 1860s: "In no respect can the [Tlingit] be considered dependent on the company; rather, it can be said that the company's very settlements on the American coast depend on them."[30] Company outposts (referred to as *faktoriia*, i.e., factories, another link with previous company-states) were scattered along the coast and the islands, with little effort to exert authority inland.[31]

The Russians experienced problems of a very different nature with the Aleuts. Unlike the Tlingits, they were formally incorporated into the empire. The Aleuts, however, preferred selling furs to British and American traders, who paid higher prices.[32] The solution for both Shelikhov-Golikov and later the Russian-American Company was coercion. All males between the ages of 15 to 50 were

23. Gibson 1978: 368; see also Dean 1995: 290; Vinkovetsky 2011: 84.
24. Vinkovetsky 2011: 22.
25. Wheeler 1971.
26. Tikhmenev 1978 [1863]: 174.
27. Marsden and Galois 1995.
28. Dean 1995.
29. Tikhmenev 1978 [1863]: 352–53.
30. Gibson 1978: 375.
31. Davidson 1941: 33.
32. Wheeler 1971: 423.

obliged to hunt otters for the Company, being paid in kind.[33] They were forbidden to sell pelts to non-Russians.[34] The Aleuts were extremely skilled hunters, being trained from boyhood with kayaks and harpoons, and as such were indispensable to the whole Company project.[35] Their society paid a horrific price for their usefulness to the Russians, however. As a result of new diseases, overwork, and violence, the most densely populated section of the Aleutians saw its population decline by almost half just in the period 1806–1817.[36] The Aleuts were later supplemented as Company hunters by the natives of Kodiak Island, who suffered a similarly catastrophic population decline of 75 percent 1792–1834.[37] Gibson rather chillingly notes that because the Aleut, Kodiak, and sea otter populations collapsed at roughly at the same rate, the Company was able to keep up its exploitation of all three.[38]

The basic economic model of the Russian-American Company was a triangular trade.[39] Sea otter pelts, supplemented with those of seals and land animals, were obtained by coercion or barter from Native Americans and islanders, and then transported to China. There, they were exchanged for porcelain, silks, but especially tea.[40] Sea otter, like opium for the East India Company, was the unlikely solution to the difficulty that all Western firms trading into China faced: what to trade with the Chinese, who had so much, but wanted so little from the outside world, except silver and gold?[41] The tea and other Chinese goods were then sold in European Russia.

While all company-states faced substantial logistical problems, those of the Russian-American Company were perhaps the most acute. The journey overland from St. Petersburg through Siberia to the Pacific coast and then across the Bering Sea to Russian America took about 17 months, one way. The alternative maritime route

33. Gibson 1978: 363.
34. Jones 2013.
35. Gibson 1980: 129.
36. Gibson 1987: 80–81.
37. Gibson 1978: 363–64.
38. Gibson 1978: 364.
39. Smith-Peter 2015.
40. Petrov 2015.
41. Wheeler 1971: 421.

evolved into a series of round-the-world trips that cut the time between these two points to "only" 11 months.[42] Shipwrecks were common.[43] Until 1858 the Russians were largely blocked from trading at Canton.[44] Instead, trade with the Chinese had to be conducted at Kyatkha, far inland on the Mongolian border, meaning long overland treks with the cargo in both directions.[45] Aside from Alaskan natives, the Company was also forced to trade with British, Spanish, and Americans to obtain sufficient fresh food and other supplies.

The finances of the Company were opaque, especially as it became progressively entwined with the state.[46] In 1850 the Tsar instructed Company officials to begin settling the Amur River region on the border with China, and in 1853 the island of Sakhalin too.[47] Though some compensation was offered from the government, it didn't come close to covering the Company's costs.[48] The Company ran up debts to the government, but there was no formal subsidy from the state until the Company's very last years.[49]

Another difficulty was a chronic labor shortage. Under serfdom, the vast majority of Russians were not free to move, and those who could were unlikely to volunteer for Russian America. Even at the end of Company rule in 1867, there were only around 800 Russians in Alaska.[50] Aside from their conscripted islander hunters, the Company bulked out its labor force with the creole descendants of Russian men and local women. These creoles came to outnumber the Russians in their Alaskan capital of New Archangel by four to one.[51] Thus the Russian-American Company staff was two or three times larger than its North American neighbor the Hudson's Bay Company, although nothing like the scale of the Dutch or British East India Companies.

42. Grinëv 2014: 414.
43. Anichtchenko 2013.
44. Gibson 1980: 133.
45. Anichtchenko 2013: 47.
46. Mazour 1944: 173.
47. Tikhmenev 1978 [1863]: 286–300.
48. Grinëv 2015: 24.
49. Petrov 2015.
50. Lain 1976: 143.
51. Easley 2008: 80.

THE INTERNATIONAL RELATIONS OF
THE RUSSIAN-AMERICAN COMPANY

The Company's first attempts at diplomacy with Asian powers in 1805 did not go well. Condescending correspondence to the Japanese explained that "Russia occupies half the world and is the greatest Empire in the Universe," and further that "the Great Russian Tsar, seeing the deficiencies suffered by other lands," was open to trade.[52] After a long wait, a would-be Company embassy was turned away by the Japanese. In revenge for this slight, and in the hope that gunboat diplomacy would convince the Japanese to open their markets to Russian trade, in 1806 two Company ships spent six months ravaging Japanese settlements in Sakhalin.[53] Evidencing the uncertain legal status of the Company's use of force, the captains leading these raids were thrown in jail on their return to the Russian Far East for taking military action without the permission of the government.[54]

What role did the Russian-American Company play in the great power competition for North America? The initial grant and settlement had come in defiance of Spain's claim to the Americas.[55] The Spanish were moved to protest in 1812 when the Russians established Fort Ross in California, but the revolt of Spain's American colonies made its claim moot.[56] The main rivals were the British, both the empire and the Hudson's Bay Company, but increasingly the United States.

Fort Ross aside, the Company's first real attempt at expansion came in Hawaii in 1816. Acting on instructions from New Archangel, a Company agent struck a deal with the main rival of the Hawaiian king. The Company promised 500 armed men and a ship to topple the incumbent, and in return the would-be monarch declared the islands a protectorate of the Tsar, granted the Russian-American Company a monopoly on sandalwood, the right to establish factories and plantations, and ceded four ports and half

---

52. Matthews 2013: 177.
53. Tikhmenev 1978 [1863]: 101–4.
54. Matthews 2013: 299.
55. Nichols 1967: 15.
56. Grinëv 2015: 19; Mazour 1936.

the land of Oahu.[57] The Tsar himself remained uncertain about the venture, however, and being concerned with the reaction of the British and Americans, he let the opportunity of a Russian Hawaii slip away.

A more serious collision loomed in 1821 after the Company's first charter renewal. Responding to problems caused by American commercial competition and gunrunning, at the Company's urging the Tsar extended the Russian sphere from the 55th parallel (slightly above the current Canadian-Alaskan border) to the 51st (just north of Vancouver Island), and for good measure banned all foreign ships from 100 miles of the coast. This created an immediate and sharply negative reaction from both the United States and the British governments.[58] The latter had just brokered the merger of the Hudson's Bay and North West Companies that extended their corporate sovereignty claims to the Pacific. Unwilling to antagonize either government, St. Petersburg quickly backed down. The resulting conventions with the United States and Britain in 1824 and 1825 set the southern boundary of Russian America at 54′40″ latitude. These agreements also opened up the waters of the area to traders from any nation, to the horror of the Russian-American Company, who lobbied vigorously but unsuccessfully against this concession by their government.[59]

As a result, the Hudson's Bay Company and the Russian-America Company clashed in the Stikine incident of June 1834.[60] The HBC was expanding its Pacific presence, while the Russians were concerned about more competition both with Tlingits for furs, and in the Chinese market. Catching wind in 1833 of an HBC plan to establish a post on the Stikine River, the Russian governor sent an armed Company ship to preempt the British and bar their way, if necessary by force.[61] The Russians successfully faced down the HBC mission, which protested first to the directors in London, and then the British government. The latter then raised the issue with the Russian government, and demanded future freedom of passage,

57. Mazour 1937: 17–18.
58. Nichols 1967.
59. Bolkhovitinov 1987: 268.
60. Davidson 1941; Shelest 1989.
61. Davidson 1941: 41.

and £22,000 compensation. In the protracted negotiations that followed, and in keeping with the hybrid nature of the company-states involved, both sides became confused as to whether they were engaged in inter-state diplomacy, or a commercial dispute between two companies. For example, HBC governor George Simpson went to St. Petersburg, only to be denied standing to negotiate because he held no government post. In the end the 1839 resolution that leased the disputed territory to the HBC was signed by the Hudson's Bay Company and the Russian government, a hybrid solution to a dispute among hybrid actors, perhaps.[62]

The negotiations revealed that for the Russian-American Company, "The prominent role played by government institutions, civilian and military, contrasted sharply with the relatively independent HBC."[63] Despite this dispute, generally relations between the Hudson's Bay and Russian-American Companies were a model of civility compared to those between the early modern English, Dutch, and French company-states. Indeed, none of the nineteenth century company-states fought with European corporate or state armies, once again reflecting the degree to which war had become the exclusive province of the sovereign state. In keeping with the generally cautious stance of the Russian government in North American disputes, the Tsar, concerned about damage to the broader Anglo-Russian relationship, consistently favored compromise with the British.[64] The resulting harmony between the two North American companies later extended to a neutrality pact while their respective home states went to war in Crimea 1853–56.[65]

THE RUSSIAN-AMERICAN
COMPANY AND THE RUSSIAN STATE

The private character of the Russian-American Company was both more and less pronounced than equivalent company sovereigns. Firstly, the charter had been given to an active merchant enterprise

62. Shelest 1989.
63. Easley 2008: 79.
64. Shelest 1989.
65. Grinëv 2014: 415.

that had already come close to achieving a monopoly, at least amongst its co-nationals. The Company was thus not simply conjured out of the air at the fiat of the Tsar. Furthermore, these merchants had already engaged in substantial exploration and conquest on their own initiative. In 1799, before news of the charter issued in St. Petersburg had reached its agents in the East, a Company expedition led by a 22-gun ship founded New Archangel.[66] As noted, the original 1799 charter was modeled on earlier company-states in creating "a symbiosis of government and private organization."[67] However the Company was quickly drawn into the government apparatus. The Correspondent position was replaced by a supervisory committee of three (later five) to handle political questions, with a status equal to the shareholders. Although two members were appointed by the Company, in practice they were senior government and naval officials.[68] The Company was formally transferred to the Ministry of the Interior in 1811, and from 1819 the Ministry of Finance. Though shareholders on occasion protested against the diminution of their control, this had little effect.[69]

The Company came to rely on the state to address the constant problem of securing enough ships and sailors.[70] Given the paucity of private options, and the restrictions serfdom put on taking labor from elsewhere in Russia, the navy was the only other option for transport (although the Company did lease foreign ships also). Ships and naval officers were seconded to the Company, but this created status uncertainty. Naval officers often refused to take orders from senior Company officials, who were merely civilians, leading on one occasion to Company forces opening fire on a Russian navy ship leaving New Archangel without permission.[71] Russia was a status-obsessed society still organized according to the Petrine table of ranks, but this same problem was experienced in many other company-states. For naval officers the solution was obvious: to put the civilian Company administration under naval control.

66. Grinëv 2014: 405.
67. Mazour 1944: 168; Vinkovetsky 2011: 8–9.
68. Mazour 1944: 169–70.
69. Grinëv 2015: 19.
70. Anichtchenko 2013; Grinëv 2014.
71. Mazour 1944: 171.

After the first Company governor of Russian America departed in 1818, all the rest were serving naval officers. The successive 20-year charter renewals tended to impose more and more government control. Mazour's conclusion is that "by the middle of the nineteenth century, the Russian-American Company became an agency of the crown rather than a free private enterprise."[72]

The final and conclusive demonstration of the powerlessness of the Company directors and shareholders occurred in 1867, when they were blindsided by the Russian government's sale of Alaska to the United States for $7.2 million.[73] Although the Company's share price initially rose on the prospect of government compensation, a request for 1.58 million rubles generated a payment of only 380,000.[74] None of the money from the US government went to the Company. Though the Company had experienced serious financial problems in the early 1860s and its efforts at settlement had stalled, there is no reason to think it was in terminal decline. The successive agreements with Britain and the United States insulated the Company from great power predation, and it had finally gained access to Canton. The charter had just been renewed, and for the first time the Company had even won an annual state subsidy of 200,000 rubles. However the Company's main political adversaries, including the younger brother of the Tsar, Grand Duke Konstantin, and the finance minister, objected in principle to combining commercial and governmental functions in the one organization.[75] A press campaign "waged mainly in the name of economic liberalism . . . painted the RAC as a vestige of monopolistic privilege and serfdom."[76] Successive Tsars' conciliatory attitude to Britain and the United States in the Northwest Pacific saved Russian America from being a great power battleground, but this stance was a product of the same indifference that ultimately made this area, and the Russian-American Company itself, expendable.

72. Mazour 1944: 173; see also Grinëv 2015: 24.
73. Lain 1976.
74. Petrov 2015.
75. Petrov 2015: 80.
76. Vinkovetsky 2011: 185.

The German Pacific Companies

Germany was a latecomer to the scramble for empire. Aside from the newness of united Germany itself, this posture also reflected Chancellor Bismarck's personal suspicion that colonies were strategically useless and economically costly. Even before unification he opined: "The advantages which people expect from colonies for the commerce and industry of the mother country are mainly founded on illusions, for the expenditure very often exceeds the gain . . . as is proved by the experience of England and France."[77] Bismarck had specifically rejected any notion of acquiring French colonies in the 1871 treaty ending the Franco-Prussian War as otiose luxuries.[78]

From the beginning of the 1880s, however, a growing political movement in Germany agitated for building a colonial empire, seen as an essential marker of great power status, but also as an outlet for German emigration, and a market for German goods. As other colonial powers accelerated their acquisitions in Africa and the South Pacific and imposed protectionist measures, German traders increasingly complained about discriminatory treatment. They raised the danger that Germans would be shut out of overseas markets.[79]

In a dramatic reversal of its previous indifference, in 1884 the German government declared protectorates in West, Southwest, and East Africa as well as the Pacific. In keeping with his prior reservations and those of a large fraction of the Reichstag, however, Bismarck's conversion to the colonial cause only went so far. In particular, he was very concerned that the costs of colonial ventures be borne by private interests, not the imperial government, and he expressly ruled out state-governed colonies on the French model.[80] He reasoned:

> I think it would be wise to leave to the companies the care of government, limiting ourselves to study the means of assuring to the European the superiority . . . always on condition of not being obliged to

77. Otto von Bismarck, quoted in Barnhart 2016: 409.
78. Churchill 1920: 85.
79. Kennedy 1972.
80. Ohff 2008: 64.

keep garrisons . . . Our intention is not first to create provinces to be administered, but to take under our protection colonial enterprises and to aid them during their development, whether against the attacks of immediate neighbors, or against the annoyances that might arise from European nations. In so doing, where such creations are unsuccessful, the Empire will not lose much and the expense will not have been considerable.[81]

Companies were thus chartered to administer the new protectorates of German East and Southwest Africa, the Marshall Islands, and New Guinea under the same general terms, inspired by recent British creations like the South Africa Company and the North Borneo Company.[82] In this way from nothing in 1883, Germany came to possess the third biggest European overseas empire by the outbreak of World War I, spanning almost 3 million square kilometers.

The logic expressed here once again echoes that which played out in previous centuries: European rulers seeking overseas expansion on the cheap by delegating sovereign powers to commercial interests. The state stood to benefit from a share of the profits and advanced its geopolitical interests, while passing on the cost and the risk to private concerns; what could go wrong? In fact, in keeping with many other chartered company ventures, the German companies quickly proved unviable, leaving the government the choice of an embarrassing retreat, or the very outcome it had sought to avoid: taking on loss-making colonies.[83] For example, the German East Africa Company sold its charter rights back to the German government after only four years in 1889.[84] It was in the Pacific that German chartered companies lasted longest and spent most, and so in line with the goals of this chapter, we use evidence from this region to examine why chartered companies were resurrected and why they had a relatively fleeting existence.

The first German traders from Hamburg had set up in the South Pacific in 1857, and by the 1860s German interests controlled up to

---

81. Otto von Bismarck, quoted in Giordani 1916: 19.
82. Churchill 1920: 88; Sack 1973: 74; Press 2017.
83. Firth 1973: 28.
84. Ohff 2008: 83.

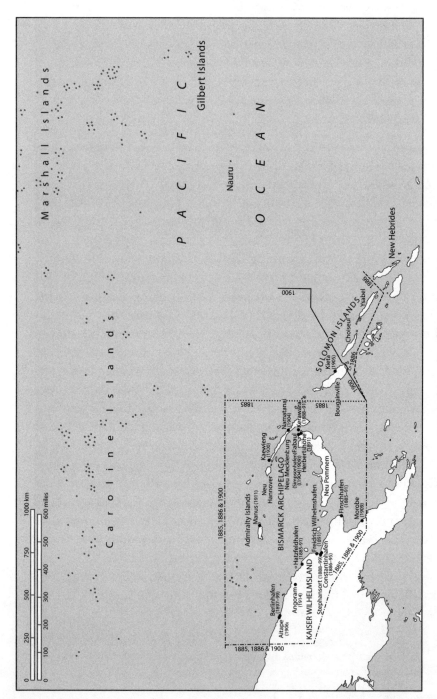

MAP 8. German Pacific Companies

70 percent of trade in the region.[85] German warships regularly visited the area from 1875.[86] In the 1870s and early 1880s, there was a steady trend to parceling out different areas of the region, with US dominance over Hawaii, the British in Fiji, and the French annexing several Polynesian island groups.[87] The largest unclaimed territory was the eastern half of New Guinea (the western half being part of the Dutch East Indies). Initial appeals by German traders to annex the area had fallen on deaf ears, but in 1883 the British colony of Queensland sought to preempt any German action by claiming eastern New Guinea. This move was disavowed in London, leading to an outraged chorus of irredentist calls from the Australian colonies.[88] Precipitating the very move they had hoped to prevent, the German government was then moved to counter the "Australian menace" by sending warships to claim the northeast portion of New Guinea in November 1884.[89] Anglo-German talks led to a formal division of the area in 1886, with Germany also gaining other possessions including the Marshall Islands.

THE GERMAN NEW GUINEA COMPANY

After the German warship had hoisted the flag to assert the Reich's claim, it was left to the newly-incorporated German New Guinea Company to get on with colonization. The Company received its imperial charter in May 1885. This delegated "local sovereign powers" to the Company, including the right to set and administer taxes, negotiate with native rulers, exercise police functions, and own all previously unclaimed land.[90] The Company was forbidden from conducting relations with "civilized" powers, and the Company's territory was under the protection of the German Empire. Judicial powers were exercised by a state-appointed judge whose salary was paid by the Company. The same investors who founded the Company also put capital into Germany's African chartered companies.

85. Kennedy 1972: 263; Firth 1973.
86. Jacobs 1951: 15.
87. Kennedy 1972: 264.
88. Overlack 1973: 132.
89. Jacobs 1951: 16.
90. *German New Guinea: The Annual Reports* 1979.

The New Guinea Company proved to be a debacle during the period of its rule 1885–1899, in both administrative and commercial terms. Initially investors had pinned their hopes on land sales to the flood of patriotic settlers expected in New Guinea from Germany and Germans in Australia, but it quickly became apparent that no such rush of intrepid Teutonic pioneers would arrive.[91] By the end of Company rule the European population was only 250.[92] The second plan was for the newly christened Kaiser Wilhelmsland to become a "German Java" through cotton and tobacco plantations worked by indentured Asian laborers.[93] This plan too failed, as the German overseers were thoroughly ignorant of how unfavorable local conditions were for these crops. For instance, only after considerable time and effort was spent putting up fences to guard crops from monkeys was it realized that there were no monkeys.[94]

Monkeys aside, a much more serious threat was the catastrophically high toll diseases inflicted on Europeans but especially the plantation laborers, who suffered a staggering annual death rate of up to 28 percent.[95] The sentiment of the Company doctor that "every tropical colony had to be manured with human bodies before it bears fruit" was presumably no consolation.[96] The Company was later accused in the Reichstag of having committed "pure mass murder."[97] Aside from the cost in human lives, in its first 27 years of operations the Company did not pay a single dividend, but required repeated recapitalizations from its long-suffering shareholders.[98] The only tax that brought in any income of note was the duty on opium imports.[99]

What of the German New Guinea Company as a company-state? In common with many others of its forebears, the hybrid nature of the enterprise caused tensions in matters large and small. According to the Company's first annual report the "supreme

91. Sack 1973: 81.
92. Sack 1973: 95.
93. Biskup 1970: 88.
94. Sack 1973: 84.
95. Firth 1982, 1985.
96. Firth 1972: 374.
97. Firth 1972: 376.
98. Ohff 2008: 74.
99. Firth 1972: 373.

plenipotentiary and legal representative" of the Company in the field was Vice-Admiral (ret.) Baron von Schleinitz.[100] Despite being "supreme head in charge of the entire Protectorate Administration" (i.e., about a dozen sickly staff), the Baron was deeply offended when German naval officers failed to salute him, on the grounds that officers did not salute those from private companies.[101]

A more substantive problem was security. The Company was slow to set up its police force, even in the face of worsening relations with the original Melanesian inhabitants, who clashed with intruding plantation owners and settlers. The Company sought to employ the German Imperial Navy as a mobile police force, landing up to 500 marines at a time and shelling villages. For its part, the navy resented being used in this way.[102] Company "policing" mainly consisted of punitive raids to kill local Melanesians and destroy their villages.[103] The Company faced an uprising from the local Tolai people, who were inspired by an ointment said to make wearers bulletproof.[104] Aside from ad hoc local arrangements, there were no political agreements between Company authorities and locals, who remained almost completely beyond the jurisdiction of the newcomers. The small Melanesian communities shunned plantation work, and instead traded with the Germans on reasonably equal terms. Attempts at micromanagement from the Company director hardly helped as he "tried to run New Guinea from his office desk in Berlin as if it were a feudal estate in Brandenburg."[105]

From only a few years after it was first chartered, the New Guinea Company sought to hand its sovereign powers back to the German government, having resolved that it was impossible to turn a profit while paying for the costs of administration (such as it was).[106] The catch, however, was that like its counterparts in German Africa, the Company wanted to be compensated for the investments it had made so far. The price had to be agreed in the

---

100. *German New Guinea: The Annual Reports* 1979.
101. Sack 1973: 82.
102. Firth 1972: 362.
103. Hempenstall 1978: 134.
104. Hempenstall 1978: 128.
105. Overlack 1973: 140.
106. Ohff 2008: 78.

Reichstag, and for years there was a deadlock over the deal. Eventually in 1899 a settlement was finalized, whereby the Company would retain some land and mining concessions, and receive 4 million marks over 10 years that had to be spent on facilities in German New Guinea.[107] German New Guinea was then run somewhat more successfully as a state colony until it was taken by Australian troops at the start of World War I.

The second, slightly longer-lived and much more profitable German chartered company in the Pacific was the Jaluit Gesellschaft, which held the rights for the Marshall Islands protectorate 1888–1906. Named after the Jaluit atoll, the Company was formed of a merger of two firms trading pearl shells and copra (dried coconut flesh). Its charter was very similar to that for New Guinea: the Company was responsible for all the costs of government, and in return it received local sovereignty, ownership of all unclaimed land, a monopoly on pearling and phosphate, and the right to raise taxes and duties. German imperial law obtained but was administered by Company officials, while the home country guaranteed diplomatic and military protection against other Westerners.[108] The great stroke of luck for the Jaluit Gesellschaft was that the phosphate island of Nauru had been unknowingly included in the German sphere, and hence in the chartered territory.[109] The German company knew nothing of mining, and so subcontracted the rights to the British Pacific Phosphate Company, then sat back and watched the profits roll in (the Nauruans themselves were excluded from this bounty).[110] But times were changing. With the withdrawal of the New Guinea Company and the expansion of the German Pacific empire with the acquisition of Samoa and the purchase of the Caroline Islands from Spain in 1899, the German state was increasingly reconciled to directly administering its colonies. After a 1906 dispute with Australia over trading access to Nauru, Berlin withdrew the Jaluit Gesellschaft's charter, but left it in possession of its valuable phosphate revenues.[111]

107. Ohff 2008: 80.
108. Firth 1973, 1978.
109. Viviani 1978: 20.
110. Viviani 1978: 28–30.
111. Firth 1978: 38–39.

THE GERMAN PACIFIC COMPANY-STATES IN CONTEXT

Given the slight achievements of the German New Guinea Company, and the supine rentier posture of the Jaluit Gesellschaft, why spend time considering these ephemeral company-states? The experiences of these companies are probably more representative of company-states in general than the oft-told tales of the British and Dutch East India Companies. Even in their seventeenth century heyday, most company-states were similarly marginal.[112] In addition, they highlight the different circumstances that obtained in the nineteenth century. While the German Companies had modest police forces, in both law and practice they had no capacity to tangle with other Western powers. There was no equivalent of the Dutch Companies fighting the Portuguese in Brazil and the Indian Ocean, the Anglo-French struggle in India, or even the much smaller scale Anglo-French clashes around the Hudson's Bay up to 1713. International war and diplomacy between "civilized" nations had become a closely guarded state monopoly. With reference to the New Guinea Company, it is notable that the Company very quickly came to the conclusion that the responsibilities of rule were incompatible with profit. Finally, just because the presence of chartered companies was small-scale and relatively brief does not preclude them having significant and durable historical legacies. Many of the colonial borders that now define the existence and current shape of sovereign states were set for or by such enterprises.

The British South Africa Company

Of the nineteenth-century chartered companies created in the mold of their seventeenth-century exemplars, perhaps none made an impact as great as the British South Africa Company (BSAC). The present-day states of Zimbabwe and Zambia, formerly Southern and Northern Rhodesia, are the direct successors of the company-state's activities. Furthermore, perhaps none of the company-states at any period were as closely associated with one man, in this case Cecil John Rhodes, whose name continues to inflame passions to

112. Steensgaard 1981.

this day.[113] The BSAC is a close fit with the general themes raised already: the co-mingling of new imperialist geopolitical ambitions with a hunger for profit among private investors, and a government keen for colonial possessions paid for by someone else.

Like the German chartered companies founded at the same time, the South Africa Company was a generic solution for the British government, following the creation of the North Borneo Company in 1881, the Royal Niger Company in 1886, and the Imperial British East Africa Company in 1888. The South Africa Company was perfectly willing to use violence and war to attain its ends, to an extent that ended up greatly embarrassing the British government. If this Company was more militaristic and durable than most second-wave chartered companies, ruling over territories for 33 years, 1890–1923, it was no more profitable. While Rhodes and several others amassed huge fortunes, often at the expense of credulous minority shareholders in his ventures, and the Company's shares were sometimes the subject of speculative frenzies, not a single dividend was paid until after the BSAC relinquished its government prerogatives.[114]

Although the politics of empire was central in the birth and development of the Company, its origins were firmly in the private sector. The Company's two most important financial backers, Rhodes himself and Albert Beit, had earlier made their fortunes in the South African Kimberley diamond mines, eventually cornering the market with the creation of De Beers. By the late 1880s, Rhodes was also a prominent politician in the British Cape Colony, becoming Prime Minister in 1890, and he was increasingly fêted in London also. Biographers and historians dispute the extent to which Rhodes was motivated by financial self-interest or the pursuit of imperial grandeur, but as was common with company-states, these goals were seen as generally complementary.[115]

In a familiar way, the British government was very reluctant to see the land that currently comprises Zimbabwe and Zambia taken by the Boers of the neighboring Transvaal republic, the Portuguese

113. Butler 1977; Newsinger 2016.
114. Mabin 1982; Phimister 2015; Butler 1977: 262.
115. Butler 1977.

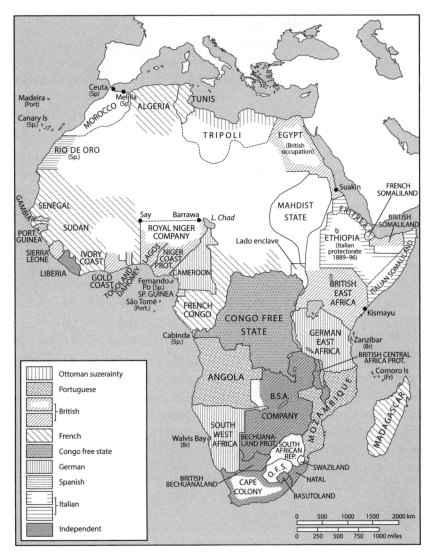

MAP 9. Congo Free State and British South Africa Company during the "scramble for Africa"

from coastal Mozambique, or the Germans, yet London was also wary of the expense of taking formal possession of the area.[116] Once again, a chartered company was seen as the way to square this circle, "thereby indulging in imperialism without responsibility

116. Glass 1966: 34–36; Galbraith 1974: 311.

and, more importantly, without expense."[117] As noted earlier, the Germans were operating on the same principle, and even the Portuguese chartered their own companies in the region in 1891, the Mozambique Company and the Nyassa Company.[118] Paralleling the geopolitical imperative was a commercial one for Rhodes and his various partners, whose investments in the Witswatersrand gold fields of Transvaal were experiencing heavy losses.[119] These and other capitalists cast a covetous eye on the land above the Limpopo and below the Zambezi Rivers as a prospective huge new source of mineral wealth, especially gold, a "Second Rand" in keeping with the fabled land of King Solomon's mines.[120]

Aside from European competitors, the main obstacle was King Lobengula, recognized by the British as ruler of the Ndebele (formerly referred to as the Matabele), who also exercised an uncertain suzerainty over the Mashona (Shona) people. By a series of diplomatic subterfuges 1887–88, those behind the would-be chartered company extracted both a written agreement that Lobengula would not conduct diplomatic relations or cede parts of his kingdom to a non-British power, and a grant exchanging all mining and mineral rights in his lands in exchange for a modest monetary stipend and 1,000 rifles.[121] Lobengula subsequently tried to repudiate the agreements, to no avail. Armed with these concessions, Rhodes and his supporters then mobilized support for a new chartered company in the Cape but particularly in London, buying out rival claimants, and accumulating aristocratic politically-connected supporters, e.g., offering a directorship to then–Prime Minister Salisbury's son.[122]

The campaign bore fruit in 1889. The boundaries of the new corporate domain were specified only in vague terms, leaving room for further opportunistic expansion. The Colonial Office insisted that the new British South Africa Company remain British in its

117. Palmer 1971: 44.

118. Neil-Tomlinson 1977; Isaacman and Isaacman 1983.

119. Blainey 1965; Phimister 1974.

120. Phimister 2015; Mseba 2016.

121. Galbraith 1974: 71–74. This latter clause was illegal, but British authorities turned a blind eye to the delivery (Mabin 1982).

122. Galbraith 1974: 120–24.

directors and headquarters.[123] The Company could acquire land via agreements with local rulers, though these treaties had to be agreed to by the British government, and a government High Commissioner retained ultimate responsibility for this territory. The High Commissioner similarly maintained a veto over any Company dealings with foreign powers.[124] The Company was responsible for maintaining "peace and order" within its territories, and was authorized to raise a police force to this end, in addition to its more general "powers necessary for the purposes of government and the preservation of public order in or for the protection of territories, lands, or property" (clause 3). The BSAC thus had a generic mix of private and sovereign powers common to company-states.

The new Company had a quoted initial capital of £1 million, an optimistic valuation resting on the uncertain basis of half the value of the as yet unknown mineral resources of the territory, and the charter itself. The actual capital available was far less. Without the backing of De Beers and Rhodes's Gold Fields company it seems unlikely that the whole venture would have got off the ground, or stayed solvent for very long. Many BSAC shares were parceled out to win influence among prominent government officials in London and the Cape, with further capital issues resting on highly misleading information as to the Company's finances.[125] Rhodes secured power of attorney from the other directors, meaning that he could largely direct the Company as he saw fit, an extraordinary concentration of power in combination with his Prime Ministership.

THE BRITISH SOUTH AFRICA COMPANY
AND THE FORMATION OF RHODESIA

Lured by the prospect of quick riches on the scale enjoyed during the gold rush in neighboring Transvaal, a column of prospectors escorted by armed officers of the new British South Africa Company Police headed north from the British Protectorate of Bechuanaland (current-day Botswana) in 1890, skirting the center of

123. Galbraith 1974: 113.
124. Galbraith 1974: 122.
125. Mabin 1982: 52–54; Phimister 2015.

Lobengula's Ndebele kingdom to establish Salisbury (now Harare), named in honor of the then–British Prime Minister.[126] They then fanned out to make their fortunes.[127]

It very quickly became apparent to those in the field (if not to investors in London), however, that the hopes of easy mineral wealth had been greatly exaggerated; there was to be no gold rush.[128] Although the Company disingenuously continued to talk up the prospects of spectacular finds, in the next couple of years it burned through its initial funds, necessitating both radical economy measures (e.g., cutting the paramilitary police from 600 to 150), and loans from De Beers and Rhodes personally.[129] Because the Company had bet on their new possession being a mining colony, the initial laws created significant disincentives for farming, leading to early tensions, and some settlers returned to South Africa.[130] As part of the general retrenchment, the Company withdrew from some of the frontiers of its new realm, and confined its "government" of the local Africans to extorting forced labor and what were allegedly tax payments.[131]

For the first few years relations with Lobengula and the Ndebele were generally cordial. Conflict arose, however, as former Shona vassals of Lobengula refused to offer up tribute, claiming that they were now under the protection of the whites. In response, Ndebele punitive missions raided the Shona close to the Company outpost of Victoria, leading to a skirmish with settlers in July 1893.[132] At this point the incident might have petered out, but the Company chief in Salisbury, Leander Jameson, and Rhodes decided that their interests were better served by war.[133] Concerns about the Company's share price were explicit in their calculations.[134] They faced both legal and practical problems in taking the offensive, however. First of all they needed the permission of the British High

---

126. Galbraith 1974: 152–53.
127. Phimister 2015: 29.
128. Phimister 1974: 75; Butler 1977: 265.
129. Phimister 1974: 78–79; Woolford 1978b: 606.
130. Palmer 1971: 43; Mseba 2016: 672.
131. Warhurst 1978.
132. Woolford 1978a: 539, 542.
133. Ranger 1971: 66; Woolford 1978a: 543.
134. Palmer 1971: 43; Woolford 1978b: 606.

Commissioner and the Colonial Office.[135] Secondly, they had disbanded most of the Company's military to save money.[136] They addressed the second concern by promising settlers extensive land grants in Lobengula's territory if they took up arms, an offer kept secret from the British government. To win the acquiescence of the Colonial Office for an offensive, Jameson sent false reports of Ndebele forces massing to threaten white settlements, reports supported by Rhodes as both Prime Minister and head of the BSAC.[137]

The British imperial authorities were skeptical, with Colonial Secretary Ripon expressing his fears to Prime Minister Gladstone about the Company's "extensive plans of conquest."[138] The High Commissioner at the time, Sir Henry Loch, had already made clear his dislike of the whole chartered company concept. In 1891 he had urged that the BSAC be subject to a government board of control on the lines of the nineteenth-century East India Company, or else the Company could draw Britain into a war with the Boers, the Portuguese, or the Ndebele.[139] The curt rejection from London reasoned that it was "difficult to see why the Crown should incur a very risky responsibility in order to further the interests of the adventurers and nobodies who have gone out prospecting."[140] In 1893 Loch now sought to establish the primacy of the Crown over the Company by sending government troops north, and insisting that he handle any negotiations with Lobengula.[141] Unfortunately for Loch and the principle of the state monopoly on armed force, a fortnight before his forces arrived the Company volunteers routed the Ndebele, aided by the combat debut of the Maxim gun, which mowed down the Ndebele ranks. After what a disillusioned Ripon referred to as this "horrid little war," the victors distributed the lands and the Company's share price enjoyed a healthy bump.[142] Despite the provisions of state control written into the charter, and telegraphic communication between London and the Cape, the

135. Denholm 1981.
136. Woolford 1978b: 606.
137. Glass 1966: 40–41.
138. Denholm 1981: 234.
139. Galbraith 1974: 318.
140. Palmer 1971: 44.
141. Glass 1966: 36, 41.
142. Denholm 1981: 234.

Company had outwitted the government in conducting its private war of conquest. Perhaps, then, it is not surprising that this success moved the same characters to an even greater gamble two years later.

THE JAMESON RAID AND THE UPRISING

Despite its defeat in the first Anglo-Boer War (1880–81), the British government had never relinquished its hopes that the Boers could be brought into a British-led South African federation.[143] The leaders of the BSAC had their own personal reasons for wanting to eject the Boer government of Transvaal. As major shareholders of gold mining concerns in the area, they hoped to rewrite the local laws in their favor, boosting profits and share prices.[144] A conspiracy began to take shape. The Company would foment a rebellion among the British population of the Boer republic (the *Uitlanders*), BSAC forces would intervene to "restore order," and then the Transvaal would be brought under the British crown. Non-Boers in the Transvaal were disenfranchised and claimed discrimination, so there was some genuine disaffection.[145] Both the British High Commissioner in the Cape and the Colonial Secretary Joseph Chamberlain gave tacit encouragement to the conspiracy, though they were also keen to maintain "plausible deniability."[146]

By December 1895 the Company had 400 of its mounted police and 200 other volunteers under the command of Jameson ready to strike. Unfortunately for the Company conspirators, plans for the uprising fell through, but unwilling to back down, the intervention went ahead anyway. It was a debacle. The British authorities immediately disavowed the raid, while the Company forces were captured by the Boers within the week.[147] The ringleaders were ransomed back to the Company for a huge payment the following year. Rhodes was forced to resign as Cape Prime Minister and as Company manager (though he retained control until his death in

143. Denholm 1981: 233.
144. Blainey 1965; Galbraith 1970; Phimister 1974; Mendelsohn 1980.
145. Makhura 1995.
146. Wilburn 1997.
147. Galbraith 1970.

1902), and he faced hostile questioning at a British parliamentary inquiry into the affair in 1897.[148] But worse was to come for the Company.

In order to raise the Jameson force, the Company had denuded its garrison in what was by then called Rhodesia.[149] Land seizures, forced labor, and arbitrary and excessive taxation had thoroughly alienated both the Ndebele and Shona.[150] They rose in rebellion in 1896, massacring those settlers they could get their hands on.[151] Company and British government troops managed to repress the revolt by the end of the next year, often starving out their enemies or dynamiting them in their caves.[152] From this point, the Company became a consistent target of the Aboriginal Protection Society and other similar humanitarian pressure groups in Britain.[153]

After the revolt, the British government was determined to exercise much closer supervision over Company rule, posting a Resident Commissioner in Salisbury and enforcing new land allocation rules, while the British South Africa Company Police became the British South Africa Police.[154] In Northern Rhodesia above the Zambezi, where the white population was always much sparser, in part thanks to Company discouragement of settlers, the Company governed through the local Lozi ruler King Lewanika.[155] Though the Company was spared both uprisings and foreign adventures across its territories after 1898 (with the suppression of the Ngoni in Northern Rhodesia in that year, again with the aid of state troops), it was still no closer to solving its basic problem: an inability to make profits given the costs of government.[156] Facing equivalent problems, the British East Africa Company lost its sovereign rights in 1894, and the charter of the Royal Niger Company was revoked in 1899.

148. Wilburn 1997.
149. Woolford 1978b: 611.
150. Warhurst 1978: 220; Phimister 2015: 34.
151. Woolford 1978b.
152. Beach 1998.
153. Glass 1966: 39.
154. Palmer 1971: 50–51.
155. Slinn 1971.
156. Butler 1977: 267.

THE END OF BRITISH SOUTH AFRICA COMPANY RULE

The Company struggled on in the twentieth century, surviving "endemic financial strain" through further share issues and taking on more debt as the share price slid and the prospect of dividends remained unrealized.[157] The Company's relationship with the Colonial Office after the Jameson Raid was at best distant, and it had a persistently bad reputation in British politics.[158] Its greatest internal opponents became the expanding settler population of Southern Rhodesia (Zimbabwe).[159] Many of their complaints revolved around the fact that the Company was simultaneously a commercial operation and the government, and that the BSAC pursued profits over development.[160] Northern Rhodesia (Zambia) had a much smaller settler population, being largely a mining territory, but was no more profitable for the Company.[161]

The BSAC looked for exit options to hand back its governing powers to the British government, but the same problem that complicated the shift from company-state to state rule from Canada to New Guinea again reared its head. The Company wanted to be compensated for its investments, and to retain lucrative land and mining concessions. At first this seemed best effected by unification of both Rhodesias with South Africa, but this solution was voted down in a 1922 referendum in Southern Rhodesia. At this time the European population of Southern Rhodesia was 36,000, compared with 890,000 Africans.[162] The Company eventually extricated itself when Southern Rhodesia became a Dominion in 1923, and Northern Rhodesia a Crown Colony in 1924. Freed from its governing responsibilities but retaining lucrative mineral, railway, and land concessions, the Company finally began to generate substantial profits, more than 30 years after receiving its charter.

To what extent does the experience of the British South African Company conform to those of the other nineteenth century

---

157. Slinn 1971: 366–67.
158. Slinn 1971: 370–71; Frederiksen 2014: 1,278.
159. Phimister 1984; Madimu 2016.
160. Mseba 2016.
161. Frederiksen 2014.
162. Musoni 2017: 313, 321.

company-states? It lasted longer as a commercial and governing entity than any of its British or German equivalents, which had either gone broke or abdicated their sovereign privileges within a few years (excepting the British North Borneo Company, displaced only by World War II). To what extent was the BSAC really sovereign? The Company raised its own military, which although small (up to 600) was powerful enough to independently defeat a significant African ruler. The sole foray into international affairs, the Jameson Raid, was a disaster, but rather than this being some rogue effort, the British government seems to have been complicit in encouraging the Company expedition. As threadbare as it was, the Company administration managed to exert some sort of authority over an area of more 1.1 million square kilometers, roughly the size of Texas and California combined. It succeeded in its basic geopolitical purpose of establishing the sovereignty of the British Empire in these territories with little cost to the government. In commercial terms the BSAC was a failure. It did little for the Europeans it governed, and oppressed and dispossessed the Africans.[163] To this extent the contemporary verdict of the *Economist* was that the British South African Company provided "the most effective object lesson which could be imagined as to the danger in our day of mixing up pecuniary adventure and politics."[164]

"A Monstrous Heresy": The Congo Free State, 1885–1908

The last public/private hybrid entity we consider here—the Congo Free State—was not a company-state. But it nevertheless demands attention as the largest and most devastating example of hybrid colonialism in the late nineteenth century. Furthermore, controversies surrounding the Congo Free State's evolution also give us insight into evolving Western views regarding the legitimacy of non-state actors' exercise of sovereign powers. By the time the Free State was established in 1885, the dominant view among international lawyers was that sovereign powers could legitimately be

163. Slinn 1971: 368.
164. Newsinger 2016: 75.

exercised solely by "civilized" states. Positivist international law in the nineteenth century divided the world between "civilized" Western states, and "barbarous" and "savage" non-European polities denied full membership of international society.[165] The majority view also held that at best, entities like chartered companies could wield powers of government on behalf and in the name of metropolitan governments, but could not by themselves claim international legal personality.[166] The controversies attending the contested emergence of the Congo Free State, and the scandals that destroyed it, thus provide a window into the prevailing climate concerning the rules of admission to the international society of the day.

THE ORIGINS OF THE CONGO FREE STATE

From 1885 through to its transfer to the Belgian state in 1908, the Congo Free State existed as the private patrimony of Belgium's King Leopold II. For the duration of his rule Leopold presided as absolute monarch and proprietor over a territory approximately the size of Western Europe. Ostensibly committed to humanitarian purposes, the Congo Free State instead saw the Congolese population ruthlessly exploited. During Leopold's rule, the Free State did not build a single hospital or school for its local subjects. Rather, the population was conscripted to harvest rubber, and threatened with torture, mutilation, and death at the first sign of resistance. Estimates of the death toll from Leopold's misrule remain hotly contested, but range from hundreds of thousands at the low end, to somewhere between eight and ten million at the high end.[167] A chorus of disapproval—the most prominent global humanitarian campaign since the push to abolish slavery—eventually culminated in the transfer of Congolese sovereignty from Leopold to the Belgian state, the latter compensating the king handsomely for his loss.[168]

---

165. See, for example, Gong 1984; Keene 2002.
166. Fitzmaurice 2010; see also generally Press 2017.
167. See Stannard 2014: 463.
168. See generally Pavlakis 2010.

It is the Free State's unusual origins that are of greatest interest here. By the late nineteenth century, there was a truly global international system. Europeans were imposing their own diplomatic practices and ways of ordering international relations onto non-European polities. A necessary adjunct of this process was the codification and consolidation of a new body of positivist international law, supposedly of universal application. This law sought to prescribe explicit and restrictive "scientific" criteria for determining which actors could legitimately enjoy international legal personality. Specifically, international lawyers from this time saw "civilized" sovereign states as the sole legitimate participants within international society.[169]

Positivist international law was not merely Eurocentric, but also emphatically state-centric as well. International lawyers increasingly conceived of sovereignty in indivisible terms, and as a set of authority claims which should legitimately attach only to states. The emergence of the second wave of chartered company-states illustrates that there was still some—but not much—wiggle room within this emerging consensus. Given the long history of colonial expansion via company-states, nineteenth-century international lawyers grudgingly allowed for the possibility that chartered companies might serve as licensed instrumentalities of their state masters.[170]

For Leopold, the emerging stigma against non-state colonization was especially confining. The Belgian establishment looked askance at colonial projects, seeing them as costly and counterproductive. The failure of early efforts to establish colonies of Belgian emigrants overseas, in places as diverse as Guatemala (Santo Tomas) and Western Africa (Rio Nunez) merely further entrenched this aversion.[171] Belgian neutrality—guaranteed in the country's constitution—indirectly provided further grounds for opposing colonial endeavors. This was due to the belief that colonial expansion risked entrapping Belgium in competition with other European states—potentially jeopardizing its neutrality, and with it, the

169. See generally Gong 1984. On the strongly statist conception of international legal personality that generally prevailed at this time, see also Wheatley 2017: 760–61.

170. See generally Press 2017.

171. Vandersmissen 2011: 11.

protection from invasion that neutrality supposedly secured from its international treaty guarantors.[172]

Having been earlier frustrated in his hopes of buying the Philippines from Spain, Leopold turned his attention to the relatively unexplored Congo River Basin. Control over the Congo was particularly attractive, given its potential importance as an artery for commerce throughout much of sub-Saharan Africa. The practice of slaving in the region provided a further humanitarian warrant for European intervention, the anti-slavery project eventually becoming a key rationale for the existence of the Congo Free State.

In 1876 Leopold established the *Association Internationale Africaine* (AIA). The first of three consecutive "geographical societies" that would later form the nucleus of the Free State, the association was a nominally an entirely private association, dedicated to scientific and philanthropic purposes.[173] Unlike company-states, geographic societies such as the AIA did not enjoy clearly codified privileges assigned by sovereign authorities.[174] Instead, they possessed an almost willful mutability, designed to confuse critics and obfuscate their true purposes. Elaborating on their obscure legal character, Benoît Henriet thus notes that the three geographic societies Leopold sponsored at times seemed to operate simultaneously, rather than one superseding its predecessor. Thus in December 1878, it was the *Comité d'Études du Haut Congo* (CEHC), the supposed successor to the AIA, that signed H. M. Stanley's contract to explore the Congo River on behalf of the association. But it was ultimately the flag of the AIA—by now supposedly defunct—that flew over the stations that Stanley progressively established as his expedition advanced upstream.[175]

The society's flag—a golden five pointed star meant to symbolize the light of civilization that would shine in the African "darkness," began to proliferate along the banks of the Congo, as Leopold's agents founded a string of stations which laid the basis for a future claim over the region.[176] From 1880–1882, the association's

---

172. Vandersmissen 2011: 11.
173. Henriet 2015: 205.
174. Henriet 2015: 206.
175. Henriet 2015: 206.
176. Vandersmissen 2011: 24.

men signed treaties with local chieftains, aiming to win territory on which to establish permanent outposts along the river, to the exclusion of all European rivals.[177] As activity from rival colonial powers accelerated, the association's claims grew more expansive, and its treaty-making with local actors more frenetic. Thus, from 1883 to 1884, the association signed no less than 195 treaties supposedly granting it land in exchange for protecting local client chieftains. So successful was this treaty-making frenzy that by the end of this short period, the association had succeeded in establishing "a chain of sovereign territorial enclaves" stretching from the mouth of the Congo River through to Lake Tanganyika—in effect founding the "spinal column" of what would eventually become the Congo Free State.[178]

For Leopold's plans to succeed, he ultimately needed both recognition from other European states, as well as the acquiescence of the Belgian state. He eventually won both at the 1885 Berlin Conference—though not without controversies that are instructive for what they reveal about late nineteenth-century attitudes toward non-state colonialism.

The king's supporters increasingly stressed the inter-linked commercial and humanitarian grounds for extending "civilization" into Central Africa. According to this line of argument, a mere neutralization of the Congo River Basin, the option that was initially favored, would fail to achieve Europeans' shared interests and values without the presence of a sovereign power capable and prepared to uphold them. Leopold's advocates stressed the additional need for an agency to collectively enforce freedom of riverine navigation and the suppression of slavery. Nevertheless, jurists by that time were explicit that sovereignty "belonged to the State to which the individual or companies owed political allegiance."[179] More generally, the majority international legal opinion held that private societies such as Leopold's associations could not legitimately acquire sovereignty.[180]

---

177. Henriet 2015: 210.
178. Henriet 2015: 210.
179. Reeves 1909: 106, quoted in Henriet 2015: 207.
180. Fitzmaurice 2010: 114; see also Koskenniemi 2002: 108; Henriet 2015: 206.

Leopold's advocates marshalled a range of historical precedents aimed to bolster the legitimacy of his claims. One of Leopold's lawyers, Sir Travers Twiss, invoked medieval examples such as the Order of St. John of Jerusalem and the Teutonic Knights to establish the longevity of non-state colonialism within the Western tradition.[181] Twiss also pointed to the fact that at least four of the contemporary states of the United States of America began as private colonies without license from any state sovereign.[182] More generally, Leopold's advocates foregrounded the more recent example of the founding of Liberia by a private society (the Society for the Colonization of Free People of Color of America) to justify their proposed course of action. From 1820, an estimated 22,000 emancipated African slaves had settled on the northwest African coast under the society's sponsorship, before eventually achieving self-rule and diplomatic recognition as the state of Liberia in 1847.[183] This last example dovetailed neatly with Leopold's philanthropic justifications for colonial expansion, and appeared to provide the firmest immediate precedent for a Congo Free State.

Leopold was successful in securing international recognition for his Congo Free State, beginning with recognition from the United States in 1884, and later through a series of bilateral treaties between the Association and the European powers as part of a general settlement of African affairs at the Congress of Berlin the following year. Nevertheless, this recognition owed more to expediency and Leopold's adroit manipulation of great power rivalries than it did to any new international consensus in favor of private colonialism. This is dramatized by the fact that neither Leopold nor the states that recognized his patrimony were aware of exactly quite what it was that was being recognized throughout the negotiation process. In their initial negotiations, the Association's agents opted for a plural denomination of "Free States" or "Free Cities" to describe the corridor of stations along the Congo River that eventually formed the Free State's foundation.[184] Only at the very end of

181. Fitzmaurice 2010: 114.
182. Fitzmaurice 2010: 114.
183. Henriet 2015: 207.
184. Henriet 2015: 211.

the Berlin Conference did the Association and the signatories generally accept the new polity as a single and unitary "Free State."[185]

While the Association's advocates won the immediate battle to establish a Congo Free State, "Twiss' proposal that private associations could exercise sovereign powers was not, in the long term, accepted by the majority of his colleagues."[186] The legal ambiguity Leopold's advocates created was however enough—in conjunction with a favorable alignment of international interests—to enable Leopold to build a private state over which he was the sole sovereign proprietor. International lawyers openly ridiculed Twiss's invocation of medieval precedents. One anonymous critic even went so far as to argue that to recognize "as a rule of international law the right of a private association to exercise sovereignty would be *a monstrous heresy*. Facts have sometimes conferred privileges on associations, but to demand today the recognition of absolute rights, without them even being exercised in fact, as in the case of the Congo, this would seem to us to leave the path of serious juridical debate."[187]

THE CONSTITUTION AND EARLY
EVOLUTION OF THE CONGO FREE STATE

The Free State was from the outset a sui generis form of polity—neither directly governed by a metropolitan government, nor by a company-state deriving its charter powers from same. In practice, the Free State "consisted of a growing but loose network of armed trading posts grafted onto African trade networks along the shores of the Congo River and its tributaries, complemented by reconnaissance expeditions which gradually expanded the state's knowledge of its territory and subjects."[188]

Leopold resorted to indirect rule via two types of intermediaries—local African collaborators and specially favored European trading companies. African intermediaries were indispensable to the Free State initially as both trading partners, and also as sources of

185. Henriet 2015: 212.
186. Fitzmaurice 2010: 121–22.
187. Anonymous, quoted in Fitzmaurice 2010: 115–16, emphasis added.
188. Roes 2010: 636–37.

muscle for the Free State's embryonic army (the *Force Publique*). Thus, "until around 1890 the colonial state generally infiltrated and manipulated rather than conquered and subjected African trade networks and polities."[189] Such a posture entailed heavy reliance on African middlemen to enable the Free State to tap into local trading networks. This was particularly important for accessing the region's ivory trade, which accounted for more than half the Free State's exports for the first decade of its existence.[190] Politically, meanwhile, the Free State initially peacefully coexisted with powerful militarized commercial actors such as the Zanzibari slave-trading networks under conditions of de facto equality.[191]

Notwithstanding its practical dependence on local collaborators, the Free State understood local African populations as "savages" in need of "civilization" through exposure to the benevolent influences of European culture and commerce. The task of extending Europe's commerce and its "civilizing" influence generally fell to favored concessionary companies. These companies, typically founded by friends and retainers of Leopold, were charged with building and maintaining the infrastructure (in particular railways and steamships) necessary to develop the Free State.[192] In return, they received sizeable land concessions reserved for their exclusive exploitation.[193]

From the outset, the subcontracted concession companies operated under a "dual mandate" of economic development and "civilizing" Africans.[194] Analogous to the governments chartering company-states, Leopold hoped to maximize his own economic returns from the Free State while offloading the costs to his commercial partners. Nevertheless, this early effort at imperialism on the cheap was generally unsuccessful. While concessionary companies could assume some of the burden of colonial development, it ultimately fell to the Free State's armed forces to quell local rebellions and punish refractory local chieftains. These costs intensified

189. Roes 2010: 637.
190. Nelson 1994: 55.
191. Nelson 1994: 56.
192. Nelson 1994: 52.
193. Nelson 1994: 53.
194. Nelson 1994: 53.

over time. The disruption the European presence generated among indigenous middlemen and warlords ultimately accelerated the disintegration of existing African patronage hierarchies, significantly worsening local insecurity.[195] The breakdown of peace between the Free State and the Zanzibari slaving networks in the 1890s further strained the Free State's finances.[196]

The fiscal strains that afflicted the Free State in its early years very nearly proved its undoing. The Belgian government had approved Leopold's colonial project on the understanding that the colony would be self-sufficient, and would not require government funding.[197] Leopold initially invested his own fortune into the Free State, confident in the expectation that local taxes and export tariffs would be more than enough to cover the colony's administrative overheads. Leopold's optimism soon proved badly misplaced, and in 1889 he was forced to secure loans from the Belgian government, which in return stipulated that it reserved the right to take over the colony.[198] Compounding Leopold's financial woes, he was generally unsuccessful in raising money on the international bonds market, private investors judging that the colony produced insufficient revenue and possessed insufficient assets to underwrite a loan.[199]

Facing the specter of personal bankruptcy, Leopold and his advisors initiated significant reforms in the early 1890s. Though the Free State had been forbidden from imposing import duties at the Berlin Conference, Leopold's diplomats finally won him the right to do so in 1892, on grounds that greater resources were needed to fund the armies necessary to suppress the local slave trade.[200] Even more important, from 1889 to 1892 Leopold embarked on a mass appropriation of land, dividing the Congo into separate territories, some to be directly exploited by the State (in essence, the king's private patrimony), and others to be exploited by concessionary companies, but with the King nevertheless retaining ultimate

195. Gordon 2017: 143.
196. Nelson 1994: 56.
197. De Roo 2017: 103.
198. De Roo 2017: 106.
199. De Roo 2017: 103; see also Nelson 1994: 85; Roes 2010: 638.
200. De Roo 2017: 106; see also Nelson 1994: 56.

ownership of the land.[201] Simultaneously, Leopold demanded taxes in-kind from his African subjects, and later also legislated a requirement for men and women to undertake up to forty hours' a month of work for the State—a limit that State and concessionary company officials later routinely disregarded.[202]

"RED RUBBER" AND THE MATURATION
OF THE CONGO FREE STATE

Regardless of the reforms, by 1895 it appeared little could be done to make the Free State a going concern. Indeed, though the Free State's financial system had improved, Leopold continued to appeal to the Belgian government for financial support. In considering additional loans at this time, the Belgian parliament put forward a bill proposing annexation of the Free State, ultimately setting it aside only because legislators did not want to see Belgium saddled with a supposedly "doomed" colony.[203]

It was the advent of a global rubber boom from the mid-1890s that temporarily revived the Free State's fortunes, and briefly rendered it the financial success Leopold had always dreamed about. Following John Dunlop's invention of the first pneumatic rubber tire in 1888, demand for rubber soared globally.[204] Having already doubled in value from 1860 to 1880, the value of rubber doubled again from 1900 to 1906.[205] For the Free State, which possessed significant reserves of rubber vines, the global rubber boom proved a financial bonanza.[206] Indeed, by the 1900s, the Free State's profits from the rubber boom were so vast that it was briefly profitable,[207] albeit as a "plundering and tribute-collecting empire."[208]

Echoing and extending earlier arrangements, the Free State provided the concessionary companies with guns, ammunition, and

201. Nelson 1994: 89–90.
202. Nelson 1994: 89; see also De Roo 2017: 107.
203. De Roo 2017: 110.
204. Nelson 1994: 82.
205. Nelson 1994: 82.
206. Harms 1975: 75. De Roo (2017: 112) notes that the Congo possessed the largest wild rubber reserves in the world after the Amazon.
207. De Roo 2017: 112.
208. Harms 1983: 125.

soldiers to help them set up trading posts, as well as being ready to deploy the *Force Publique* to crush rebellions and punish villages that fell behind on their assigned rubber quotas.[209] Beyond its role as the ultimate coercive backstop, however, the Free State generally left day-to-day governance to the concessionary companies. Within each concession area, the local director assumed ultimate responsibility for maximizing rubber production, and with it, company profits and Free State tax revenues.[210]

Below the director, European agents manned the rubber stations, and sustained production through reliance on locally recruited African sentries armed with modern rifles.[211] Hired on three-year contracts and paid a meager salary, company agents made the vast majority of their income from commissions awarded from the amount of rubber collected—and so faced powerful incentives to maximize production through all means necessary.[212] Sentries—local enforcers of the company system—meanwhile also benefited from their affiliation with the company. Company employment enabled them "to reign over the villages as absolute masters," accumulating wealth and power through the systematic extortion of villagers already hard-pressed by the company's incessant demands for rubber. [213]

Coercion lay at the very heart of this system, with company agents relying on systematic torture, hostage-taking, mutilations, and punitive expeditions to maximize rubber extraction. For at least one rubber post in neighboring French Congo, the graph of rubber production there corresponded directly with the amount of ammunition expended by company agents, with production falling away once the agents were forced to adopt less violent methods.[214] The violence of the Free State ultimately attained genocidal proportions, with millions of Congolese estimated to have died by the 1908 transfer of Leopold's sovereignty to Belgium.

209. Harms 1983: 128–32.
210. Harms 1983: 132.
211. Harms 1983: 132.
212. Harms 1983: 132.
213. Harms 1983: 133.
214. Harms 1975: 76.

Historian Aldwin Roes argues that we can explain the Free State's extreme violence at least partially by reference to the immense difficulty the Free State and its company partners faced in controlling labor. The combination of state weakness, low population densities, and the vast area over which the rubber reserves sprawled made "direct control of labour impossible."[215] Consequently, State and company agents adapted "through a process of copying, adapting, extending and intensifying the economic organisation of the Eastern slave frontier."[216] Through this system, sustained coercive labor mobilization was ensured through a combination of a highly mobile military (the *Force Publique*), in addition to a network of African auxiliaries stationed more permanently in villages.[217]

THE DEMISE OF THE CONGO FREE STATE

Though the Congo Free State briefly enjoyed huge profits, like the second-wave company-states, it ultimately proved a financial failure; Leopold was bailed out and transferred sovereignty of the Free State to the Belgian government in 1908. A transnational civil society movement against the Free State played a critical role in publicizing the widespread atrocities of the rubber system, and thus in delegitimizing Leopold's rule.[218] Nevertheless, by the time of annexation, the Free State was already in crisis, and for a far more prosaic reason—it was running out of rubber.[219]

The Congo rubber reserves were both more limited and far more vulnerable to overexploitation than Leopold and his advisors assumed. Belated Free State efforts to conserve the rubber vines proved unsuccessful, due to company agents' widespread defiance of conservation measures. Operating on short-term contracts and working mainly on commission, company agents had no incentive to preserve or build up rubber vine plantations.[220] Over time, then, the rubber vines on which the Free State's economy was built

215. Roes 2010: 639.
216. Roes 2010: 639.
217. Roes 2010: 639.
218. See, for example, Hochschild 1998; Clay 2016.
219. Harms 1975: 77.
220. Harms 1975: 82.

were rapidly exhausted, along with large numbers of the impressed workers beaten and coerced into harvesting them.

In the short term, the Free State momentarily outshone all other colonies—both those administered directly by metropolitan governments and those ruled by second-wave company-states—in being able to turn a profit.[221] But even setting aside questions of sustainability, the exploitation of wild rubber was profitable only when rubber prices soared.[222] Conversely, when prices fell (e.g., after the massive contraction in US demand for rubber following the 1907 financial panic), the Free State's business model proved unviable.[223]

For the concessionary companies, the depletion of rubber, and the intensified violence that came with it as various actors sought to profit from dwindling supplies, was apparent long before the Free State properly comprehended the situation. The largest company, Abir, managed to sell its exhausted concession back to Leopold in 1906, as Leopold falsely labored under the illusion that there was still ample rubber left to harvest there once rebellions had been put down.[224] As evident elsewhere in our cases, the Free State ended up bearing the costs of imperial administration following the failure of feckless corporate imperialists. In this case, however, the Free State itself managed to effect a similar escape from responsibility two years later, when Belgian taxpayers reluctantly assumed control, while Leopold received generous compensation. In this respect, the Free State's final failure mirrors that of the second-wave company-states.

Conclusion

The much tighter rein governments maintained over the second wave of chartered companies indicates a fundamental change in both the allocation of political authority and the constitution of international society relative to the early modern period. In their seventeenth-century heyday, company-states disposed of a full

221. Nelson 1994: 112.
222. De Roo 2017: 113.
223. De Roo 2017: 112.
224. Harms 1975: 87.

range of sovereign prerogatives in law and practice, and sometimes rivaled and even exceeded their sponsoring governments in wealth and military power. Although designed for encounters with alien civilizations, these first-wave company-states routinely clashed with other Europeans, from raiding and privateering to full-scale wars. The second-wave companies of the nineteenth century by contrast were far more constrained, far weaker economically and militarily relative to their chartering governments, and were much less durable. Reflecting the new state monopoly on war and peace, these company-states never fought with other Westerners, and even their clashes with non-Europeans were comparatively small-scale. Company-states had become increasingly redundant in functional terms, and increasingly illegitimate in terms of the shared conceptions of international society. They were usually willing participants in their own dissolution, freely handing back what sovereign powers they had been granted, and selling their claims back to the governments that had created them.

That company-states were revived at all in the late nineteenth century is a testament to the mirage of conquest on the cheap they seemed to offer the greedy and the gullible. To an extent, they did indeed bring major new territories under the sway of Western rule, from North America to Africa, Southeast Asia and the South Pacific, even though this period of corporate sovereignty (and the sui generis Free State arrangement) was but a brief precursor to formal imperial rule. But the revival of the company-states is also a powerful tribute to their familiarity. By the time of their resurrection, chartered company-states had for centuries been the primary institutional solution used by Europeans to organize the coercion and capital necessary for long-distance commerce and conquest. As such, it is in some ways unsurprising that European governments briefly returned to this model when the impulse to colonial expansion again stirred. The failure of both the Free State and the second-wave company-states at the dawn of the twentieth century nevertheless sealed the fate of non-state, hybrid forms of colonialism, and thereby paved the way for the subsequent universal sovereign state monoculture.

Conclusion

COMPANY-STATES ARE VITAL but previously neglected actors in world politics. We have told the story of their rise, worldwide diffusion, and fall, from the seventeenth through twentieth centuries. Here, we reprise our key arguments, before teasing out the larger lessons our study offers for understanding the evolution of the modern international system. We finish with a brief speculative coda, reflecting on the prospects for a return to corporate sovereignty.

Recapping the Argument

Company-states matter for some of the biggest questions in the study of history and international politics because of what they were, what they did, and how they reflected and drove fundamental trends that produced the modern world.

Company-states were a distinct form of institution defined by their hybrid private/public nature. As with sovereign states, there were certainly variations between different company-states from the seventeenth to the nineteenth century. But this variation should not obscure the fact that they were all instances of a recognizable general class. This basic similarity was not (or not just) because rulers faced similar problems that gave rise to similar institutional solutions. Rather, this form became a transferrable template that was deliberately copied from country to country, and from century to century. Though other earlier expedients like privateers and adventurers, as well as one-offs like the Congo Free State, had their own particular mix of public and private features and prerogatives, the company-states were distinctive. They cannot be relegated to a grab-bag historical residual category of non-state oddities and also-rans.

Neither can the identity of the company-states be reduced to simply a private merchant company, or a mere administrative appendage of the states that chartered them. Company-states were a powerful institutional alternative to both private companies and sovereign states. Their particular hybrid identity is important in that it disabuses us of the idea that the current division of labor between states and companies, whereby the former monopolize war and the latter practice commerce, is somehow natural or inevitable. On the contrary, for most of the modern era, this separation of functions was provisional, contested, or entirely absent.

Company-states are so important not just because of what they *were* institutionally, but also because of what they *did* historically. They blazed the trail of European world empires in almost every region. That we can now speak of a world economy at all was in the first instance thanks in large part to company-states' inter-continental trade. From spices to tea to textiles, they drove a consumer revolution in Europe. In their business structures and practices they helped lay the basic foundations of financial capitalism. The company-state form was so widely emulated in Europe because for very long periods of time these hybrids worked so well as engines of self-financing corporate imperialism.

For much of the rest of the world, the company-states mediated other cultures' first sustained encounters and interactions with Europeans. Whether their corporate reign was lengthy or brief, it often left key legacies that are still with us today, especially in the progression from company-state rule, to formal European imperialism, to postcolonial statehood. Current borders from Alaska to Zimbabwe were directly set by company-states, and dozens of countries across the world owe their current shape or even their very existence to the earlier role of the company-states.

As well as being hugely consequential in the aggregate, just as notable was the variation in company-states' performance within and across regions and eras. In itself, the fact that different members of the same class of institutions perform differently is no great surprise: some sovereign states are prosperous and secure, others are failed states, some contemporary corporations are wildly successful, many more quickly go bust. Although there are no hard-and-fast rules that uniformly predict the fortunes of company-states, some patterns do emerge.

First and most notable is variation over historical eras. In terms of both the creation and the fortunes of company-states, their golden age began at the dawn of the 1600s and waned in the second half of the 1700s. The late eighteenth and first half of the nineteenth century saw the company-states either go broke and disappear, or become incrementally subordinated to their respective governments. This long decline was to a large extent a product of the increased scope and intensity of European geopolitical competition that disrupted the delicate compromise all company-states had to strike in balancing profit and power.

By the 1870s company-states had become extinct. The brief period ca. 1880–95, however, saw a very temporary revival, associated with the fevered search for new colonies. As much as these new incarnations were directly modeled on early modern precedents, their performance was consistently disappointing, often to the point of farce. Taking an institutional model from one historical context to a very different one gave rise to radically different results. Partly, this reflected the fact that Western great powers were by then much more able to fight and rule at a distance than their early modern predecessors. As a result, company-states were both less necessary as extra-European proxies for states, and less able to compete on the international stage with newly empowered sovereign states. But the ephemeral nature of the second wave of chartered companies also reflected changes in shared beliefs about the appropriate role of states as the exclusive locus of public authority, and companies as the primary institutional embodiment of private commerce. Western states assiduously guarded their relatively new monopoly on war, especially inter-state war. For their part, with only minor exceptions, the chartered corporate captains of the late nineteenth century had neither the will nor the means to contest this state monopoly of organized violence.

Even during the early modern heyday of the company-states, however, there was huge variation in their fortunes. The regional patterns are less clear-cut than the temporal ones, but it is possible to find some rough trends. The first is that the standout successes, the Dutch and English East India Companies, were in Asia, whereas almost identical institutions launched by these and other countries in Atlantic Africa and the Americas did far less well. The relatively shorter distances in the Atlantic compared with the East made for more competition from private interloper traders, and more direct exposure to great power struggles, both of which made company-states more susceptible to interference by their sponsor governments. As the Atlantic exception that may support the rule, the Hudson's Bay Company, one of the longest-lived company-states, kept a very modest commercial and military profile, and benefited from the isolation of the frozen sea, which often insulated it from geopolitical competition.

Company-States and World Politics

Beyond their intrinsic historical importance, company-states also matter for the lessons they offer in understanding the development of the modern international system. In particular, this relates to the management of inter-polity relations across deep cultural differences, the evolution of the public/private dichotomy, and the centrality of company-states in laying the early modern foundations for the later emergence of the world's first genuinely global international system.

COMPANY-STATES AS MEDIATORS
OF CROSS-CULTURAL RELATIONS

Company-states were the main managers and mediators of inter-polity relations across vast geographic distances and cultural differences, especially in the early modern period. Traditionally, international relations has referred only to relations between sovereign (most often Western) states. The prominence of company-states in European projects of long-distance commerce and conquest invalidates this state-centrism. And the company-states' diverse forms of interaction with non-European polities—often engaging with non-European polities on terms of equality or even European inferiority—necessitate a shift away from Eurocentric perspectives. We cannot hope to understand how cross-cultural relations functioned for much of the past half millennium without jettisoning both state-centrism and Eurocentrism.

This argument builds upon work that has sought to understand how Europeans mediated their relations with non-Western polities before the late nineteenth century. Influential accounts have paid considerable attention to Western efforts to apply, extend, and adapt natural international law to their dealings with non-Western polities.[1] This work has tended to fixate heavily on the European experience in the Americas, however, where pandemics and the resulting collapse of local societies created huge asymmetries of power between Western colonial powers and local polities. Even more geographically broad-ranging accounts have tended to stress Western hierarchy as the default mode of engagement with non-European societies, for example contrasting a uniform "logic of civilization" against the more egalitarian "logic of toleration" mediating relations among Western states.[2] The result has been a tendency to exaggerate the impact and significance of purely Western institutions in mediating cross-cultural relations, and hence of unilateral imposition, instead of more complex practices of negotiation, accommodation, and ingratiation in this process.

By contrast, this book argues that it was company-states—not sovereign states—that were in most instances the vanguards of European encounters with non-Europeans from the seventeenth through nineteenth centuries. They arose at a time when no worldwide system of international law or diplomatic practice existed, and when it was both legitimate and practical for European rulers to delegate portions of their sovereignty to corporate actors that were tailor-made to pursue long-distance commerce and conquest without direct government finance or control.

Company-states' commitment to territorially non-exclusive rule, and their origins in a conception of sovereignty as divisible rather

1. See, for example, Williams 1992; Keal 2003.
2. Keene 2002.

than absolute, made it possible for them to infiltrate into a diverse array of commercial and political networks in the extra-European world. The charters that licensed company-states granted them the management of relations with distant and culturally dissimilar societies, a role that was a central warrant for their existence. Their encounters with non-Europeans generally differed markedly from traditional tales of European military dominance.[3] Company-states often relied on violence. Sometimes this culminated in genocidal conquest (e.g., the Spice Islands).[4] But company-states interacted with non-European polities across incredibly varied contexts, which more often than not favored non-European hosts over European interlopers.[5] From the Atlantic African coast, through to maritime Asia and the frozen expanses of Prince Rupert's land, company-states were usually supplicants, suzerains, allies, or de facto partners with indigenous power-brokers, rarely their masters. Rather than driving a unilateral Western *domination* of supine non-European societies, company-states were more often *incorporated* into existing economic and political systems, their success dependent on the sufferance and support of locals.

Traditional European expansion stories portray the modern period as one of accelerating Western dominance. They argue for the progressive global spread of Western institutions for mediating inter-polity relations. The focus is most often on the late nineteenth century, and the spread of Western diplomatic practices and a system of positive international law.[6] But this story typically takes as its lead-in the prior diffusion of Western notions of natural international law, and the West's imposition of diplomatic and commercial practices in the wider world.

In contrast, by foregrounding the company-states, our treatment puts a very different perspective on these early modern cross-cultural encounters. Specifically, we highlight the dynamics of bargaining and ingratiation that marked the company-states' interactions with non-European hosts. The often tenuous outposts

---

3. On traditional narratives of military superiority as the primary engine of European overseas conquest, see, for example, Parker 1996.

4. Raben 2012: 487.

5. See, for example, Clulow 2014: 17.

6. See, for example, Gong 1984.

that company-states secured rested on bespoke bargains, very different from the purportedly universal Western systems of international law and diplomacy that feature so prominently in traditional accounts. It was these customized compacts that underwrote early modern globalization, and that must be understood if we are to properly trace the emergence of the world's first genuinely global international system.

Far from simply embroidering detail onto the story of Europeans' early efforts at cross-cultural diplomacy, our argument challenges prominent narratives of early modern Western global expansion. As canvassed above, we refute claims that Western military superiority was the driving force of European expansion.[7] True, company-states benefited from their niche advantages in blue water naval warfare, which were critical to their success as militarized long-distance trade monopolies.[8] But Europeans' terrestrial military weakness nearly always compelled them to strike deals with indigenous host polities. The company-states operated thousands of kilometers from home, with their tiny handful of European employees often weakened and perpetually at risk of dying from deadly tropical illnesses to which they had no natural immunity. Cost-cutting company directors meanwhile jealously sought to minimize military and administrative overheads wherever possible. Given these constraints, the company-states had little choice but to rely on diplomatic dexterity over martial prowess to win over local on-shore allies.

If the company-states' story largely invalidates military explanations, what of alternatives stressing institutional superiority as the key to Europe's overseas expansion? Scholars have extensively debated the claim that preindustrial Western Europe possessed domestic institutions that placed it in prime position for industrialization.[9] Comprehensive engagement with this discussion lies beyond the scope of this book, though we note in passing that the "California School" of East Asian historians has convincingly

7. McNeill 1982; Parker 1996.
8. Marshall 1980.
9. See for example Landes 1969; North and Thomas 1973.

unsettled claims that the early modern West was uniquely preco-
cious in its degree of commercialization.[10]

Yet the company-state was a uniquely Western phenomenon,
with no direct analogues elsewhere in the early modern world. The
unarmed resident trading diasporas that historically dominated
Eurasia's long-distance trade bore no comparison to company-
states. Likewise, there is no meaningful room for comparison with
the rare coastal kingdoms in early modern Africa and Asia that did
seek to marry military power with maritime commercial might.
Polities like the Omani Sultanate did sponsor local maritime protection rackets that merit some comparisons with European high
seas predation.[11] Others, such as the Zheng confederacy that ruled
Taiwan in the mid-seventeenth century, leveraged local naval dominance to briefly control a maritime empire in the South China Sea
that exceeded the value of the Dutch East India Company.[12] Note-
worthy as these achievements were, these polities lacked the corporate structure and hybrid combination of power and profit-seeking
characteristic of company-states. Neither did they yield a reproduc-
ible institutional form capable of universal imitation or worldwide
diffusion, unlike the company-states.

Contemporary readers are now rightly leery of claims for Western uniqueness, and of single-origin stories regarding the historical roots of modernity's master institutions. Recent studies have
discredited the claim that the idea of sovereignty is of exclusively
Western provenance.[13] Likewise, East Asianists have rightly cri-
tiqued the view that the centralized, bureaucratically administered,
and clearly bordered sovereign state was a uniquely Western invention.[14] Polities roughly matching this description first developed
in Northeast Asia by the late centuries of the first millennium of
the Common Era, at a time when most of Europe still dwelled in
the Dark Ages.[15] This discrepancy alone between the "myth of

10. See for example Pomeranz 2000.
11. Andrade 2010: 166.
12. Andrade and Hang 2016: 12.
13. Zarakol 2018.
14. Kang 2003.
15. Lieberman 2009.

Westphalia"[16] and historical reality refutes most accounts of the origins of the modern international system. These cast the sovereign state as an exclusively Western creation, and track modernity's ascent by the spread of the sovereign state from Europe.

The institutional advantages that company-states combined reflected the West's medieval inheritance. And they also addressed a range of problems that were particularly acute for feuding Europeans. Vast distances separated Western Europeans from Eurasia's demographic and commercial heartlands of South and East Asia. Formidable transportation and information-obtaining costs, and potentially crippling principal-agent problems, both flowed from this tyranny of distance.[17] Portugal's prior militarization of the Europe-Asia maritime trade likewise raised protection costs. Added to this, finally, cultural differences and the lack of a Eurasia-wide diplomatic infrastructure further impeded Western European efforts to participate in the first Asia-centric wave of globalization.

Nevertheless, for all of the company-states' world-changing significance, we do not suggest that company-states *alone* made the modern world, nor by extension that the West deserves either exclusive credit or blame for the emergence of the world's first global international system. In the early 1600s, the Dutch and English had little to sell the world apart from wool and cod—commodities hardly in high demand in the prosperous ports and courts of South and East Asia.[18] Company-states provided these otherwise marginal polities with a means of insinuating their way into the world's biggest and wealthiest economies, and then selling exotic Asian luxuries at a premium back home.

The company-states' historic success depended on the serendipitous convergence between the company-states' distinctive attributes and the particularly congenial environment of maritime Asia. It was the pull of Asian prosperity that first helped inspire company-states' creation. Subsequently, comparable traditions of territorially non-exclusive rule permitted company-states' enmeshment along the Indian Ocean and East Asian littorals. The

16. Teschke 2003.
17. Harris 2018: 113.
18. Harris 2018: 113.

forbearance of Asia's most powerful rulers, and the company-states' willingness and capacity to become vassals and junior partners to these suzerains, finally then helped to cement the latter's place as pivotal arbitrageurs within Eurasia's long-distance trading circuits.

THE PUBLIC/PRIVATE DIVIDE AND THE EVOLVING DISTRIBUTION OF AUTHORITY IN THE MODERN INTERNATIONAL SYSTEM

In his groundbreaking examination of the origins of the modern international system, John Ruggie placed equal store on two grand dichotomies: the inside/outside divide demarcating international and domestic politics, and the public/private divide distinguishing public qua state power from the private sphere.[19] According to Ruggie, the emergence and consolidation of *both* were essential to the constitution of a modern system of sovereign states. The rise of territorially exclusive rule (the inside/outside divide) was key to the sovereign state's triumph over rival forms of political authority, such as the Catholic Church and the Holy Roman Empire.[20] But the codification of a divide between sovereign "public" power and "private" market relations was equally important for the transition from medieval to modern international orders in Europe.[21] This was in part because the revival of Roman conceptions of exclusive private property provided a useful analogue for rulers asserting sovereign supremacy within their own jurisdictions.[22] But this was also because—at least in Europe—the "breakthrough" to modernity depended on a dismantling of feudalism, and with it, an accompanying disentanglement of property rights from political authority.[23]

While hugely influential, this account has been challenged. Even within its original European context, some have argued that the

---

19. Ruggie 1993.
20. Ruggie 1993: 151.
21. Ruggie 1993: 151.
22. Ruggie 1993: 157.
23. Ruggie 1993: 157.

process of establishing this inside/outside distinction was a much longer and more contested process than Ruggie suggests.[24] Though it has received much less attention, dissenters have also complicated efforts to trace the emergence of a crisp public/private.[25]

A proper awareness of the company-states bolsters these critiques, which apply with even greater force beyond Europe. That a public/private divide clearly separated sovereigns from non-sovereigns makes little sense in the early modern period, when company-states routinely mediated the West's relations with large portions of the non-European world. Even later, during the late nineteenth-century scramble for colonies, this separation remained permeable and contested, as the rise of the second-wave company-states and the Congo Free State illustrates. Indeed, it is only from the early decades of the twentieth century that we begin to see a firm system-wide presumption against hybrid forms of sovereign authority.

Accordingly, one of this book's chief findings is that—at least in Europe's relations with the non-European world—the public/private dichotomy differentiating sovereigns from commercial actors evolved extremely slowly, and did not definitively consolidate before the twentieth century. An analysis of the company-states enables us to capture a centuries-long progression across three broad epochs. In their attitudes toward hybrid forms of sovereign authority such as the company-states, these epochs may be respectively characterized as permissive, restrictive, and prohibitive.

COMPANY-STATES IN HISTORICAL CONTEXT: PERMISSIVE, RESTRICTIVE, AND PROHIBITIVE ERAS

The permissive era entailed widespread acceptance of hybrid forms of sovereign authority, and an accompanying willingness of rulers to delegate extensive sovereign prerogatives to what we would now (anachronistically) deem non-state actors. Recalling chapter 1, this permissive attitude toward hybrid sovereigns had deep medieval roots. The idea of the corporation was itself a medieval one, and

24. See, for example, Branch 2013.
25. See, for example, Teschke 2003; Owens 2008; Barkawi 2010.

reflected the necessity of conferring legal personality on "artificial persons" (e.g., municipalities, guilds, universities) at a time of growing social complexity.[26]

That late medieval Europe was a laboratory for the development of diverse forms of governance is well established.[27] What remains less recognized is how important the legacies of this diversity were for Europeans' subsequent global expansion. Europeans were far from the only ones to embark on long-distance commerce and conquest at this time. Indeed, for much of the early modern epoch, they were not even the most successful conquerors, relative to their most powerful Asian contemporaries.[28] Nevertheless, Europeans did roam farthest, and European rulers were likewise unique in investing non-state actors with such extensive powers of sovereignty to facilitate trade and plunder.

In rethinking the conventional chronology of modernity, then, our findings illustrate that the mixing of public and private, inside and outside, should not be seen as something confined either to the medieval period, or to Europe. Instead, Europe's heteronomous heritage imbued its political, commercial, and cultural elites with a shared understanding of the ways in which authority might be organized to facilitate trade and rule over the oceans. Accordingly, once European rulers did join in Eurasia-wide processes of expansion, they already had at their disposal the institutional models from which company-states could be fashioned. The VOC and EIC's spectacular successes in Asia then proved the utility of the company-state form, spurring its later widespread emulation by European traders and would-be conquerors in the Americas and Africa. This pattern of cross-regional diffusion of company-states then dramatically reconfigured the distribution of political authority globally for the next one and a half centuries. For this critical period, hybrid polities combining the profit motive with sovereign authority were at the vanguard of European expansion.

The period from the mid-eighteenth down to the mid-nineteenth century saw sustained, if uneven, moves toward marginalizing and

26. See generally Berman 1983; Cavanagh 2016.
27. See, for example, Poggi 1978; Strayer 1970; Spruyt 1994.
28. Sharman 2019.

eventually eliminating the company-state form. During this second period, company-states' innate vulnerabilities and growing redundancy were exacerbated by shifting conceptions of legitimate authority. As European geopolitical rivalries globalized from the mid-eighteenth century, company-states in Asia began to suffer from the same challenges that had long troubled their counterparts in the Americas in reconciling profit and power. This pushed some to bankruptcy (e.g., the VOC), while forcing others to essentially transform into de facto sovereign states themselves (e.g., EIC), the latter inviting creeping nationalization.

There was a growing normative presumption against hybrid forms of sovereignty and the delegation of sovereign powers to non-state actors within European international society. The new prejudice was by no means exclusively targeted at company-states. But it was company-states that often proved an especially prominent focal point for controversy during this time. Thus, the EIC's conquests in India after 1765 scandalized British opinion and eventually led to a series of ever more restrictive charters that eventually subordinated the EIC as an administrative extension of the British metropolitan state.[29]

By the late eighteenth century, the new British "science" of political economy posited an increasingly sharp distinction between the "public" and the "private" spheres, which did not easily accommodate hybrid actors.[30] But even beyond Britain, more prosaic considerations of power and profit in any case counseled against company-states. The Dutch made no effort to resuscitate the VOC once its last charter expired in 1799. Following the stabilization of Europe after the Congress of Vienna, would-be European traders and colonialists showed no desire to launch company-states to spearhead imperial expansion.

The resurrection of company-states toward the end of the century dramatizes the fact that the company-state precedent was not forgotten, and that the prospect of overseas conquest on the cheap remained attractive. Nevertheless, when company-states were temporarily revived, alongside other hybrid polities such as

29. Dirks 2008.
30. Grewal 2016: 417–33.

the Congo Free State, what is striking is the practical restrictions that governments imposed on their exercise of sovereign powers. European rulers were deeply reluctant to allow newly-formed nineteenth century company-states to participate in international relations to anything like the degree of their early modern predecessors. This reluctance reveals a larger shift within the modern international system, from a permissive environment in which a multitude of different types of sovereign actors co-existed, to an ever more restrictive one in which prerogatives of government were presumed to lie exclusively with sovereign states.

Finally, we come to the twentieth century—in our chronology, the prohibitive era, in which company-states disappeared entirely, and the modern international system became a universal sovereign state monoculture. The second-wave company-states were conspicuously unsuccessful, both commercially and also as surrogate imperialists for miserly metropolitan states. Metropolitan national governments were very quickly forced to bail out or nationalize the company-states of the late nineteenth century, taking their territories into direct imperial administration. No new company-states were formed in the twentieth century.

Throughout the early part of the twentieth century, governments continued to occasionally blur the public/private boundary with experiments in hybrid forms of governance on a subnational scale. International concessions—in part a form of "extraterritoriality in miniature for foreign investors"[31]—often granted international investors considerable immunities from tariffs and local laws of host states, and in some instances even empowered them to forcibly conscript unpaid indigenous labor to work on their plantations and in their factories.[32] Where possible, colonial administrations also still tried to offload the overheads of financing economic development to international concessions at a provincial level throughout the interwar period.[33] But by then, the era of investing corporations with quintessentially sovereign powers of war-making, diplomacy,

---

31. Veeser 2013: 1,142.
32. Veeser 2013: 1,143; see also generally Grandin 2010.
33. Veeser 2013: 1,143.

and the large-scale administration of civil and criminal justice was well and truly over.

The mid-century wave of decolonization swept away the forms of racial and civilizational hierarchy that had formerly supported colonial empires. Within the new order, sovereignty is conceived as the exclusive property of juridically equal sovereign states. The divisible idea of sovereignty—which had formerly been so central to both European projects of civilizational hierarchy and to the company-states that mediated relations between Europeans and other cultures—is no more.[34] Decolonization did not delegitimate and destroy the company-states, for they were already gone by the time that African and Asian states won their independence. But the global spread of ideas of national self-determination did provide a powerful retrospective warrant against their possible resurrection, and continues to do so. As we will shortly see, contemporary proposals to revive corporate sovereignty in even very limited forms— for example through privately run "chartered cities" in developing countries—are routinely ridiculed and reviled as stalking horses for neocolonialism.[35] Almost a century after their disappearance, company-states retain the stigma of their intimate association with colonialism. The disintegration of formal distinctions between "civilized" and "uncivilized" peoples, on which company-states rested, has reinforced an increasingly sharply drawn and enforced distinction between the public and the private realms. The reorganization of these constitutive divisions (the abolition of the former, and the sharper delineation of the latter) today holds fast, and poses a forbidding barrier to the revival of company-states.

COMPANY-STATES, GLOBAL TRANSFORMATIONS, AND THE EVOLVING INTERNATIONAL ORDER

Many scholars have portrayed the modern international system as the product of a relatively continuous centuries-long diffusion of the sovereign state system from its Western heartland.[36] In contrast

---

34. Keene 2002: 119.
35. See, for example, *The Economist* 2017.
36. The classic work on this topic remains Bull and Watson 1985.

to these traditional accounts, which posit basic continuities from the early modern period to the present, Barry Buzan and George Lawson have recently argued that the modern international system only dates from approximately 1860, emerging from a "global transformation" that sharply distinguished the post-1860 world. This transformation, driven by industrialization, rational state-building, and the rise of ideologies of progress, was characterized by revolutionary increases in global interaction capacity, and culminated in the West's late rise to worldwide dominance.[37]

Our argument challenges the thesis that the international system was constructed through the diffusion of the sovereign state: we have shown that it was company-states that largely initiated, constructed, consolidated, and sustained these networks in the first instance. Conversely, the nineteenth century did indeed see a global transformation, marked in part by "rational state-building" and the accompanying shift from indirect toward more bureaucratic forms of direct rule.[38] Yet the post-1860 global international system remained dependent on the dense networks of inter-continental diplomatic and commercial relations that the company-states had pioneered. Furthermore, a key part of the global rationalization of political authority was the delegitimation, dismantling, and eventual forgetting of the earlier form of hybrid company-state sovereignty.

In examining the composition of the contemporary international order, John Ikenberry notes: "International order is composed of an accumulation of artefacts from various historical eras, deposited like layers of geological strata. There are artefacts that date to the classical age, the early modern period, the age of European imperialism, and the two centuries of the liberal ascendancy."[39] Our findings argue for the excavation of the long buried company-state stratum of the global international order. This gives us a clearer sense of the agents, processes, and products of early modern European expansion; a better understanding of the origins of the public/private divide; and a much more

37. Buzan and Lawson 2015.
38. Buzan and Lawson 2015: 127; see also more generally Maier 2014.
39. Ikenberry 2020: 137.

comprehensive understanding of the development of the international system. But it is also important politically, in two quite different senses.

First, an awareness of company-states' centrality in the forging of the early modern world constitutes an important corrective to state-centric hagiographies of the modern liberal international order. Folk wisdom in the field continues to fixate on the Peace of Westphalia in 1648 as an origin myth for the sovereign state system, and sees Westphalia as the foundation for the liberal international order that subsequently evolved.[40] From a world historical rather than a parochially European perspective, however, it was the seventeenth-century innovation of the company-state that was most important for the development of international relations at a global level. In their hybrid constitution, company-states confounded the public/private separation at the core of liberalism. Company-states thus offer an important corrective to ahistorical accounts of the Westphalian moment and the presumed genealogy of the liberal international order.

Second, our examination of the company-states' rise and fall also cautions against the more extreme current denunciations of corporate power. Corporations remain central to capitalism, and dispose of significant political influence worldwide. But an understanding of corporate sovereignty rapidly reveals the limits of modern companies' political power, and discredits comparisons between these companies and the early modern company-states. A historical perspective shows that companies today exert much less political power than their early modern hybrid predecessors.

Coda: The Future of Corporate Sovereignty in a World of Sovereign States

This book's concerns and focus have been primarily historical. But in an era of expanding public/private partnerships and private security companies, are we now or might we shortly be in the midst of a third wave of company-states? Is the international system now witnessing the re-emergence of hybrid entities combining

40. See, for example, Jackson 2000: 181.

the pursuit of profit with the exercise of sovereign power, potential harbingers of a coming age of "neo-medievalism"?[41] In assessing such conjectures, it is crucial to be aware of the long view. Although there is certainly a good deal of mixing of private and public prerogatives in a variety of domains today, a historical perspective gives grounds for skepticism. In assessing the evolution of the contemporary international system, it is productive to apply some of the same benchmarks used so far to establish the significance of the company-states to would-be contemporary hybrids: what are they? What have they done? Finally, how important are they for the constitution and operation of international society?

It is certainly true that over the last few decades there has been an explosive growth in the private security industry.[42] These new for-profit firms currently engage in security functions conventionally seen as core sovereign prerogatives: domestic policing and foreign war-making. If, as argued here, the defining feature of company-states' hybrid nature was their combined focus on power and profit, doesn't this suggest that we are seeing more and more twenty-first-century chartered companies, and perhaps a corresponding retreat of the sovereign state as well? Unless they are intended only as loose "back to the future" similes, however, such claims do not stand up.

As discussed, company-states had a standard suite of legal powers: making war and peace and engaging in international diplomacy (albeit usually only with non-Western polities); claiming and ruling territory; administering criminal and civil justice; and of course various monopolies on trade or resources. Jointly these prerogatives made company-states what they were as a class of institution. By comparison, none of the twenty-first-century private security companies possesses even a fraction of these sweeping legal prerogatives. Instead, they are legally subject to the sovereign power of states in which they operate and are incorporated. To this extent, they relate to the state in the same way as any other private company.

41. See, for example, Bull 1995: 258–60; Cerny 2000: 623–46.
42. Singer 2003; Avant 2005; Chesterman and Lehnardt 2007; Krahmann 2010; Abrahamsen and Williams 2011.

Indeed, it is precisely within the private military and security sector that the contrast between company-states and contemporary reality is most starkly evident. Western private military companies remain tightly controlled and subordinate handmaidens to Western states, having neither sought nor claimed the level of independent authority and autonomy that company-states historically enjoyed. The brief unregulated burst of private military entrepreneurship that punctuated the immediate post–Cold War era moreover spurred rapid and comprehensive international efforts to consolidate the anti-mercenary norm and reaffirm the state's monopoly on the legitimate use of violence.[43]

The discrepancy between company-states and contemporary private military companies is even more pronounced when we look beyond the liberal West, to those originating from authoritarian states like China and Russia. As China's Belt and Road Initiative has gained momentum, the prominence of Chinese security firms in securing this infrastructure has evoked fears that these companies will serve as vanguards for a form of Eurasia-wide Chinese informal empire. The intimately close ties between these military companies, Chinese State-Owned Enterprises, and the Chinese Communist Party may stoke such apprehension. But the extraordinarily tight control Beijing exerts over such Chinese companies nevertheless does militate against the idea that the latter exert any independent influence as actors within the current international system, in contrast to the company-states.[44] This lack of autonomy—and even meaningful institutional separation from national states—applies with even greater force to Russia, which has used informal "semi-state" security forces such as the Wagner Group to covertly pursue its interests in Syria, Eastern Ukraine, and elsewhere while maintaining a veneer of plausible deniability.[45] That Russia refuses to even legalize such groups, much less invest them with the suite of sovereign powers that characterized company-states, further undermines the presumptive analogy with private military companies.

43. Percy 2007.
44. Arduino 2017.
45. Marten 2019.

If one reason to care about a certain class of actors (or not) is what they are, the significance of their identity, another reason is because of what they do, the significance of their achievements (or lack thereof). Earlier company-states made substantial conquests in their own right and with their own resources, for example half of Brazil and half of Indonesia for the Dutch companies, and most famously the whole of South Asia for the EIC. Today, even in theaters like Iraq and Afghanistan where there have been tens of thousands of private military contractors present, these have operated strictly in accord with basic strategic, operational, and tactical goals set by their state employers. In law and in fact, these firms enjoy nothing like the autonomy of either second- or first-wave chartered companies.

It could of course be said that historically the VOC and EIC were very much the exceptions; the holdings of the average company-state might not extend beyond a couple of ramshackle trading posts. Yet even ephemeral company-states like the Scottish Darien Company, the Danish East India Company, or the various French company-states utilized the most capital- and technology-intensive weapon systems of their day, deploying groups of multidecked cannon-armed sailing ships. In contrast, even with the most powerful contemporary military companies, there is no equivalent: there are no private aircraft carriers, attack submarines, armored divisions, or fighter squadrons. The difference between then and now is legal, but also very practical.

Following the same comparison of historical company-states with their purported equivalents today, the last question concerns the implications for our understanding of international society. What is the systemic significance of private military and security companies for world politics since they appeared around the closing stages of the Cold War? As we have argued, company-states fundamentally broaden our view of the changing constitution of international society over time since ca. 1600. They do so by undermining a myopic focus on European international politics as the only game in town, and sovereign states as the only players. Functionally, the importance of the company-states is in terms of their role in forming one of the mainstays of cross-cultural diplomacy during the initial centuries of globalization. It is hard to see any equivalent transformation signified or brought about by the advent of multinational corporations providing policing or military support services.

None of this is to deny that there may be an increasing variety of institutions that mixes public and private prerogatives, from State-Owned Enterprises to company towns.[46] Yet just as early modern privateers and adventurers were hybrids that were nevertheless not the same thing as company-states, so too it is a basic category mistake to see private military companies and their ilk as latter-day versions of historical company-states.

It is also worth noting that treatments emphasizing the new or perhaps even unprecedented character of organizations that straddle the public/private divide in performing policing, security, or governance functions often underrate the extent to which the state monopoly of these missions is itself very recent and incomplete. The first modern police force appeared only in 1829.[47] For most countries in the nineteenth century, non-state policing was very much the rule. Writing about private firms in the business of war, Parrott argues convincingly that up until recently scholars have been in thrall to a powerful teleology whereby the public monopoly of violence is seen as the natural and inevitable end-point of historical progress toward modernity. Accordingly, the vital role of private and hybrid actors in war-making even in the recent past has been systematically downplayed or ignored, leading to misleading conclusions about the novelty and importance of current revivals along these lines.[48]

HYBRID DREAMS AND FUTURES

Finally, what of more speculative proposals whereby private actors either create a new state themselves, or are alternatively incorporated into emergent forms of rule reminiscent of yesterday's company-states? The seasteading movement—a libertarian project that proposes the establishment of floating "free" cities on the high

46. In the security realm, see, for example, Abrahamsen and Williams 2011.
47. Reiner 2010: 42.
48. Parrott 2012.

seas beyond the fiscal grasp of nation-states—constitutes the most prominent example of the former. Plans to establish foreign-run chartered cities to kick-start economic growth within fragile states are representative of the latter. At first glance, both seasteading and chartered cities reflect a new openness to experimenting with sovereignty. But on closer examination, in neither their conception nor in their reception do seasteading or chartered cities portend the revival of corporate sovereigns.

The seasteading movement constitutes one of the most radical attempts to revive a form of corporate sovereignty within the international system. In its conception, seasteading's advocates conceive their floating cities as a way of escaping the predation and corruption of national governments.[49] More positively, they envisage that privately run city-colonies would be more efficient in nourishing entrepreneurship, and more capable of guaranteeing personal freedoms, than existing forms of national government. Seasteading has found influential proponents, including Patri Friedman (grandson of Milton Friedman) and Silicon Valley venture capitalist and PayPal co-founder Peter Thiel.[50]

The prominence and wealth of these patrons notwithstanding, seasteading bears few parallels with historical forms of corporate sovereignty. This contrasts with historical company-states, which typically worked in conjunction with national governments in pursuit of complementary goals of long-distance commerce or conquest, rather than as direct challengers to the sovereign state. Likewise, whereas company-states explicitly combined functions of sovereignty and profit-making in the one hybrid form, it is unclear from seasteading proposals exactly who or what would be invested with sovereign powers, or whether seasteading governments would themselves be full-fledged corporations directly dedicated to profit maximization.

This lack of clarity helps account for the generally negative reception to seasteading outside of libertarian circles. Critics have seized on the wealth of some seasteading proponents to cast the movement as an incipient form of plutocratic secession, which

49. Steinberg et al. 2012: 1542.
50. Steinberg et al. 2012: 1536.

if successful would enable the "one percent" to evade their civic responsibilities by decamping to their own privileged offshore enclaves. Even among themselves, seasteaders have failed to resolve questions concerning the nature and location of sovereign prerogatives within seasteading communities, or the character of the diplomatic and trading relationships seasteading communities would maintain with erstwhile national sovereigns. Indeed, some have gone so far as to suggest that seasteading's real value may be as a utopian catalyst for rethinking forms of governance within existing states, rather than standing as a concrete practical alternative.[51]

Seasteading proposals have generally been dismissed as either utopian or dystopian fantasies. This testifies to the degree to which "private" sovereignty has become anathema within mainstream political thought and practice—a clear contrast to the condition that prevailed prior to the twentieth century. Proposals for charter cities have, however, received more serious attention, perhaps suggesting *some* potential for a return to more hybrid forms of rule. Though individual proposals vary, charter city proposals generally call for fragile states to charter new cities within their territories that would be open to the free flow of goods, capital, and people, and would guarantee migrants and investors the rights necessary to help catalyze economic development.[52] Strikingly, charter city proposals call for foreign nations to serve as the ultimate guarantors for the city's charter, potentially taking responsibility for the exercise of quintessentially sovereign functions such as law enforcement, defense, and the administration of civil and criminal justice.[53]

Superficially, chartered cities are reminiscent of the hybrid sovereignty arrangements of earlier eras. This is evident in the granting of sovereign privileges to foreign entities. Nevertheless, none of the models of chartered cities currently being championed envision delegation of sovereign powers to entities other than foreign national governments. That is, the commingling of sovereign and

51. Steinberg et al. 2012: 1,545.
52. Sagar 2016: 512–13.
53. Sagar 2016: 512.

commercial attributes that defined the company-states is entirely absent from contemporary proposals for charter cities.

The hostility that proposed charter cities have consistently provoked again illustrates the normative stickiness of the state, and the deep resistance to deviations from this form. Abortive attempts to establish a charter city in Madagascar partially motivated a coup against the incumbent government in 2009, dramatizing the idea's polarizing potential.[54] Likewise, in 2012, the Honduran Supreme Court deemed an effort to establish a charter city there unconstitutional.[55] Subsequent efforts to resurrect the initiative—this time with a supervisory board including Michael Reagan (Ronald Reagan's son), libertarian anti-tax activist Grover Norquist, and even a descendent of the Habsburg royal family—proved equally unsuccessful.[56] In both instances, charter cities attracted criticism for being stalking horses for neocolonialism. Popular opposition rapidly doomed these enterprises, despite initial interest from prospective host polities.

The poor reception accorded to hybrid dreams like seasteading and charter cities testifies to the degree to which ideas and practices even vaguely evocative of company-states are now beyond the pale. Corporate sovereignty was once commonplace. But now its afterlife can be found not in the real world practice of international politics, but in libertarian venture capitalist fantasies, and in the dark dystopian fears of their progressive critics. This in itself is a tribute to the current universal dominance of the sovereign state, and to the unimaginability of a return to a not-so-distant world where companies were once kings.

54. Sagar, 2016: 527.
55. Kroth 2014: 63.
56. Kroth 2014: 63.

REFERENCES

Abrahamsen, Rita, and Michael C. Williams. 2011. *Security Beyond the State: Private Security in International Politics*. Cambridge: Cambridge University Press.

Abu-Lughod, Janet L. 1991. *Before European Hegemony: The World System A.D. 1240–1350*. Oxford: Oxford University Press.

Adams, Julia. 1994. "Trading States, Trading Places: The Role of Patrimonialism in Early Modern Dutch Development." *Comparative Studies in Society and History* 36 (2): pp. 319–55.

Adams, Julia. 1996. "Principals and Agents, Colonialists and Company Men: The Decay of Colonial Control in the Dutch East Indies." *American Sociological Review* 61 (1): pp. 12–28.

Adams, Julia. 2005. *The Familial State: Ruling Families and Merchant Capitalism in Early Modern Europe*. Ithaca, NY: Cornell University Press.

Anderson, J. L. 1995. "Piracy and World History: An Economic Perspective on Maritime Predation." *Journal of World History* 6 (2): 175–99.

Andrade, Tonio. 2004. "The Company's Chinese Pirates: How the Dutch East India Company Tried to Lead a Coalition of Pirates to War Against China, 1621–1662." *Journal of World History* 15 (4): pp. 415–44.

Andrade, Tonio. 2010. "Beyond Guns, Germs, and Steel: European Expansion and Maritime Asia 1400–1750." *Journal of Early Modern History* 14 (1): pp. 165–86.

Andrade, Tonio. 2018. "The Dutch East India Company in Global History: A Historiographical Reconnaissance." In *The Dutch and English East India Companies: Diplomacy, Trade and Violence in Early Modern Asia*, edited by Adam Clulow and Tristan Mostert, pp. 239–56. Amsterdam: University of Amsterdam Press.

Andrade, Tonio, and Xing Hang. 2016. "The East Asian Maritime Realm in Global History, 1500–1700." In *Sea Rovers, Silver, and Samurai: Maritime East Asia in Global History, 1550–1700*, edited by Tonio Andrade and Xing Hang, pp. 1–27. Oxford: Blackwell.

Andrews, Clarence L. 1927. "Russian Plans for American Dominion." *Washington Historical Quarterly* 18 (2): pp. 83–92.

Anichtchenko, Evguenia. 2013. "The Fleet of the Russian-American Company." *Alaska Journal of Anthropology* 11 (1–2): pp. 37–50.

Anonymous. 1772. *An Enquiry into the Rights of the East-India Company of Making War and Peace, and of Possessing their Territorial Acquisitions without the Participation or Inspection of the British Government, in a Letter to the Proprietors of East-India Stock*. London: Walter Shropshire and Samuel Bladon.

Arduino, Alessandro. 2017. "China's Belt and Road Initiative Security Needs. The Evolution of Chinese Private Security Companies." RSIS Working Paper 306. https://www

.rsis.edu.sg/rsis-publication/rsis/wp306-chinas-belt-and-road-initiative-the
-evolution-of-chinese-private-security-companies/#.XegUndWnw2w.

Avant, Deborah. 2005. *The Market for Force: The Consequences of Privatizing Security.*
Cambridge: Cambridge University Press.

Barkawi, Tarak. 2010. "State and Armed Force in International Context." In *Mercenaries, Pirates, Bandits, and Empires,* edited by Alejandro Colas and Bryan Mabee,
pp. 33–54. New York: Columbia University Press.

Barkey, Karen. 2008. *Empire of Difference: The Ottomans in Comparative Perspective.*
Cambridge: Cambridge University Press.

Barnhart, Joslyn. 2016. "Status Competition and Territorial Aggression: Evidence from
the Scramble for Africa." *Security Studies* 25 (3): pp. 385–419.

Barrow, Ian J. 2017. *The East India Company, 1600–1858: A Short History with Documents.* Indianapolis, IN: Hackett Publishing Company, Inc.

Bartlett, Robert. 1994. *The Making of Europe: Conquest, Colonization and Cultural
Change, 950–1350.* Princeton, NJ: Princeton University Press.

Bassett, D. K. 1998. "Early English Trade and Settlement in Asia, 1602–1690." In *The
East India Company: 1600–1858,* vol. 4, *Trade, Finance and Power,* edited by Patrick
Tuck, pp. 1–25. London: Routledge.

Bayly, C. A. 1983. *Rulers, Townsmen and Bazaars: North Indian Society in the Age of
British Expansion, 1770–1870.* Cambridge: Cambridge University Press.

Bayly, C. A. 1998. "The First Age of Global Imperialism, c. 1760–1830." *Journal of
Imperial and Commonwealth History* 26 (2): pp. 28–47.

Beach, D. N. 1998. "An Innocent Woman, Unjustly Accused? Charwe, Medium of the
Nehanda Mhondoro Spirit, and the 1896–97 Central Shona Rising in Zimbabwe."
History in Africa 25: pp. 27–54.

Bean, Richard. 1973. "War and the Birth of the Nation State." *Journal of Economic
History* 33 (1): pp. 203–21.

Benner, Margareta. 2003. "The Digital Archive of the Swedish East India Company,
1731–1813: A Joint Project of a University Library and a History Department."
Online Information Review 27 (5): pp. 328–32.

Benton, Lauren. 1999. "Colonial Law and Cultural Difference: Jurisdictional Politics
and the Formation of the Colonial State." *Comparative Studies in Society and
History* 41 (3): pp. 563–88.

Berg, Maxine, Timothy Davies, Meike Fellinger, Felicia Gottmann, Hanna Hodacs, and
Chris Nierstrasz. 2015. "Private Trade and Monopoly Structures: The East India
Companies and the Commodity Trade to Europe in the Eighteenth Century." In
Chartering Capitalism: Organizing Markets, States, and Publics, edited by Emily
Erikson, pp. 123–45. Bingley: Emerald Group Publishing.

Berman, Harold J. 1983. *Law and Revolution: The Formation of the Western Legal
Tradition.* Cambridge, MA: Harvard University Press.

Bertrand, Alicia Marie. 2011. "The Downfall of the Royal African Company on the
Atlantic African Coast in the 1720s." Master's thesis, Trent University.

Bick, Alexander. 2012. "Governing the Free Sea: The Dutch West India Company and
Commercial Politics, 1618–1645." PhD diss., Princeton University.

Biedermann, Zoltán. 2009. "The Matrioshka Principle and How it was Overcome: Portuguese and Habsburg Imperial Attitudes in Sri Lanka and the Responses of the Rulers of Kotte (1506–1598)." *Journal of Early Modern History* 13 (4): pp. 265–310.

Biskup, Peter. 1970. "Foreign Coloured Labour in German New Guinea" *Journal of Pacific History* 5 (1): pp. 85–107.

Blainey, G. 1965. "Lost Causes of the Jameson Raid." *Economic History Review* 18 (2): pp. 350–66.

Blockmans, Wim. 2002. *Emperor Charles V, 1500–1558*. London: Arnold.

Blussé, Leonard. 2014. "Peeking into the Empires: Dutch Embassies to the Courts of China and Japan." *Itinerario* 37 (3): 14–29.

Blussé, Leonard, and Femme Gaastra, eds. 1981. *Companies and Trade: Essays on Overseas Trading Companies during the Ancien Régime*. Leiden: Leiden University Press.

Bobbio, Norberto. 1997. *Democracy and Dictatorship: The Nature and Limits of State Power*. Hoboken, NJ: Wiley.

Bolkhovitinov, N. N. 1987. "Russian America and International Relations." In *Russia's American Colony*, edited by S. Frederick Starr, pp. 251–70. Durham, NC: Duke University Press.

Bowen, H V. 2006. *The Business of Empire: The East India Company and Imperial Britain, 1756–1833*. Cambridge: Cambridge University Press.

Bowen, Huw V. 2011. "Trading with the Enemy: British Private Trade and the Supply of Arms to India." In *The Contractor State and Its Implications, 1659–1815*, edited by Richard Harding and Sergio Solbes Ferri, pp. 32–54. Las Palmas, Spain: Contractor State Group.

Bown, Stephen R. 2009. *Merchant Kings: When Companies Ruled the World, 1600–1900*. New York: St. Martin's Press.

Boxer, C. R. 1957. *The Dutch in Brazil, 1624–1654*. Oxford: Clarendon Press.

Boxer, C. R. 1965. *The Dutch Seaborne Empire 1600–1800*. New York: Alfred A. Knopf.

Branch, Jordan. 2013. *The Cartographic State: Maps, Territory, and the Origins of Sovereignty*. Cambridge: Cambridge University Press.

Braudel, Fernand. 1984. *Civilization and Capitalism, 15th–18th Century: Perspective of the World*. New York: HarperCollins.

Bryant, G. J. 2013. *The Emergence of British Power in India, 1600–1784: A Grand Strategic Interpretation*. London: Boydell and Brewer Ltd.

Bull, Hedley. 1995. *The Anarchical Society: A Study of Order in World Politics*. London: Macmillan Press.

Bull, Hedley, and Adam Watson, eds. 1985. *The Expansion of International Society*. Oxford: Oxford University Press.

Burbank, Jane, and Frederick Cooper. 2010. *Empires in World History: Power and the Politics of Difference*. Princeton, NJ: Princeton University Press.

Burke, Edmund. 2003 [1788]. "Edmund Burke on the Impeachment of Warren Hastings, 15–19 February 1788." *Archives of Empire*, vol. 1, *From the East India Company to the Suez Canal*, edited by Barbara Harlow and Mia Carter, pp. 143–55. Durham, NC: Duke University Press.

Butler, Jeffrey. 1977. "Review Article: Cecil Rhodes." *International Journal of African Historical Studies* 10 (2): pp. 259–81.

Butman, John, and Simon Targett. 2018. *New World, Inc.: The Making of America by England's Merchant Adventures.* London: Atlantic Books.

Buzan, Barry, and George Lawson. 2015. *The Global Transformation: History, Modernity and the Making of Modern International Relations.* Cambridge: Cambridge University Press.

Carlos, Ann M. 1991. "Agent Opportunism and the Role of Company Culture: The Hudson's Bay and Royal African Companies Compared." *Business and Economic History* 20: pp. 142–51.

Carlos, Ann M. 1994. "Bonding and the Agency Problem: Evidence from the Royal African Company, 1672–1691." *Explorations in Economic History* 31 (3): pp. 313–35.

Carlos, Ann M., Jennifer Key, and Jill L. Dupree. 1998. "Learning and the Creation of Stock-Market Institutions: Evidence from the Royal African and Hudson's Bay Companies, 1670–1700." *Journal of Economic History* 58 (2): pp. 318–44.

Carlos, Ann M., and Jamie Brown Kruse. 1996. "The Decline of the Royal African Company: Fringe Firms and the Role of the Charter." *Economic History Review* 49 (2): pp. 291–313.

Carlos, Ann M., and Frank D. Lewis. 2001. "Trade, Consumption, and the Native Economy: Lessons from York Factory, Hudson Bay." *Journal of Economic History* 61 (4): pp. 1,037–64.

Carlos, Ann M., and Frank D. Lewis. 2002. "Marketing in the Land of Hudson Bay: Indian Consumers and the Hudson's Bay Company." *Enterprise and Society* 3 (2): pp. 285–317.

Carlos, Ann M., and Frank D. Lewis. 2010. *Commerce by a Frozen Sea: Native Americans and the European Fur Trade.* Philadelphia: University of Pennsylvania Press.

Carlos, Ann M., and Stephen Nicholas. 1988. "'Giants of an Earlier Capitalism': The Chartered Trading Companies as Modern Multinationals." *Business History Review* 62 (3): pp. 398–419.

Carlos, Ann M., and Stephen Nicholas. 1990. "Agency Problems in Early Chartered Companies: The Case of the Hudson's Bay Company." *Journal of Economic History* 50 (4): pp. 853–75.

Carlos, Ann M., and Stephen Nicholas. 1993. "Managing the Manager: An Application of the Principal Agent Model to the Hudson's Bay Company." *Oxford Economic Papers* 45 (2): pp. 243–56.

Cavanagh, Edward. 2011. "A Company with Sovereignty and Subjects of Its Own? The Case of the Hudson's Bay Company, 1670–1763." *Canadian Journal of Law and Society* 26 (1): pp. 25–50.

Cavanagh, Edward. 2016. "Corporations and Business Associations from the Commercial Revolution to the Age of Discovery: Trade, Jurisdiction and the State, 1200–1600." *History Compass* 14 (10): pp. 493–510.

Cavanagh, Edward. 2017. "The Atlantic Prehistory of Private International Law: Trading Companies of the New World and the Pursuit of Restitution in England and France, 1613–43." *Itinerario* 41 (3): pp. 452–83.

Cerny, Philip G. 2000. "The New Security Dilemma: Divisibility, Defection and Disorder in the Global Era." *Review of International Studies* 26 (4): pp. 623–46.

Chase, Kenneth. 2003. *Firearms: A Global History to 1700*. Cambridge: Cambridge University Press.

Chaudhuri, K. N. 1978. *The Trading World of Asia and the English East India Company 1660–1760*. Cambridge: Cambridge University Press.

Chaudhuri, K. N. 1985. *Trade and Civilization in the Indian Ocean: An Economic History from the Rise of Islam to 1750*. Cambridge: Cambridge University Press.

Chesterman, Simon, and Chia Lehnardt, eds. 2007. *From Mercenaries to Market: The Rise and Regulation of Private Military Companies*. Oxford: Oxford University Press.

Churchill, William. 1920. "Germany's Lost Pacific Empire." *Geographical Review* 10 (2): pp. 84–90.

Clay, Dean. 2016. "Transatlantic Dimensions of the Congo Reform Movement, 1904–1908." *English Studies in Africa* 59 (1): pp. 18–28.

Clulow, Adam. 2007. "Unjust, Cruel and Barbarous Proceedings: Japanese Mercenaries and the Amboyna Incident of 1623." *Itinerario* 31 (1): pp. 14–34.

Clulow, Adam. 2014. *The Company and the Shogun: The Dutch Encounter with Tokugawa Japan*. New York: Columbia University Press.

Clulow, Adam, and Tristan Mostert, eds. 2018. *The Dutch and English East India Companies: Diplomacy, Trade and Violence in Early Modern Asia*. Amsterdam: Amsterdam University Press.

Cook, Weston F. 1994. *The Hundred Years War for Morocco: Gunpowder and the Military Revolution in the Early Modern Muslim World*. Boulder, CO: Westview.

Crowley, Roger. 2015. *Conquerors: How Portugal Seized the Indian Ocean and Forged the First Global Empire*. New York: Faber and Faber.

Curtin, Philip D. 1984. *Cross-Cultural Trade in World History*. Cambridge: Cambridge University Press.

Darwin, John. 2012. *Unfinished Empire: The Global Expansion of Britain*. London: Penguin.

da Silva, Filipa Ribeiro. 2014. "African Islands and the Formation of the Dutch Atlantic Economy: Arguin, Gorée, Cape Verde and São Tomé, 1590–1670." *International Journal of Maritime History* 26 (3): pp. 549–67.

Davidson, Donald C. 1941. "Relations of the Hudson's Bay Company with the Russian American Company on the Northwest Coast, 1829–1867." *British Columbia Historical Quarterly* 5 (1): pp. 33–51.

Davies, K. G. 1957. *Royal African Company*. London: Longmans, Green and Co.

Davies, K. G. 1966. "From Competition to Union." *Minnesota History* (Winter): pp. 166–77.

Dean, Jonathan R. 1995. "'Uses of the Past' on the Northwest Coast: The Russian American Company and Tlingit Nobility, 1825–1867." *Ethnohistory* 42 (2): pp. 265–302.

Dean, Jonathan R. 1997. "The Hudson's Bay Company and Its Use of Force, 1828–1829." *Oregon Historical Quarterly* 98 (3): pp. 262–95.

Denholm, A. F. 1981. "Lord Ripon and Liberal Party Policy in Southern Africa 1892–1902." *Australian Journal of Politics and History* 27 (2): pp. 232–40.

De Roo, Bas. 2017. "Taxation in the Congo Free State, An Exceptional Case? (1885–1908)." *Economic History of Developing Regions* 32 (2): pp. 97–126.

Deshpande, Anirudh. 2012. "Wars of the East India Company (1748–1849)." In *The Encyclopedia of War*, edited by Gordon Martel, pp. 2,489–96. London: Blackwell.

Devecka, Martin. 2015. "Raisins d'Etat: Trade, Politics, and Diplomacy in the History of the Levant Company." In *Chartering Capitalism: Organizing Markets, States, and Publics*, edited by Emily Erikson, pp. 77–94. Bingley: Emerald Group Publishing.

Dirks, Nicholas B. 2008. *The Scandal of Empire: India and the Creation of Imperial Britain*. Cambridge, MA: Belknap Press.

Disney, A. R. 1977. "The First Portuguese India Company, 1628–33." *Economic History Review* 30 (2): pp. 242–58.

Disney, A. R. 2009. *A History of Portugal and the Portuguese Empire*, vol. 2, *The Portuguese Empire*. Cambridge: Cambridge University Press.

Drelichman, Mauricio, and Hans-Joachim Voth. 2014. *Lending to the Borrower from Hell: Debt, Taxes, and Default in the Age of Philip II*. Princeton, NJ: Princeton University Press.

Duby, Georges. 1978. *The Three Orders: Feudal Society Imagined*, trans. Arthur Goldhammer. Chicago: University of Chicago Press.

Easley, Roxanne. 2008. "Demographic Borderlands: People of Mixed Heritage in the Russian American Company and the Hudson's Bay Company, 1670–1870." *Pacific Northwest Quarterly* 99 (2): pp. 73–91.

Economist. 2017. "Honduras Experiments with Charter Cities." 12 August. https://www.economist.com/the-americas/2017/08/12/honduras-experiments-with-charter-cities.

Emmer, Peter C. 2003. "The First Global War: The Dutch versus Iberia in Asia, Africa and the New World, 1590–1609." *e-Journal of Portuguese History* 1 (1): pp. 1–14.

Emmer, Pieter C., and Wim Klooster. 1999. "The Dutch Atlantic, 1600–1800: Expansion without Empire." *Itinerario* 23 (2): pp. 48–69.

Erikson, Emily. 2014. *Between Monopoly and Free Trade: The English East India Company, 1660–1757*. Princeton, NJ: Princeton University Press.

Erikson, Emily, and Valentina Assenova. 2015. "Introduction: New Forms of Organization and the Coordination of Political and Commercial Actors." In *Chartering Capitalism: Organizing Markets, States, and Publics*, edited by Emily Erikson, pp. 1–13. Bingley, UK: Emerald Group Publishing.

Erikson, Emily, and Peter Bearman. 2006. "Malfeasance and the Foundations for Global Trade: The Structure of English Trade in the East Indies, 1601–1833." *American Journal of Sociology* 112 (1): pp. 195–230.

Feldbæk, Ole. 1986. "The Danish Trading Companies of the Seventeenth and Eighteenth Centuries." *Scandinavian Economic History Review* 34 (3): pp. 204–18.

Finnemore, Martha. 1996. *National Interests in International Society*. Ithaca, NY: Cornell University Press.

Firth, Stewart. 1972. "The New Guinea Company, 1885–1899: A Case of Unprofitable Imperialism." *Historical Studies* 15 (59): pp. 361–77.

Firth, Stewart. 1973. "German Firms in the Western Pacific Islands, 1857–1914." *Journal of Pacific History* 8 (1): pp. 10–28.

Firth, Stewart. 1978. "German Labour Policy in Nauru and Angaur, 1906–1914." *Journal of Pacific History* 13 (1): pp. 36–52.

Firth, Stewart. 1982. *New Guinea Under the Germans*. Melbourne: Melbourne University Press.

Firth, Stewart. 1985. "German New Guinea: The Archival Perspective." *Journal of Pacific History* 20 (2): pp. 94–103.

Fisch, Jorg. 1992. "Law as a Means and as an End: Some Remarks on the Function of European and Non-European Law in the Process of European Expansion." In *European Expansion and Law: The Encounter of European and Indigenous Law in 19th- and 20th-Century Africa and Asia*, edited by W. J. Mommsen and J. A. De Moor, pp. 15–38. Oxford: Berg Publishers.

Fitzmaurice, Andrew. 2010. "The Justification of King Leopold II's Congo Enterprise by Sir Travers Twiss." In *Law and Politics in British Colonial Thought: Transpositions of Empire*, edited by Shaunnagh Dorsett and Ian Hunter, pp. 109–26. New York: Palgrave Macmillan.

Fitzmaurice, Andrew. 2014. *Sovereignty, Property and Empire, 1500–2000*. Cambridge: Cambridge University Press.

Flynn, Dennis O., and Arturo Giráldez. 1995. "Born with a 'Silver Spoon': The Origin of World Trade in 1571." *Journal of World History* 6 (2): pp. 201–21.

Folz, Robert. 1969. *The Concept of Empire in Western Europe: From the Fifth to the Fourteenth Century*, translated by Sheila Ann Ogilvie. London: Edward Arnold.

Frederiksen, Tomas. 2014. "Authorizing the 'Natives': Governmentality, Dispossession, and the Contradictions of Rule in Colonial Zambia." *Annals of the Association of American Geographers* 104 (6): pp. 1,273–90.

Gaastra, Femme. 1981. "The Shifting Balance of Trade of the Dutch East India Company." In *Companies and Trade: Essays on Overseas Trading Companies during the Ancien Régime*, edited by Leonard Blussé and Femme Gaastra, pp. 47–69. Leiden: Leiden University Press.

Gaastra, Femme S. 2003. *The Dutch East India Company*. Leiden: Walburg Pers.

Galbraith, John S. 1949. "The Hudson's Bay Land Controversy, 1863–1869." *Mississippi Valley Historical Review* 36 (3): pp. 457–78.

Galbraith, John S. 1951. "Land Policies of the Hudson's Bay Company, 1870–1913." *Canadian Historical Review* 32 (1): pp. 1–21.

Galbraith, John S. 1957. *The Hudson's Bay Company as an Imperial Factor, 1821–1869*. Berkeley: University of California Press.

Galbraith, John S. 1970. "The British South Africa Company and the Jameson Raid." *Journal of British Studies* 10 (1): pp. 145–61.

Galbraith, John S. 1974. *Crown and Charter: The Early Years of the British South Africa Company*. Berkeley: University of California Press.

Gelderblom, Oscar, Abe de Jon, and Joost Jonker. 2013. "The Formative Years of the Modern Corporation: The Dutch East India Company VOC, 1602–1623." *Journal of Economic History* 73 (4): pp. 1,050–76.

Gelderblom, Oscar, and Joost Jonker. 2004. "Completing a Financial Revolution: The Finance of the Dutch East India Trade and the Rise of the Amsterdam Capital Market, 1595–1612." *Journal of Economic History* 64 (3): pp. 641–72.

German New Guinea: The Annual Reports. 1979. Edited and translated by Peter Sack and Dymphna Clark. Canberra: Australian National University Press.

Gibson, James R. 1978. "European Dependence upon American Natives: The Case of Russian America." *Ethnohistory* 25 (4): pp. 359–85.

Gibson, James R. 1980. "Russian Expansion in Siberia and America." *Geographical Review* 70 (2): pp. 127–36.

Gibson, James R. 1987. "Russian Dependence upon the Natives of Alaska." In *Russia's American Colony*, edited by S. Frederick Starr, pp. 7–104. Durham, NC: Duke University Press.

Giordani, Paolo. 1916. *The German Colonial Empire: Its Beginning and Ending.* London: G. Bell and Sons.

Glamann, Kristof. 1981. *Dutch-Asiatic Trade, 1620–1740.* The Hague: Martinus Nijhoff.

Glass, S. 1966. "The Outbreak of the Matabele War (1893) in the Light of Recent Research." *Rhodesiana* 14 (July): pp. 34–43.

Glete, Jan. 2000. *Warfare at Sea: 1500–1650: Maritime Conflicts and the Transformation of Europe.* London: Routledge.

Gong, Gerrit W. 1984. *The Standard of "Civilization" in International Society.* Oxford: Oxford University Press.

Goodman, Brian. 2010. "The Dutch East India Company and the Tea Trade." In *Emory Endeavors in World History*, vol. 3, *Navigating the Great Divergence*, edited by Brian Goodman, pp. 60–68. Atlanta, GA: Department of History, Emory University.

Gordon, David M. 2017. "Precursors to Red Rubber: Violence in the Congo Free State, 1885–1895." *Past and Present* 236 (1): pp. 133–68.

Gottmann, Felicia. 2013. "French-Asian Connections: The Compagnies des Indes, France's Eastern Trade, and New Directions in Historical Scholarship." *Historical Journal* 56 (2): pp. 537–52.

Government of India Act. 1853. Accessed 19 March 2019. https://www.legalcrystal.com /act/133615/government-of-india-act-1853-complete-act.

Grandin, Greg. 2010. *Fordlandia: The Rise and Fall of Henry Ford's Forgotten Jungle City.* London: Picador.

Great Britain. Parliament. House of Commons. 1857. *Report from the Select Committee on the Hudson's Bay Company; Together with the Proceedings of the Committee, Minutes of Evidence, Appendix and Index.* London: House of Commons.

Green, Toby. 2011. *The Rise of the Transatlantic Slave Trade in Africa, 1300–1589.* Cambridge: Cambridge University Press.

Greene, Jack P. 1986. *Peripheries and Center: Constitutional Development in the Extended Polities of the British Empire and the United States, 1607–1788.* Athens: University of Georgia Press.

Greenwald, Erin Michelle. 2011. "Company Towns and Tropical Baptisms: From Lorient to Louisiana on a French Atlantic Circuit." PhD diss., Ohio State University.

Grewal, David Singh. 2016. "The Political Theology of *Laissez-Faire*: From *Philia* to Self-Love in Commercial Society." *Political Theology* 17 (5): pp. 417–33.

Grinëv, Andrei V. 2014. "Foreign Ships in the Fleet of the Russian-American Company (1799–1867)." *The Mariner's Mirror* 100 (4): pp. 405–21.

Grinëv, Andrei V. 2015. "Russia's Emperors and Russian America (for the Four Hundredth Anniversary of the Romanov Dynasty)." *Russian Studies in History* 54 (1): pp. 5–35.

Halliday, Paul D. 2013. "Laws' Histories: Pluralisms, Pluralities, Diversity." In *Legal Pluralism and Empires, 1500–1850*, edited by Lauren Benton and Richard J. Ross, pp. 261–77. New York: New York University Press.

Harms, Robert. 1975. "The End of Red Rubber: A Reassessment." *Journal of African History* 16 (1): pp. 73–88.

Harms, Robert. 1983. "The World Abir Made: The Margina-Lopori Basin, 1885–1903." *African Economic History* 12: pp. 125–39.

Harris, Ron. 2009. "The Institutional Dynamics of Early Modern Eurasian Trade: The *Commenda* and the Corporation." *Journal of Economic Behavior and Organization* 71 (3): pp. 606–22.

Harris, Ron. 2018. "Trading with Strangers: The Corporate Form in the Move from Municipal Governance to Overseas Trade." In *Research Handbook on the History of Corporate and Company Law*, edited by Harwell Wells, pp. 88–118. Cheltenham: Edward Elgar.

Headrick, Daniel R. 2010. *Power Over Peoples: Technology, Environments, and Western Imperialism, 1400 to the Present*. Princeton, NJ: Princeton University Press.

Heijmans, Elisabeth. 2019. "Investing in French Overseas Companies: A Bad Deal? The Liquidation Processes of Companies Operating on the West Coast of Africa and in India (1664–1719)." *Itinerario* 43 (1): pp. 107–21.

Hellman, Lisa. 2019. "Scandinavia." In *The Corporation as a Protagonist in Global History, c. 1550–1750*, edited by William A. Pettigrew and David Veevers, pp. 279–90. Leiden: Brill.

Hempenstall, Peter J. 1978. *Pacific Islanders Under German Rule: A Study in the Meaning of Colonial Resistance*. Canberra: Australian National University Press.

Henige, David. 1977. "John Kabes of Komenda: An Early African Entrepreneur and State Builder." *Journal of African History* 18 (1): pp. 1–19.

Henley, David. 2004. "Conflict, Justice, and the Stranger-King Indigenous Roots of Colonial Rule in Indonesia and Elsewhere." *Modern Asian Studies* 38 (1): pp. 85–144.

Henriet, Benoît. 2015. "Colonial Law in the Making: Sovereignty and Property in the Congo Free State (1876–1908)." *Legal History Review* 83 (1–2): pp. 202–25.

Hill, Lisa. 2006. "Adam Smith and the Theme of Corruption." *Review of Politics* 68 (4): pp. 636–62.

Hochschild, Adam. 1998. *King Leopold's Ghost: A Story of Greed, Terror and Heroism in Colonial Africa*. New York: Houghton Mifflin Company.

Hodges, Leonard. 2019. "France." In *The Corporation as a Protagonist in Global History, c. 1550–1750*, edited by William A. Pettigrew and David Veevers, pp. 290–300. Leiden: Brill.

Horwitz, Morton J. 1982. "The History of the Public/Private Distinction." *University of Pennsylvania Law Review* 130 (6): pp. 1,423–28.

Howard, Michael. 1976. *War in European History*. Oxford: Oxford University Press.

Hsueh, Vicki. 2010. *Hybrid Constitutions: Challenging Legacies of Law, Privilege, and Culture in Colonial America*. Durham, NC: Duke University Press.

Hughes, William Michael. 2016. "Inventing 'Crime' in a Lawless Land: Legal Conflict, Racial Formation, and Conquest in the North American Interior." PhD diss., University of Illinois at Urbana-Champaign.

Ikenberry, John, G. 2020. "Liberal Internationalism and Cultural Diversity." In *Culture and Order in World Politics*, edited by Andrew Phillips and Christian Reus-Smit, pp. 137–58. Cambridge: Cambridge University Press.

Isaacman, Allen F., and Barbara Isaacman. 1983. *Mozambique: From Colonialism to Revolution: 1900–1982*. Boulder, CO: Westview Press.

Israel, Jonathan I. 1995. *The Dutch Republic: Its Rise, Greatness, and Fall, 1477–1806*. Oxford: Oxford University Press.

Jackson, Robert. 2000. *The Global Covenant: Human Conduct in a World of States*. Oxford: Oxford University Press.

Jacobs, Marjorie G. 1951. "Bismarck and the Annexation of New Guinea." *Historical Studies* 5 (17): pp. 14–26.

Jones, Ryan Tucker. 2013. "A. F. Kashevarov, the Russian-American Company, and Alaska Conservation." *Alaska Journal of Anthropology* 11 (1–2): pp. 51–68.

Jones, S. R. H., and Simon P. Ville. 1996. "Efficient Transactors or Rent-Seeking Monopolists? The Rationale for Early Chartered Trading Companies." *Journal of Economic History* 56 (4): pp. 898–915.

Kamen, Henry. 2002. *Empire: How Spain Became a World Power 1492-1763*. London: Penguin.

Kang, David C. 2003. "Getting Asia Wrong: The Need for New Analytical Frameworks." *International Security* 27 (4): pp. 57–85.

Keal, Paul. 2003. *European Conquest and the Rights of Indigenous Peoples: The Moral Backwardness of International Society*. Cambridge: Cambridge University Press.

Keay, John. 2000. *India: A History*. New York: Grove Press.

Keene, Edward. 2002. *Beyond the Anarchical Society: Grotius, Colonialism and Order in World Politics*. Cambridge: Cambridge University Press.

Keirn, Tim. 1988. "Daniel Defoe and the Royal African Company." *Historical Research* 61 (145): pp. 243–47.

Keith, H. Lloyd. 2007. "'A Place so Dull and Dreary': The Hudson's Bay Company at Fort Okanagan, 1821–1860." *Pacific Northwest Quarterly* 98 (2): pp. 78–94.

Kennedy, P. M. 1972. "Bismarck's Imperialism: The Case of Samoa, 1880–1890." *Historical Journal* 15 (2): pp. 261–83.

Kian, Kwee Hui. 2008. "How Strangers Became Kings: Javanese-Dutch Relations in Java, 1600–1800." *Indonesia and the Malay World* 36 (105): pp. 293–307.

Klein, P. W. 1981. "The Origins of Trading Companies." In *Companies and Trade: Essays on Overseas Trading Companies during the Ancien Régime*, edited by Leonard Blussé and Femme Gaastra, pp. 17–28. Leiden: Leiden University Press.

Koekkoek, René, Anne-Isabelle Richard, and Arthur Weststeijn. 2017. "Visions of Dutch Empire: Towards a Long-Term Global Perspective." *Low Countries Historical Review* 132 (2): pp. 79–96.

Koenigsberger, H. G. 1955. "The Organization of Revolutionary Parties in France and the Netherlands during the Sixteenth Century." *Journal of Modern History* 27 (4): pp. 335–51.

Koninckx, Christian. 1978. "The Maritime Routes of the Swedish East India Company during its First and Second Charter (1731–1766)." *Scandinavian Economic History Review* 26 (1): pp. 36–65.

Koshy, K. O. 1989. *The Dutch Power in Kerala (1729–1758)*. New Delhi: Mittal.

Koskenniemi, Martti. 2002. *The Gentle Civilizer of Nations: The Rise and Fall of International Law 1870–1960*. Cambridge: Cambridge University Press.

Krahmann, Elke. 2010. *States, Citizens and the Privatization of Security*. Cambridge: Cambridge University Press.

Kroth, Maya. 2014. "Under New Management." *Foreign Policy* 208 (September–October): pp. 60–65.

Kyriazis, Nicholas, and Theodore Metaxas. 2011. "Path Dependence, Change and the Emergence of the First Joint-Stock Companies." *Business History* 53 (3): pp. 363–74.

Kyriazis, Nicholas, Theodore Metaxas, and Emmanouil M. L. Economou. 2018. "War for Profit: English Corsairs, Institutions and Decentralised Strategy." *Defence and Peace Economics* 29 (3): 335–51.

Lain, B. D. 1976. "The Decline of Russian America's Colonial Society." *Western Historical Quarterly* 7 (2): pp. 143–53.

Lambert, Andrew. 2018. *Seapower States: Maritime Culture, Continental Empires and the Conflict that Made the Modern World*. New Haven, CT: Yale University Press.

Landes, David S. 1969. *Prometheus Unbound: Technological Change and Industrial Development in Western Europe from 1750 to the Present*. Cambridge: Cambridge University Press.

Lane, Frederic C. 1958. "Economic Consequences of Organized Violence." *Journal of Economic History* 18 (4): pp. 401–17.

Lane, Frederic C. 1966. *Venice and History: The Collected Papers of Frederic C. Lane*. Baltimore: Johns Hopkins University Press.

Law, Robin. 2007. "The *Komenda* Wars, 1694–1700: A Revised Narrative." *History in Africa* 34: pp. 133–68.

Lawson, Philip. 1993. *The East India Company: A History*. New York: Longman.

Lieberman, Victor. 2009. *Strange Parallels: Southeast Asia in Global Context, c. 800–1830*, vol. 2: *Mainland Mirrors: Europe, Japan, China, South Asia, and the Islands*. Cambridge: Cambridge University Press.

Lloyd, T. H. 2002. *England and the German Hanse, 1157–1611: A Study of Their Trade and Commercial Diplomacy*. Cambridge: Cambridge University Press.

Locher–Scholten, Elsbeth. 1994. "Dutch Expansion in the Indonesian Archipelago around 1900 and the Imperialism Debate." *Journal of Southeast Asian Studies* 25 (1): pp. 91–111.

Lynn, John A. 2003. "Heart of the Sepoy: The Adoption and Adaptation of European Military Practice in South Asia, 1740–1805." In *The Diffusion of Military Technology and Ideas*, edited by Emily O. Goldman and Leslie C. Eliason, pp. 33–62. Stanford: Stanford University Press.

Mabin, Eleanor Mary Olgilvie. 1982. "'Truth' and the British South Africa Company: The Development of a Radical's Opposition to Capitalist Imperialism in a Southern African Context." PhD diss., University of Witswatersrand.

Madimu, Tapiwa. 2016. "Responsible Government and Miner-Farmer Relations in Southern Rhodesia, 1923–1945." *South African Historical Journal* 68 (3): pp. 366–89.

Maier, Charles S. 2014. *Leviathan 2.0: Inventing Modern Statehood*. Cambridge: Cambridge University Press.

Makhura, Tlou John. 1995. "Another Road to the Raid: The Neglected Role of the Boer-Bagananwa War as a Factor in the Coming of the Jameson Raid, 1894–1895." *Journal of South African Studies* 21 (2): pp. 257–67.

Mann, Michael. 1986. *The Sources of Social Power*, vol. 1, *A History of Power from the Beginning to AD 1760*. Cambridge: Cambridge University Press.

Margerison, Kenneth. 2006. "The Shareholders' Revolt at the Compagnie des Indes: Commerce and Political Culture in Old Regime France." *French History* 20 (1): pp. 25–51.

Marsden, Susan and Robert Galois. 1995. "The Tsimshian, the Hudson's Bay Company, and the Geopolitics of the Northwest Coast Fur Trade, 1787–1840." *Canadian Geographer* 39 (2): pp. 169–83.

Marshall, P. J. 1980. "Western Arms in Maritime Asia in the Early Phases of Expansion." *Modern Asian Studies* 14 (1): pp. 13–28.

Marshall, P. J. 1987. *The New Cambridge History of India*, vol. 2, *Bengal: The British Bridgehead: Eastern India, 1740–1828*, Part 2. Cambridge: Cambridge University Press.

Marshall, P. J. 1993. "Retrospect on J. C. van Leur's Essay on the Eighteenth Century as a Category in Asian History." *Itinerario* 17 (1): pp. 45–58.

Marshall, P. J. 1998. "The British in Asia: Trade to Dominion, 1700–1765." In *The Oxford History of the British Empire*, vol. 2, *The Eighteenth Century*, edited by P. J. Marshall and A. Low, pp. 487–507. Oxford: Oxford University Press.

Marshall, P. J. 2005. *The Making and Unmaking of Empires: Britain, India and America c. 1750–1783*. Oxford: Oxford University Press.

Marten, Kimberly. 2019. "Russia's Use of Semi-State Security Forces: The Case of the Wagner Group." *Post-Soviet Affairs* 35 (3): pp. 181–204.

Mather, James. 2009. *Pashas: Traders and Travellers in the Islamic World*. New Haven, CT: Yale University Press.

Matsukata, Fuyuko. 2018. "East India Company Letters to the Shogun." In *The Dutch and English East India Companies: Diplomacy, Trade and Violence in Early*

Modern Asia, edited by Adam Clulow and Tristan Mostert, pp. 79–98. Amsterdam: University of Amsterdam Press.

Matthews, Owen. 2013. *Glorious Misadventures: Nikolai Rezanov and the Dream of a Russian America*. New York: Bloomsbury.

Mazour, Anatole G. 1936. "Dimitry Zavalishin: Dreamer of a Russian-American Empire." *Pacific Historical Review* 5 (1): pp. 26–37.

Mazour, Anatole G. 1937. "Doctor Yegor Scheffer: Dreamer of a Russian Empire in the Pacific." *Pacific Historical Review* 6 (1): pp. 15–20.

Mazour, Anatole G. 1944. "The Russian-American Company: Private or Government Enterprise?" *Pacific Historical Review* 13 (2): pp. 168–73.

McKendrick, John. 2016. *Darien: A Journey in Search of Empire*. Edinburgh: Birlinn.

McNeil, Kent. 1999. "Sovereignty and the Aboriginal Nations of Rupert's Land." *Manitoba History* 37: pp. 2–8.

McNeill, William H. 1977. *Plagues and Peoples*. New York: Anchor Books.

McNeill, William H. 1982. *The Pursuit of Power: Technology, Armed Force, and Society since A.D. 1000*. Chicago: University of Chicago Press.

Mendelsohn, Richard. 1980. "Blainey and the Jameson Raid: The Debate Renewed." *Journal of Southern African Studies* 6 (2): pp. 157–70.

Meurer, Sebastian. 2012. "Approaches to State-Building in Eighteenth Century Bengal." In *Structures on the Move: Technologies of Governance in Transcultural Encounter*, edited by Antje Flüchter and Susan Fischer, pp. 219–41. Heidelberg: Springer.

Mitchell, Matthew D. 2012. "Joint-Stock Capitalism and the Atlantic Commercial Network: The Royal African Company, 1672–1752." PhD diss., University of Pennsylvania.

Mitchell, Matthew David. 2013a. "'Legitimate Commerce' in the Eighteenth Century: The Royal African Company of England Under the Duke of Chandos, 1720–1726." *Enterprise and Society* 14 (3): pp. 544–78.

Mitchell, Matthew David. 2013b. "Three English Cloth Towns and the Royal African Company." *Journal of the Historical Society* 13 (4): pp. 421–47.

Moore, R. J. 1983. "John Stuart Mill at East India House." *Historical Studies* 20 (81): pp. 497–519.

Morris, Susan L., Glenn J. Farris, Steven J. Schwartz, Irina Vladi L. Wender, and Boris Dralyuk. 2014. "Murder, Massacre, and Mayhem on the California Coast, 1814–1815: Newly Translated Russian American Company Documents Reveal Company Concern over Violent Clashes." *Journal of California and Great Basin Anthropology* 34 (1): pp. 81–100.

Morriss, Richard. 2011. *The Foundations of British Maritime Ascendancy: Resources, Logistics and the State, 1755–1815*. Cambridge: Cambridge University Press.

Mostert, Tristan. 2007. "Chain of Command: The Military System of the Dutch East India Company 1655–1663." Master's thesis, University of Leiden.

Mseba, Admire. 2016. "Law, Expertise, and Settler Conflicts over Land in Early Colonial Zimbabwe, 1890–1923." *Environment and Planning A* 48 (4): pp. 665–80.

Müller, Leos. 2003. "The Swedish East India Trade and International Markets: Re-exports of Teas, 1731–1813." *Scandinavian Economic History Review* 51 (3): pp. 28–44.

Musoni, Francis. 2017. "Contested Foreignness: Indian Migrants and the Politics of Exclusion in Early Colonial Zimbabwe, 1890 to 1923." *African and Asian Studies* 16 (4): pp. 312–35.

Neil-Tomlinson, Barry. 1977. "The Nyassa Chartered Company: 1891–1929." *Journal of African History* 18 (1): pp. 109–28.

Nelson, Samuel H. 1994. *Colonialism in the Congo Basin, 1880–1940.* Athens, OH: Ohio University Press.

Newman, Peter C. 1998. *Empire of the Bay: The Company of Adventurers that Seized a Continent.* New York: Penguin.

Newsinger, John. 2016. "Why Rhodes Must Fall." *Race and Class* 58 (2): pp. 70–78.

Nexon, Daniel H. 2009. *The Struggle for Power in Early Modern Europe: Religious Conflict, Dynastic Empires, and International Change.* Princeton, NJ: Princeton University Press.

Nichols Jr., Irby C. 1967. "The Russian Ukase and the Monroe Doctrine: A Re-Evaluation." *Pacific Historical Review* 36 (1): pp. 13–26.

Nierstrasz, Chris. 2012. *In the Shadow of the Company: The Dutch East India Company and Its Servants in the Period of Its Decline (1740–1796).* Leiden: Brill.

Nierstrasz, Chris. 2015. *Rivalry for Trade in Tea and Textiles: The English and Dutch East India Companies (1700–1800).* Basingstoke: Palgrave Macmillan.

Nierstrasz, Chris. 2019. "Dutch." In *The Corporation as a Protagonist in Global History, c. 1550–1750,* edited by William A. Pettigrew and David Veevers, pp. 317–25. Leiden: Brill.

Nijman, Jan. 1994. "The VOC and the Expansion of the World-System 1602–1799." *Political Geography* 13 (3): pp. 211–27.

Nordlander, David. 1995. "Innokentii Veniaminov and the Expansion of Orthodoxy in Russian America." *Pacific Historical Review* 64 (1): pp. 19–36.

North, Douglass C. 1990. "Institutions, Transaction Costs, and the Rise of Merchant Empires." In *The Political Economy of Merchant Empires: State Power and World Trade, 1350–1750,* edited by James D. Tracy, pp. 22–40. Cambridge: Cambridge University Press.

North, Douglass C., and Robert Paul Thomas. 1973. *The Rise of the Western World: A New Economic History.* Cambridge: Cambridge University Press.

Norton, Matthew. 2015. "Principal Agent Relations and the Decline of the Royal African Company." In *Chartering Capitalism: Organizing Markets, States, and Publics,* edited by Emily Erikson, pp. 45–76. Bingley: Emerald Group Publishing.

Odegard, Erik. 2014. "Fortifications and the Imagination of Colonial Control: The Dutch East India Company in Malabar 1663–1795." Conference paper, presented at the Urban History Conference, Lisbon.

Odegard, Erik. 2019. "Recapitalization or Reform? The Bankruptcy of the First Dutch West India Company and the Formation of the Second West India Company." *Itinerario,* 43 (1): pp. 88–106.

Ohff, Hans-Jürgen. 2008. "Empires of Enterprise: German and English Commercial Interests in East New Guinea 1884 to 1994." PhD diss., University of Adelaide.

Oostindie, Gert. 2012. "'British Capital, Industry and Perseverance' versus Dutch 'Old School'? The Dutch Atlantic and the Takeover of Berbice, Demerara and Essequibo, 1750–1815." *Low Countries Historical Review* 127 (4): pp. 28–55.

Overlack, Peter. 1973. "German New Guinea: A Diplomatic, Economic and Political Survey." Paper presented to the Royal Historical Society of Queensland, 26 July, pp. 128–51.

Owens, Patricia. 2008. "Distinctions, Distinctions: 'Public' and 'Private' Force?" *International Affairs* 84 (5): pp. 977–90.

Palmer, Robin H. 1971. "War and Land in Rhodesia." *Transafrican Journal of History* 1 (2): pp. 43–62.

Parker, Geoffrey. 1996. *The Military Revolution: Military Innovation and the Rise of the West, 1500–1800*. Cambridge: Cambridge University Press.

Parker, Geoffrey. 2000. *The Grand Strategy of Philip II*. New Haven, CT: Yale University Press.

Parrott, David. 2012. *The Business of War: Military Enterprise and Military Revolution in Early Modern Europe*. Cambridge: Cambridge University Press.

Paul, Helen Julia. 2009. "The Darien Scheme and Anglophobia in Scotland." Discussion Paper No. 925. Southampton: University of Southampton, https://www.southampton.ac.uk/economics/research/discussion_papers/year/2009/0925_the_darien_scheme_and_anglophobia_in_scotland.page.

Pavlakis, Dean. 2010. "The Development of British Overseas Humanitarianism and the Congo Reform Campaign." *Journal of Colonialism and Colonial History* 11 (1).

Pearson, M. N. 1990. "Merchants and States." In *The Political Economy of Merchant Empires: State Power and World Trade, 1350–1750*, edited by James D. Tracy, pp. 41–116. Cambridge: Cambridge University Press.

Peifer, Douglas C. 2013. "Maritime Commerce Warfare: The Coercive Response of the Weak?" *Naval War College Review* 66 (2): pp. 83–109.

Percy, Sarah. 2007. *Mercenaries: The History of a Norm in International Relations*. Oxford: Oxford University Press.

Perdue, Peter. 2005. *China Marches West: The Qing Conquest of Central Asia*. Cambridge, MA: Harvard University Press.

Pereira, Edgar. "Iberia." 2019. In *The Corporation as a Protagonist in Global History, c. 1550–1750*, edited by William A. Pettigrew and David Veevers, pp. 301–16. Leiden: Brill.

Perry, Adele. 2001. "The State of Empire: Reproducing Colonialism in British Columbia, 1849–1871." *Journal of Colonialism and Colonial History* 2 (2).

Perry, Adele. 2015. "Designing Dispossession: The Select Committee on the Hudson's Bay Company, Fur-Trade, Governance, Indigenous Peoples and Settler Possibility." In *Indigenous Communities and Settler Colonialism: Land Holding, Loss and Survival in an Interconnected World*, edited by Zoë Laidlaw and Alan Lester, pp. 158–72. Basingstoke, UK: Palgrave Macmillan.

Peters, Marie. 2010. "State, Parliament and Empire in the Mid 18th Century: Hudson's Bay and the Parliamentary Enquiry of 1749." *Parliamentary History* 29 (2): pp. 171–91.

Petrov, Aleksandr Iu. 2015. "The Activity of the Russian-American Company on the Eve of the Sale of Alaska to the United States (1858–67)." *Russian Studies in History* 54 (1): pp. 61–90.

Pettigrew, William A. 2013. *Freedom's Debt: The Royal African Company and the Politics of the Atlantic Slave Trade, 1672–1752*. Chapel Hill: University of North Carolina Press.

Pettigrew, William A. 2015. "Corporate Constitutionalism and the Dialogue between the Global and Local in Seventeenth-Century English History." *Itinerario* 39 (3): pp. 487–501.

Pettigrew, William A. 2018. "The Changing Place of Fraud in Seventeenth-Century Debates about International Trading Corporations." *Business History* 60 (3): pp. 305–20.

Pettigrew, William A., and George W. Van Cleve. 2014. "Parting Companies: The Glorious Revolution, Company Power, and Imperial Mercantilism." *Historical Journal* 57 (3): pp. 617–38.

Pettigrew, William A., and David Veevers. 2019. "Introduction" In *The Corporation as a Protagonist in Global History, c. 1550–1750*, edited by William A. Pettigrew and David Veevers, pp. 1–39. Leiden: Brill.

Phillips, Andrew, and J. C. Sharman. 2015. *International Order in Diversity: War, Trade and Rule in the Indian Ocean*. Cambridge: Cambridge University Press.

Phimister, Ian. 1974. "Rhodes, Rhodesia and the Rand." *Journal of Southern African Studies* 1 (1): pp. 74–90.

Phimister, Ian. 1984. "Accommodating Imperialism: The Compromise of the Settler State in Southern Rhodesia, 1923–1929." *Journal of African History* 25 (3): pp. 279–94.

Phimister, Ian. 2015. "Late Nineteenth-Century Globalization: London and Lomagundi Perspectives on Mining Speculation in Southern Africa, 1894–1904." *Journal of Global History* 10 (1): pp. 27–52.

Po, Ronald C. 2018. *The Blue Frontier: Maritime Vision and Power in the Qing Empire*. Cambridge: Cambridge University Press.

Poggi, Gianfranco. 1978. *The Development of the Modern State: A Sociological Introduction*. Stanford: Stanford University Press.

Pomeranz, Kenneth. 2000. *The Great Divergence: China, Europe, and the Making of the Modern World Economy*. Princeton, NJ: Princeton University Press.

Prakash, Om. 1998. *European Commercial Enterprise in Pre-Colonial India*. Cambridge: Cambridge University Press.

Prange, Sebastian R. 2013. "The Contested Sea: Regimes of Maritime Violence in the Pre-Modern Indian Ocean." *Journal of Early Modern History* 17 (1): 9–33.

Press, Steven. 2017. *Rogue Empires: Contracts and Conmen in Europe's Scramble for Africa*. Cambridge, MA: Harvard University Press.

Quirk, Joel, and David Richardson. 2014. "Europeans, Africans and the Atlantic World, 1450–1850." In *International Orders in the Early Modern World: Before the Rise of the West*, edited by Shogo Suzuki, Yongjin Zhang, and Joel Quirk, pp. 138–58. Routledge: Abingdon.

Raben, Remco. 2012. "On Genocide and Mass Violence in Colonial Indonesia." *Journal of Genocide Research* 14 (3–4): pp. 485–502.

Ranger, T. O. 1971. "The Historiography of Southern Rhodesia." *Transafrican Journal of History* 1 (2): pp. 63–76.

Reeves, Jesse S. 1909. "The Origin of the Congo Free State, Considered from the Standpoint of International Law." *American Journal of International Law* 3 (1): pp. 99–118.

Reiner, Robert. 2010. *The Politics of the Police*. Oxford: Oxford University Press.

Restall, Matthew. 2003. *Seven Myths of the Spanish Conquest*. Oxford: Oxford University Press.

Rich, E. E. 1960a. *Hudson's Bay Company, 1670–1870*, vol. 1, 1670–1763. New York: Macmillan Press.

Rich, E. E. 1960b. "Trade Habits and Economic Motivation among the Indians of North America." *Canadian Journal of Economics and Political Science* 26 (1): pp. 35–53.

Rich, E. E. 1961. *Hudson's Bay Company, 1670–1870*, vol. 3, *1821–1870*. Glasgow: Macmillan Press.

Richards, John F. 1993. *The Mughal Empire*. Cambridge: Cambridge University Press.

Ricklefs, M. C. 1993. *War, Culture and the Economy in Java, 1677–1726*. Sydney: Allen and Unwin.

Robins, Nick. 2006. *The Corporation that Changed the World: How the East India Company Shaped the Modern Multinational*. London: Pluto.

Rodger, N.A.M. 2014. "The Law and Language of Private Naval Warfare." *The Mariner's Mirror* 100 (1): 5–16.

Roes, Aldwin. 2010. "Towards a History of Mass Violence in the Etat Indépendant du Congo, 1885–1908." *South African Historical Journal* 62 (4): pp. 634–70.

Rönnbäck, Klas. 2016. "Transaction Costs of Early Modern Multinational Enterprise: Measuring the Transatlantic Information Lag of the British Royal African Company and its Successor, 1680–1818." *Business History* 58 (8): pp. 1,147–63.

Roper, L. H. 2017. *Advancing Empire: English Interests and Overseas Expansion*. Cambridge: Cambridge University Press.

Rovira, Mónica García-Salmones. 2013. *The Project of Positivism in International Law*. Oxford: Oxford University Press.

Roy, Kaushik. 2008. "The Armed Expansion of the English East India Company, 1740s–1849." In *A Military History of India and South Asia: From the East India Company to the Nuclear Era*, edited by Daniel P. Marston and Chandar S. Sundaram, pp. 1–15. Bloomington: Indiana University Press.

Roy, Kaushik. 2011. "The Hybrid Military Establishment of the East India Company in South Asia: 1750–1849." *Journal of Global History* 6 (2): pp. 195–218.

Roy, Kaushik. 2012. "Horses, Guns and Governments: A Comparative Study of the Military Transition in the Manchu, Mughal, Ottoman and Safavid Empires, circa 1400 to circa 1750." *International Area Studies Review* 15 (2): pp. 99–121.

Roy, Tirthankar. 2012. *The East India Company: The World's Most Powerful Corporation*. New Delhi: Penguin Books.

Roy, Tirthankar. 2013. "Rethinking the Origins of British India: State Formation and Military-Fiscal Undertakings in an Eighteenth Century World Region." *Modern Asian Studies* 47 (4): pp. 1,125–56.

Royle, Stephen. 2011. *Company, Crown and Colony: The Hudson's Bay Company and Territorial Endeavour in Western Canada.* London: IB Taurus, 2011.

Rubinstein, W. D. 1983. "The End of 'Old Corruption' in Britain 1780–1860." *Past and Present* 101 (1): pp. 55–86.

Ruggie, John Gerard. 1993. "Territoriality and Beyond: Problematizing Modernity in International Relations." *International Organization* 47 (1): pp. 139–74.

Ryan, Magnus J. 2011. "Corporation Theory." In *Encyclopedia of Medieval Philosophy: Philosophy Between 500 and 1500,* edited by Henrik Lagerlund, pp. 236–40. Amsterdam: Springer Netherlands.

Sack, Peter G. 1973. *Land between Two Laws: Early European Land Acquisitions in New Guinea.* Canberra: Australian National University Press.

Sagar, Rahul. 2016. "Are Charter Cities Legitimate?" *The Journal of Political Philosophy* 24 (4): pp. 509–29.

Sánchez, Rafael Torres. 2016. *Military Entrepreneurs and the Spanish Contractor State in the Eighteenth Century.* Oxford: Oxford University Press.

Scammell, G. V. 1989. *The First Imperial Age: European Overseas Expansion c. 1400–1715* London: Unwin Hyman.

Schnurmann, Claudia. 2003. "'Wherever Profit Leads Us, To Every Sea and Shore . . .': The VOC, the WIC, and Dutch Methods of Globalization in the Seventeenth Century." *Renaissance Studies* 17 (3): pp. 474–93.

Scott, Jonathan. 2011. *When the Waves Ruled Britannia: Geography and Political Identities, 1500–1800.* Cambridge: Cambridge University Press.

Scott, W. R. 1903. "The Constitution and Finance of the Royal African Company of England from its Foundation till 1720." *American Historical Review* 8 (2): pp. 241–59.

Sgourev, Stoyan V., and Wim van Lent. 2015. "Balancing Permission and Prohibition: Private Trade and Adaptation at the VOC." *Social Forces* 93 (3): pp. 933–55.

Sharman, J. C. 2019. *Empires of the Weak: The Real Story of European Expansion and the Creation of the New World Order.* Princeton, NJ: Princeton University Press.

Shelest, J. W. 1989. "The *Dryad* Affair: Corporate Warfare and Anglo-Russian Rivalry for the Alaskan Lisière." Paper presented at the Borderlands Conference, Whitehorse, 2–4 June. http://explorenorth.com/library/history/shelest.html#intro.

Singer, Peter. 2003. *Corporate Warriors: The Rise of the Privatized Military Industry.* Ithaca, NY: Cornell University Press.

Sivramkrishna, Sashi. 2014. "From Merchant to Merchant-Ruler: A Structure-Conduct-Performance Perspective of the East India Company's History, 1600–1764." *Business History* 56 (5): pp. 789–815.

Slinn, Peter. 1971. "Commercial Concessions and Politics during the Colonial Period: The Role of the British South Africa Company in Northern Rhodesia 1890–1964." *African Affairs* 70 (281): pp. 365–84.

Smandych, Russell, and Rick Linden. 1996. "Administering Justice without the State: A Study of the Private Justice System of the Hudson's Bay Company to 1800." *Canadian Journal of Law and Society* 11 (1): pp. 21–61.

Smith, David Chan. 2018. "The Hudson's Bay Company, Social Legitimacy, and the Political Economy of Eighteenth-Century Empire." *William and Mary Quarterly* 75 (1): pp. 71–108.

Smith, Edmond J. 2013. "Naval Violence and Trading Privileges in Early Seventeenth-Century Asia." *International Journal of Maritime History* 25 (2): pp. 147–58.

Smith, Edmond J. 2018. "Reporting and Interpreting Legal Violence in Asia: The East India Company's Printed Accounts of Torture, 1603–24." *Journal of Imperial and Commonwealth History* 46 (4): pp. 603–26.

Smith-Peter, Susan. 2015. "Russian Colonization in North America." *Russian Studies in History* 54 (1): pp. 1–4.

Southall, Aidan. 1988. "The Segmentary State in Africa and Asia." *Comparative Studies in Society and History* 30 (1): pp. 52–82.

Spruyt, Hendrik. 1994. *The Sovereign State and Its Competitors: An Analysis of Systems Change.* Princeton, NJ: Princeton University Press.

Stannard, Matthew G. 2014. "Violence and Empire: The Curious Case of Belgium and the Congo." In *The Routledge History of Western Empires*, edited by Robert Aldrich and Kirsten McKenzie, pp. 454–67. London: Routledge.

Starkey, David J. 2011. "Voluntaries and Sea Robbers: A Review of the Academic Literature on Privateering, Corsairing, Buccaneering and Piracy." *The Mariner's Mirror* 97 (1): 127–147.

Steele, Ian K. 1994. *Warpaths: Invasions of North America.* Oxford: Oxford University Press.

Steensgaard, Niels. 1973. *The Asian Trade Revolution of the Seventeenth Century: The East India Companies and the Decline of the Caravan Trade.* Chicago: University of Chicago Press.

Steensgaard, Niels. 1981. "Companies as a Specific Institution in the History of European Expansion." In *Companies and Trade: Essays on Overseas Trading Companies during the Ancien Régime*, edited by Leonard Blussé and Femme Gaastra, pp. 245–64. Leiden: Leiden University Press.

Steinberg, Philip E., Elizabeth Nyman, and Mauro J. Caraccioli. 2012. "Atlas Swam: Freedom, Capital, and the Floating Sovereignties in the Seasteading Vision." *Antipode* 44 (4): pp. 1532–50.

Stern, Philip J. 2006. "British Asia and British Atlantic: Connections and Comparisons." *William and Mary Quarterly* 63 (4): pp. 693–712.

Stern, Philip J. 2008. "'A Politie of Civill and Military Power': Political Thought and the Late Seventeenth-Century Foundations of the East India Company-State." *Journal of British Studies* 47 (2): pp. 253–83.

Stern, Philip J. 2009. "History and Historiography of the English East India Company: Past, Present, and Future!" *History Compass* 7 (4): pp. 1,146–80.

Stern, Philip J. 2011. *The Company-State: Corporate Sovereignty and the Early Modern Foundations of the British Empire in India.* Oxford: Oxford University Press.

Stern, Phillip J. 2015. "The Ideology of the Imperial Corporation: 'Informal' Empire Revisited." In *Chartering Capitalism: Organizing Markets, States, and Publics*, edited by Emily Erikson, pp. 15–43. Bingley: Emerald Group Publishing.

Strayer, Joseph R. 1970. *On the Medieval Origins of the Modern State*. Princeton, NJ: Princeton University Press.

Subrahmanyam, Sanjay. 1988. "On the Significance of Gadflies: The Genoese East India Company of the 1640s." *Journal of European Economic History* 17 (3): pp. 559–81.

Subrahmanyam, Sanjay. 1989. "The Coromandel Trade of the Danish East India Company, 1618–1649." *Scandinavian Economic History Review* 37 (1): pp. 41–56.

Subrahmanyam, Sanjay. 2002. "Frank Submissions: The Company and the Mughals between Sir Thomas Roe and Sir William Norris." In *The Worlds of the East India Company*, edited by H. V. Bowen, Margarette Lincoln, and Nigel Rigby, pp. 69–96. Woodbridge, UK: Boydell.

Subrahmanyam, Sanjay. 2012. *The Portuguese Empire in Asia, 1500–1700: A Political and Economic History*. Chichester, UK: Wiley-Blackwell.

Sundmark, Bjorn. 2015. "Anders Ljungsted and the Swedish East India Company," translated from the Chinese in *Macau Studies* 80. Available at http://muep .mau.se/bitstream/handle/2043/19488/Anders%20Ljungstedt%20English2 .pdf;jsessionid=B1927F87B0B0FF860C9DB394D167B3F4?sequence=2.

Sutton, Anne F. 2002. "The Merchant Adventurers of England: Their Origins and the Mercers' Company of London." *Historical Research* 75 (187): pp. 25–46.

Teschke, Benno. 2003. *The Myth of 1648: Class, Geopolitics and the Making of Modern International Relations*. London: Verso.

Thompson, William R. 1999. "The Military Superiority Thesis and the Ascendancy of Western Eurasia in the World System." *Journal of World History* 10 (1): pp. 143–78.

Thomson, Janice E. 1994. *Mercenaries, Pirates, and Sovereigns: State-Building and Extraterritorial Violence in Early Modern Europe*. Princeton, NJ: Princeton University Press.

Thornton, John K. 1999. *Warfare in Atlantic Africa, 1500–1800*. London: Routledge.

Thornton, John K. 2011. "Firearms, Diplomacy, and Conquest in Angola." In *Empires and Indigenes: Intercultural Alliances, Imperial Expansion, and Warfare in the Early Modern World*, edited by Wayne E. Lee pp. 167–92. New York: New York University Press.

Tikhmenev, P. A. 1978 [1863]. *A History of the Russian-American Company*, edited and translated by Richard A. Pierce and Alton S. Donnelly. Seattle: University of Washington Press.

Tilly, Charles. 2005. *Trust and Rule*. Cambridge: Cambridge University Press.

Tracy, James D. 1991. "Introduction." In *The Political Economy of Merchant Empires: State Power and World Trade, 1350–1750*, edited by James D. Tracy, pp. 1–21. Cambridge: Cambridge University Press.

Travers, Robert. 2004. "'The Real Value of the Lands': The *Nawabs*, the British and the Land Tax in Eighteenth-Century Bengal." *Modern Asian Studies* 38 (3): pp. 517–58.

Travers, Robert. 2007. *Ideology and Empire in Eighteenth-Century India: The British in Bengal*. Cambridge: Cambridge University Press.

Truschke, Audrey. 2016. *Culture of Encounters: Sanskrit at the Mughal Court*. New York: Columbia University Press.

Vandersmissen, Jan. 2011. "The King's Most Eloquent Campaigner . . . Emile de Laveleye, Leopold II and the Creation of the Congo Free State." *Journal of Belgian History* 41 (1–2): pp. 7–57.

Vandervort, Bruce. 1998. *Wars of Imperial Conquest in Africa, 1830–1914*. Bloomington: Indiana University Press.

Vanek, Morgan. 2015. "The Politics of the Weather: The Hudson's Bay Company and the Dobbs Affair." *Journal for Eighteenth-Century Studies* 38 (3): pp. 395–411.

van Goor, J. J. 1985. "A Madman in the City of Ghosts: Nicolaas Kloek in Pontianak." *Itinerario* 9 (2): pp. 196–211.

van Ittersum, Martine. 2018. "Empire by Treaty." In *The Dutch and English East India Companies: Diplomacy, Trade and Violence in Early Modern Asia*, edited by Adam Clulow and Tristan Mostert, pp. 153–77. Amsterdam: University of Amsterdam Press.

van Meersbergen, Guido. 2016. "Dutch and English Approaches to Cross-Cultural Trade in Mughal India and the Problem of Trust, 1600–1630." In *Beyond Empires: Global, Self-Organizing, Cross-Imperial Networks, 1500–1800*, edited by Cátia A. P. Antunes and Amelia Polónia, pp. 69–87. Leiden: Brill.

van Meersbergen, Guido. 2019. "The Diplomatic Repertoires of the East Indian Companies in Mughal South Asia, 1608–1717." *Historical Journal* 62 (4): pp. 875–98.

Veeser, Cyrus. 2013. "A Forgotten Instrument of Global Capitalism? International Concessions, 1870–1930." *International History Review* 35 (5): pp. 1,136–55.

Veevers, David. 2013. "'The Company as Their Lords and the Deputy as a Great Rajah': Imperial Expansion and the English East India Company on the West Coast of Sumatra, 1685–1730." *Journal of Imperial and Commonwealth History* 41 (5): 687–709.

Verlinden, Charles. 2008. "The Transfer of Colonial Techniques from the Mediterranean to the Atlantic." In *The Medieval Frontiers of Latin Christendom: Expansion, Contraction, Continuity*, edited by Felipe Fernandez-Armesto and James Muldoon, pp. 191–220. London: Routledge.

Vigneswaran, Darshan. 2013. "A Corrupt International Society: How Britain was Duped into Its First Indian Conquest." In *International Orders in the Early Modern World: Before the Rise of the West*, edited by Shogo Suzuki, Yongjin Zhang, and Joel Quirk, pp. 94–117. London: Routledge.

Vink, Markus. 2003. "'The World's Oldest Trade': Dutch Slavery and Slave Trade in the Indian Ocean in the Seventeenth Century." *Journal of World History* 14 (2): pp. 131–77.

Vink, Markus. 2019. "From the Cape to Canton: The Dutch Indian Ocean World, 1600–1800—A Littoral Census." *Journal of Indian Ocean World Studies* 3 (1): pp. 13–37.

Vinkovetsky, Ilya. 2011. *Russian America: An Overseas Colony of a Continental Empire, 1804–1867*. Oxford: Oxford University Press.

Viviani, Nancy. 1978. *Nauru: Phosphate and Political Progress*. Canberra: Australian National University Press.

Wagner, Michael. 2012. "Managing to Compete: The Hudson's Bay, Levant and Russia Companies, 1714–1763." *Business and Economic History On-Line* 10: pp. 1–11.

Wagner, Michael. 2018. *The English Chartered Trading Companies, 1688–1763: Guns, Money and Lawyers*. New York: Routledge.

Wagner, Mike. 2014. "Asleep by a Frozen Sea or a Financial Innovator? The Hudson's Bay Company, 1714–63." *Canadian Journal of History* 49 (2): pp. 179–202.

Wallerstein, Immanuel. 1980. *The Modern World-System*, vol. 2, *Mercantilism and the Consolidation of the European World-Economy, 1600–1750*. New York: Academic Press.

Ward, Kerry. 2009. *Networks of Empire: Forced Migration in the Dutch East India Company*. Cambridge: Cambridge University Press.

Ward, Peter. 2013. *British Naval Power in the East, 1794–1805: The Command of Admiral Peter Rainier*. Woodbridge: Boydell Press.

Warhurst, Philip. 1978. "A Troubled Frontier: North-Eastern Mashonaland, 1898–1906." *African Affairs* 77 (307): pp. 214–29.

Watt, Douglas. 2007. *The Price of Scotland: Darien, Union and the Wealth of Nations*. Edinburgh: Luath Press.

Wellen, Kathryn. 2015. "The Danish East India Company's War against the Mughal Empire, 1642–1698." *Journal of Early Modern History* 19 (5): pp. 439–61.

Weststeijn, Arthur. 2014. "The VOC as a Company-State: Debating Seventeenth Century Dutch Colonial Expansion." *Itinerario* 38 (1): 13–34.

Wezel, Filippo Carlo, and Martin Ruef. 2017. "Agents with Principles: The Control of Labor in the Dutch East India Company, 1700 to 1796." *American Sociological Review* 82 (5): pp. 1,009–36.

Wheatley, Natasha. 2017. "Spectral Legal Personality in Interwar International Law: On New Ways of Not Being a State." *Law and History Review* 35 (3): pp. 753–87.

Wheeler, Mary E. 1971. "Empires in Conflict and Cooperation: The 'Bostonians' and the Russian-American Company." *Pacific Historical Review* 40 (4): pp. 419–41.

Wheeler, Mary E. 1987. "The Russian American Company and the Imperial Government: Early Phase." In *Russia's American Colony*, edited by S. Frederick Starr, pp. 43–62. Durham, NC: Duke University Press.

Wickremesekera, Channa. 2015. "European Military Experience in South Asia: The Dutch and British Armies in Sri Lanka in the Eighteenth Century." In *Chinese and Indian Warfare: From the Classical Age to 1870*, edited by Kaushik Roy and Peter Lorge, Abingdon: Routledge, pp. 289–301.

Wilburn, Kenneth. 1997. "The Drift Crisis, the 'Missing Telegrams,' and the Jameson Raid: A Centennial Review." *Journal of Imperial and Commonwealth History* 25 (2): pp. 219–39.

Willan, Thomas S. 1956. *Early History of the Russia Company, 1553–1603*. Manchester: Manchester University Press.

Williams, Glyn. 1996. "'To Make Discoveries of Countries Hitherto Unknown': The Admiralty and Pacific Exploration in the Eighteenth Century." *The Mariner's Mirror* 82 (1): pp. 14–27.

Williams, Glyndwr. 1970. "The Hudson's Bay Company and Its Critics in the Eighteenth Century." *Transactions of the Royal Historical Society* 20: pp. 149–71.

Williams Jr., R. A. 1992. *The American Indian in Western Legal Thought: The Discourses of Conquest.* Oxford: Oxford University Press.

Wills, John E. 1993. "Maritime Asia, 1500–1800: The Interactive Emergence of European Domination." *American Historical Review* 98 (1): pp. 83–105.

Wilson, Charles. 1965. *England's Apprenticeship, 1603–1763.* London: Longman.

Winius, George Davison. 1971. *The Fatal History of Portuguese Ceylon: Transition to Dutch Rule.* Cambridge, MA: Harvard University Press.

Woolford, J. V. 1978a. "The Matabele War: Part 1." *History Today* 28 (8): pp. 537–43.

Woolford, J. V. 1978b. "The Matabele War: Part 2." *History Today* 28 (9): pp. 605–11.

Zahedieh, Nuala. 2010. "Regulation, Rent-Seeking, and the Glorious Revolution in the English Atlantic Economy." *Economic History Review* 63 (4): pp. 865–90.

Zarakol, Ayse. 2018. "A Non-Eurocentric Approach to Sovereignty." *International Studies Review* 20 (3): pp. 506–9.

Zook, George Frederick. 1919. *The Company of Royal Adventurers Trading into Africa.* Lancaster, PA: New Era Printing Company.

INDEX

Page numbers in *italics* indicate illustrations.

A NOTE ON THE TYPE

THIS BOOK has been composed in Miller, a Scotch Roman typeface designed by Matthew Carter and first released by Font Bureau in 1997. It resembles Monticello, the typeface developed for The Papers of Thomas Jefferson in the 1940s by C. H. Griffith and P. J. Conkwright and reinterpreted in digital form by Carter in 2003.

Pleasant Jefferson ("P. J.") Conkwright (1905–1986) was Typographer at Princeton University Press from 1939 to 1970. He was an acclaimed book designer and AIGA Medalist.

The ornament used throughout this book was designed by Pierre Simon Fournier (1712–1768) and was a favorite of Conkwright's, used in his design of the *Princeton University Library Chronicle*.